CW01044065

SOUTH EASTERN
AND
CHATHAM RAILWAYS

A marriage of convenience

Adrian Gray M.A.

MP Middleton Press

Cover picture: Sandling Junction, with a main line local train on the back cover and a Hythe branch train on the front. (Wakeman Collection, Ashford Library)

For R.W. Kidner, who published my first efforts
in railway history, has written more than
anyone about the SECR, and who has been a
great help in the preparation of this work.

Published April 1998

ISBN 1 901706 08 7

© *Middleton Press, 1998*

Design Deborah Goodridge

Published by
  Middleton Press
  Easebourne Lane
  Midhurst, West Sussex
  GU29 9AZ
Tel: 01730 813169
Fax: 01730 812601

Printed in Hong Kong through World Print Ltd.

Contents

Route Diagrams

Author's notes

All prices in this book are given in contemporary sums, but this may be confusing for the modern reader due to the very rapid inflation between 1914 and 1919, as well as the inflation in more recent years. In order to compare costs it is therefore useful to use a standardising system based on £100 in 1914, as follows:

1898=£85; 1900=£91; 1914=£100; 1920=£249; 1996=£4200

There are various conventions in recording railway closure dates. When referred to as *closed on* ...., this means the last date of normal services, while *closed from* .... means the first date *without* services, i.e. the first day of being a closed station. It it necessary to make this point as several SECR stations closed from a Monday, but had no Sunday services.

The name of the South Eastern & Chatham Railways Managing Committee is abbreviated to SECR throughout this book. However it should be noted that the SE&CR was used by the Committee itself.

SECR System

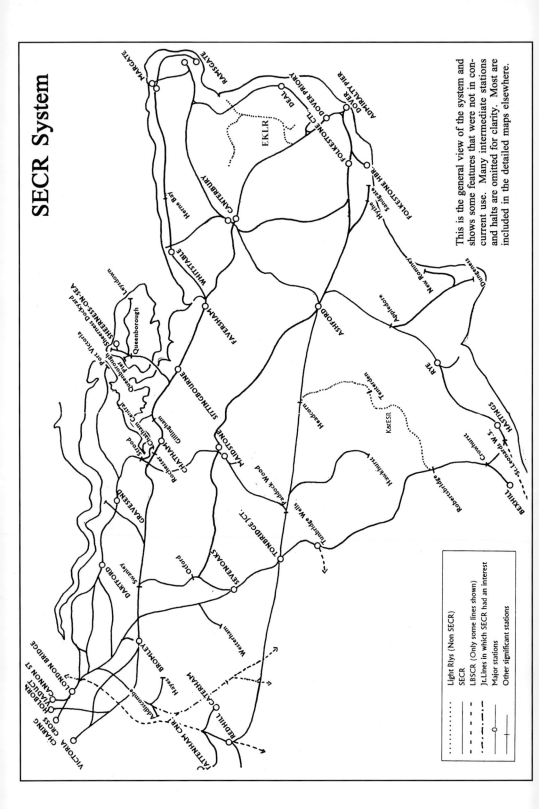

This is the general view of the system and shows some features that were not in concurrent use. Many intermediate stations and halts are omitted for clarity. Most are included in the detailed maps elsewhere.

Light Rlys (Non SECR)
SECR (Only some lines shown)
LBSCR (Only some lines shown)
Jt.Lines in which SECR had an interest
Major stations
Other significant stations

Suburban Lines

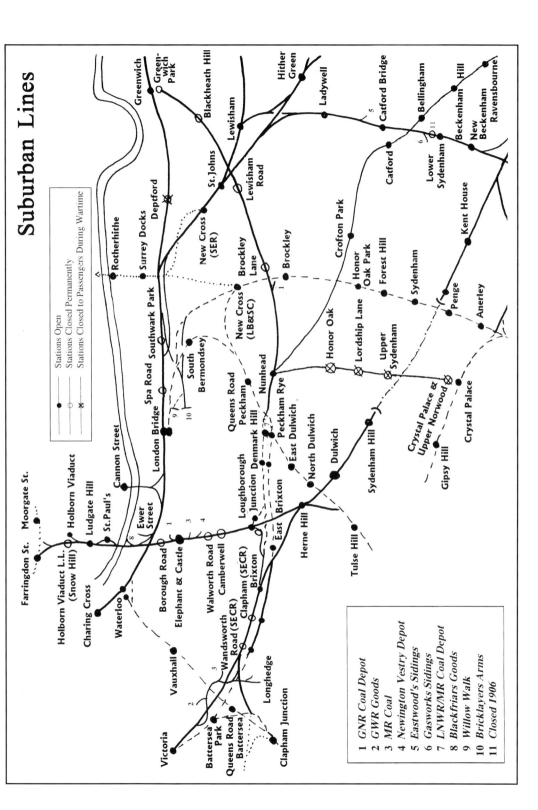

Stations Open
Stations Closed Permanently
Stations Closed to Passengers During Wartime

1 GNR Coal Depot
2 GWR Goods
3 MR Coal
4 Newington Vestry Depot
5 Eastwood's Sidings
6 Gasworks Sidings
7 LNWR/MR Coal Depot
8 Blackfriars Goods
9 Willow Walk
10 Bricklayers Arms
11 Closed 1906

Industrial Sidings in N.W. Kent

Note: Only sidings connected to the SECR are shown

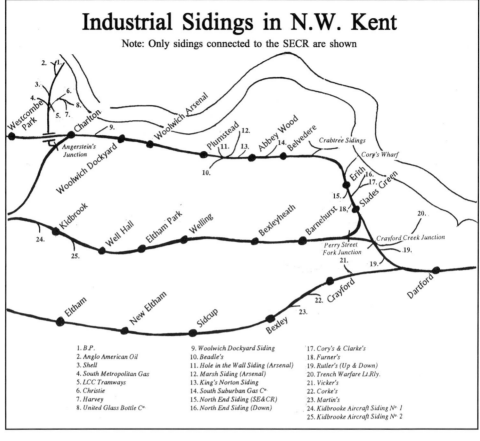

1. *B.P.*	9. *Woolwich Dockyard Siding*	17. *Cory's & Clarke's*
2. *Anglo American Oil*	10. *Beadle's*	18. *Furner's*
3. *Shell*	11. *Hole in the Wall Siding (Arsenal)*	19. *Rutler's (Up & Down)*
4. *South Metropolitan Gas*	12. *Marsh Siding (Arsenal)*	20. *Trench Warfare Lt.Rly.*
5. *LCC Tramways*	13. *King's Norton Siding*	21. *Vicker's*
6. *Christie*	14. *South Suburban Gas Cᵒ·*	22. *Corke's*
7. *Harvey*	15. *North End Siding (SE&CR)*	23. *Martin's*
8. *United Glass Bottle Cᵒ*	16. *North End Siding (Down)*	24. *Kidbrooke Aircraft Siding Nᵒ· 1*
		25. *Kidbrooke Aircraft Siding Nᵒ· 2*

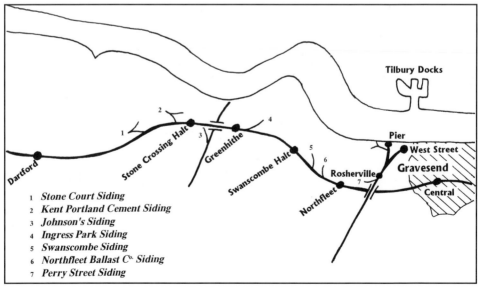

1 **Stone Court Siding**
2 **Kent Portland Cement Siding**
3 **Johnson's Siding**
4 **Ingress Park Siding**
5 **Swanscombe Siding**
6 **Northfleet Ballast Cᵒ· Siding**
7 **Perry Street Siding**

Medway Area Lines

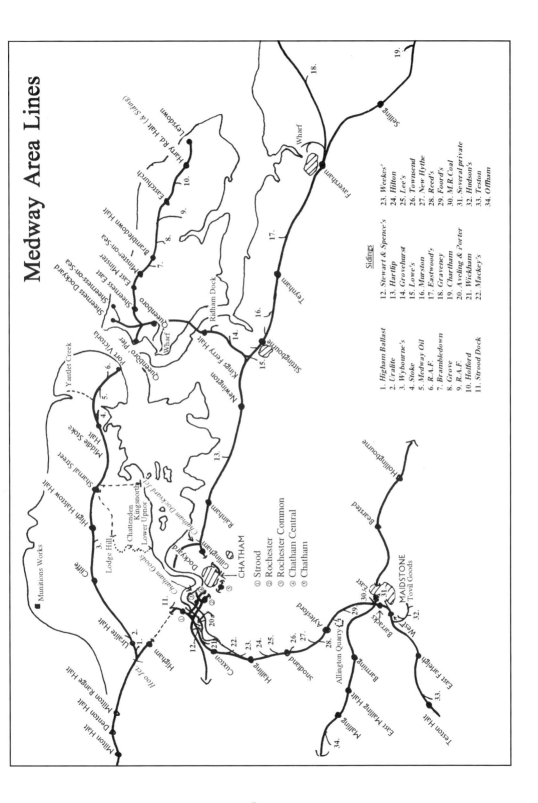

Sidings

12. Stewart & Spence's
13. Hartlip
14. Grovehurst
15. Lowe's
16. Murston
17. Eastwood's
18. Graveney
19. Chartham
20. Aveling & Porter
21. Wickham
22. Mackey's

23. Weekes'
24. Hilton
25. Lee's
26. Townsend
27. New Hythe
28. Reed's
29. Foord's
30. M.R.Coal
31. Several private
32. Hudson's
33. Teston
34. Offham

1. Higham Ballast
2. Uralite
3. Wybourne's
4. Stoke
5. Medway Oil
6. R.A.F.
7. Brambledown
8. Grove
9. R.A.F.
10. Holford
11. Strood Dock

① Strood
② Rochester
③ Rochester Common
④ Chatham Central
⑤ Chatham

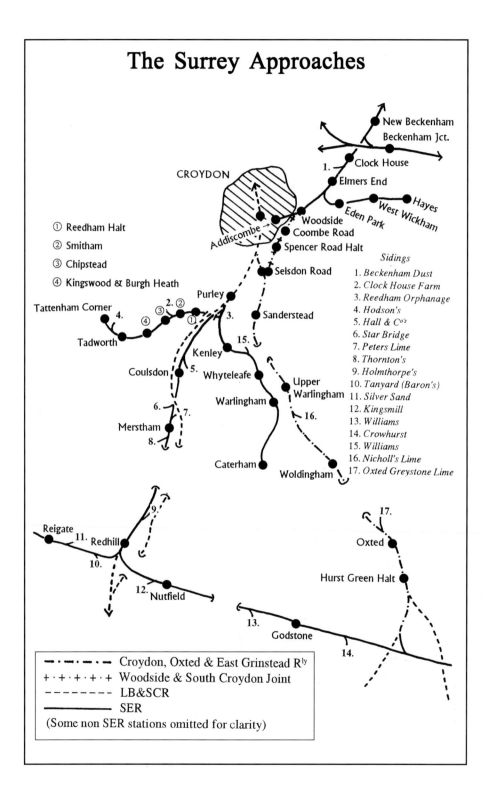

The Surrey Approaches

CROYDON

New Beckenham
Beckenham Jct.
1. Clock House
Elmers End
Hayes
West Wickham
Eden Park
Woodside
Coombe Road
Addiscombe
Spencer Road Halt

① Reedham Halt
② Smitham
③ Chipstead
④ Kingswood & Burgh Heath

Selsdon Road

Purley
2. ②
Tattenham Corner
③
4.
③
④
①
3.
Sanderstead
Tadworth
15.
Kenley
Coulsdon
5.
Whyteleafe
Upper
Warlingham
Warlingham
6.
7.
16.
Merstham
8.
Caterham
Woldingham

Sidings
1. *Beckenham Dust*
2. *Clock House Farm*
3. *Reedham Orphanage*
4. *Hodson's*
5. *Hall & Co's*
6. *Star Bridge*
7. *Peters Lime*
8. *Thornton's*
9. *Holmthorpe's*
10. *Tanyard (Baron's)*
11. *Silver Sand*
12. *Kingsmill*
13. *Williams*
14. *Crowhurst*
15. *Williams*
16. *Nicholl's Lime*
17. *Oxted Greystone Lime*

Reigate
11.
Redhill
9.
10.
12.
Nutfield

17.
Oxted
Hurst Green Halt

13.
Godstone
14.

—·—·—·— Croydon, Oxted & East Grinstead R^{ly}
+·+·+·+·+ Woodside & South Croydon Joint
– – – – – – LB&SCR
————— SER
(Some non SER stations omitted for clarity)

Chapter One:

Introduction

The conventions of railway history relate that the Edwardian period, at least before the outbreak of the First World War, was something of a "golden age" before the railways were hit by economic problems and road competition in the 1920s. Yet the South Eastern & Chatham Railways fought a losing battle against road competition virtually from the inception of the Managing Committee in 1898. In this respect 13 March 1907 can be seen as a turning point in the history of the railways of south-east England, for on that day the Board of the SECR agreed to close Borough Road station in London due to remorseless tramway competition - which it did with effect from 1 April 1907.

The death of Borough Road was the result of a continuing failure of the railways to handle the cheap and intensive competition proferred by London's tramways. In January 1909 Cosmo Bonsor, the SECR's Chairman, conceded that it was "impossible to compete" with the trams and admitted that the SECR had lost 14 million passengers a year to the tramways in the space of ten years. The Company abandoned the inner suburban traffic in a territory within six miles of central London, yet ten years later found a distance three times further into the outer suburbs could also be threatened by motor buses. Of all the southern companies, it was the slowest to consider electrification.

The danger of motor cars was also apparent before the outbreak of war in 1914. In January 1907 Bonsor complained of "a new fashion of travelling in motors instead of by the much more comfortable means of railway carriages..." in order to go to the seaside, but "He did not think, however, that this fashion would last for ever." In the face of such complacency, the SECR did little to win back the new generation of wealthy motorists.

The SECR's response to growing competition for passenger traffic was weak before the War, consisting largely of well-tried and tired responses such as altering the fares structure, amending the timetable and building new carriages. It failed to make sufficient progress on fundamental problems such as the tangle of stations and trackwork in the London Bridge, Charing Cross and Cannon Street triangle and was slow to improve the dingy stations of the former LCDR Metropolitan extension line through Ludgate. The whole system was famously incapable of handling a punctual service whenever there was fog and the problems caused by steam traction were not really debated until after the War - when little money was available. Huge capital sums were invested in widening heavily used lines, notably the infamous "Peek Freans widening", but this was the conventional 1880s answer to what was to be the problem of the 1920s.

On occasions the SECR enjoyed good periods of punctuality and these seem to have encouraged its reluctance to follow the growing fashion for electrification, which would have simplified immensely the working of Charing Cross and Can-

THE RAILWAY MAGAZINE.

OFFICERS OF CENTRE.

VINCENT W. HILL, ESQ. M.V.O.

F. H. DENT ESQ

W. THOMSON ESQ. M.V.O.

H. COSMO. O. BONSOR ESQ
PRESIDENT

H. S. WAINWRIGHT ESQ

P. C. TEMPEST ESQ

C. SHEATH ESQ

SOUTH EASTERN AND CHATHAM RAILWAY CENTRE, ST. JOHN AMBULANCE ASSOCIATION.

These are some of the key individuals in the life of the SECR, as represented through their patronage of the St John Ambulance Association. Cosmo Bonsor was Chairman for virtually the whole period; Sheath was SECR Secretary and later a director of the Southern Railway, his railway career extending from 1864 to 1939; Hill, Dent and Tempest were successive general managers; Thomson was a superintendent of the line until replaced by Edwin Cox.

non Street. Its appointment of Alfred Raworth as electrical engineer in 1918 was an encouraging step, but late in 1921 the SECR still felt that electrification depended on government support and did not see it as essential at any price. Only in February 1922 does the SECR seem to have accepted that only electric trains could maintain an adequate service, the planning for which it then turned into a political embarassment.

The pace of change was no greater in the goods traffic market. SECR attitudes before the War were still historic - private sidings were being added in a vain hope that the railway could provide a "door to door" service without the punitive costs of transhipment though some progress was made in winning over the Thames cement works to rail transport. Some of the new sidings were economically dubious at the best of times - farm sidings and builder's yards, but the SECR also exacted capital investment from the customers and guarantees of traffic. The flood of cheap lorries after the War spelt doom for many of these marginal pre-war initiatives.

It is hard to find one good and new idea that occurred within the SECR Goods Department between 1898 and 1922, apart from the development of Hither Green instead of the restricted facilities at places such as Herne Hill. One senses a forlorn hope that the success of the Kent coalfield - always a distant glimmer in the Chairman's speech at every General Meeting - would provide a harvest of gold for the SECR shareholders; it was not to be, of course, as the coalfield foundered with problems of poor quality coal and flooding.

The Edwardian period was also the last era of railway building in Britain as the Light Railways Act encouraged a spate of hopelessly uneconomic rural schemes intended to help develop remote regions. Yet the citizens of Kent embraced the idea enthusiastically and the SECR supported them, though it was careful with its own money. Any costing of rural branch lines would have shown the foolishness of these schemes and the error of the Sheppey Light can only be excused by the fact that the Southern Railway made a worse mistake with the Allhallows line thirty years later. The SECR supported the Headcorn to Tenterden line with a guarantee of interest and dithered endlessly over extensions in the Romney and Herne Bay areas. Did anyone doubt whether huge investments of fixed capital were appropriate in such circumstances?

Not every decision was a mistake, however. In 1906 the SECR was worried about the financial risks of the Kent & East Sussex Railway extending to Rye and in 1912 it bought two omnibuses of its own for use out of Hythe. However the opportunity to run a proper bus service between Canterbury and Herne Bay was never properly developed.

With regard to the Continental services, the SECR acted speedily in replacing all its paddle steamers with turbine, screw-driven vessels. Yet it was always an opponent of the train ferry idea, arguing that it was impractical despite its use in many other parts of the world. Here was an obvious way of improving the economics of the continental goods traffic, but the SECR refused to accept that such a service could be accomodated at Dover and invested massively in a new Marine station which did nothing for goods traffic. The War gifted it a train ferry service from Richborough, but the chance was lost to the Great Eastern Railway after hostilities ceased. The introduction of Pullman services hardly seems to balance

The new SECR was always best known for its cross-Channel services, for which it built a new fleet of turbine steamers - one of which is seen leaving the SECR's own port of Folkestone in about 1910.

this monumental lack of vision, and virtually as soon as the War had ended French fruit importers were championing the cause of the lorry.

In staff conditions and wages the SECR had a good record, its workers receiving higher pay before the War than was common on many lines. This protected it in the first railway strike, but not in the changed atmosphere of post-War Britain when there was a national strike in 1919. But there were also blemishes - the continued existence of porters at London termini who received no pay but existed purely on tips from the public, and the slow safety improvements at sidings. The War itself increased staff costs vastly and weakened savagely the SECR's position in the post-War years: labour intensive railway practices (such as the handling of continental goods on both sides of the Channel) built up in the years of cheap labour left the SECR dangerously exposed to competition in 1920. In the light of this, steadily rising figures for net profits hid the real malaise and management response was to tinker with costs by closing a few signalboxes.

Thus it was possible for the SECR to have the outward appearance of "first-class railway management". This was, perhaps, despite the efforts of Bonsor rather than because of his influence; his other career, in brewing, was marked by early promise and later stagnation with the same pattern being repeated at the SECR. The early years of the SECR were spent rebuilding the main-lines, which were too dated or lightly built to accomodate modern expresses, and from this costly enterprise it had hardly recovered before war broke out. It is one of the ironies of the SECR that as it struggled to the close of its short life, it bequeathed to the Southern Railway a number of fine professional railwaymen such as Raworth and Maunsell who were to shape that larger business's future.

Chapter Two:

A Marriage of Convenience

There was never any such creature as a "South Eastern & Chatham Railway", for the South Eastern Railway and the London, Chatham & Dover Railway remained legally separate entities until the last days before the Southern Railway was born. Instead, what was formed was the South Eastern & Chatham Railways Managing Committee, by which the principal transport affairs of the two businesses were run by one management with an agreed division of traffic profits and liabilities. The two railway companies continued to exist and make decisions for themselves, especially in the area of property interests; there was no amalgamation of capital. According to Bonsor himself, speaking in 1921, it was decided not to have a full amalgamation in order to avoid a hefty amount of stamp duty.

So it was never a case of "the two shall become one flesh" but a marriage of convenience, hedged around with legal barriers and controls yet surviving despite some animosity between the parties. That the marriage happened at all seems to have been due in large part to Cosmo Bonsor, the Chairman of the SER from March 1898, whose taking up of the reins coincided remarkably with a new period of bridge-building to the old enemy. At some stage in the Spring of 1898 there occurred what Forbes called a "chance conversation" between him and Bonsor, which soon flowered into a positive romance.

On 25 June 1898 *The Times* reported that three directors of each company were now preparing a "Parliamentary application". Though this was not quite correct, the newspaper was right in saying that "a better understanding [has] latterly been arrived at in the conduct of the two undertakings....both Boards have come to the conclusion that there is a wasteful expenditure which nothing can arrest short of a working arrangement." It estimated savings at £100,000 a year, much of which could come from the axing of duplicate services - Chatham had over forty London trains a day. As will be seen, some of the economies were never made and SER shares, in particular, suffered for the next few years.

What was being proposed, though, was not an amalgamation, and this was explained for readers of *The Times* on 30 June:

"The individuality of the companies will remain undisturbed, but the working staffs will be fused, and in every instance where the traffic of the separate systems is competitive it will become part of the new combined working."

However the newspaper hardly saw this as an idyllic union of the beautiful. "Both companies have been by-words for squalid indifference to the public convenience" was its view on 1 July. It felt that the union would end "a long and suicidal struggle, carried on rather to gratify the vanity of rival chairmen than to benefit the companies or the public."

By July 1898 much of the groundwork had been done, agreement on terms was reached on 21 July and the date of 1 January 1899 agreed as the date when the marriage should commence; this became the actual start of the SECR, though Parliamentary sanction came a few months later. In reality, a certain amount of cohabiting took place before the actual wedding, for the Joint Committee began sitting on 10 August 1898 with Bonsor in the Chair. Aretas-Akers Douglas of the LCDR became deputy chairman. The Committee had fourteen members, including Forbes of the LCDR as "General Adviser to the two companies," who was guaranteed payment for the next ten years although he died in 1904.

When agreement between the two companies had been sealed, the crucial figure was the division of receipts between the two - the SER to get 59% of pooled traffic and the LCDR to get 41%. These terms sparked some discussion that continued for most of the working union. An analysis of the traffic returns for the early weeks of 1898 shows that, in a combined company, the SER would have been contributing about 60% of the profits compared to the LCDR's 40%. However this disguises the fact that the LCDR was a more efficient concern giving a return of £142.60 per track mile per week compared to the SER's £87.90. 51.74% of the LCDR's income was swallowed up in its operating costs, compared to 54.61% of the SER's in the second half of 1898, though the LCDR had an advantage in fewer rural branches. Additionally the LCDR suffered from a poor seasonal balance to its traffic, so that in looking at the figures for the second half of 1897 we find that the LCDR would have earnt 38.6% of combined profits. *The Times* shared the view of growing Chatham strength, despite "persistent errors of management", for the SER had "distinctly lost ground" and was inferior in the condition of its equipment. The terms were certainly better for the Chatham than they had been in negotiations during previous rounds. However the agreement only affected traffic receipts, and the LCDR had strong property interests - earning about £54,000 per year from rentals and up to £64,000 by 1902.

Bonsor's view of it was "the bargain must be a good one, because neither side was absolutely satisfied." Forbes, however, claimed a disappointment in not winning a 42% share but felt that 41% was at least one point better than the real performance of 39.4% in 1898 and thus earnt his shareholders "£33,000 clean money."

This public house stood close to the former LCDR bridge across the ex-SER Strood to Paddock Wood line in Strood, and near the site of Rochester Bridge station which was an obvious candidate for closure once the Managing Committee had been formed. The pub's name is erroneous - the SECR was not an "amalgamation" as such. (Author)

The question of management was dealt with first - Alfred Willis was to be General Manager, Percy Tempest the Engineer and Captain Dixon Marine Superintendent. William Kirtley was paid off with a pension of £600 a year and Harry Wainwright became Locomotive, Carriage & Wagon Superintendent on £1250 a year.

One of the most telling arguments in favour of the working union was that much could be saved by rationalising competitive services - thus increasing profits. An immediate start was made on reorganising the Continental services by putting all "Grande Vitesse" and French goods via the Folkestone-Boulogne route with Folkestone-Calais for Belgian goods. In October 1898 it was decided to get rid of twelve mail or passenger boats, a goods boat and a life-saving vessel.

To rationalise the passenger services was not so easy. The passenger carriages of the two companies had different systems of brakes, lights and heating, so that interworking and pooling of stock was very difficult and so in October 1898 the conversion of LCDR stock to vacuum brakes was agreed. In November 1898 it was decided, presumably as a temporary step, to fit Westinghouse brakes to four SER locomotives so that they could work LCDR carriages down the Folkestone Harbour branch. In June 1899 it was at least decided to unite the carriages in one livery - the top "quarter panels" were to be varnished, the lower parts to be crimson lake. An elaborate livery was adopted for the locomotives, essentially of Brunswick green with brown-red underframes, liberally lined-out with red, white and light green.

In September Alfred Willis, the General Manager, suggested a number of new links to help create a combined system. His list of immediate priorities included a connection at Margate, improvements at Sevenoaks, and relaying the south to east spur at Otford. Longer term measures included new construction at Ramsgate to St Lawrence, Chislehurst, Halstead to Otford, to link the two lines at Canterbury, and doubling of the Mid Kent line spur to Beckenham Junction. A connection between Northfleet, on the North Kent line, and the former LCDR Gravesend branch was also included in the Bill of 1900.

Another valued aspect of the union was that passengers had more choice in their London destination. Season ticket holders could use Victoria or Charing Cross without penalties.

Despite this initial commitment to improve the system, there were some doubts about the monopoly position the newly married companies would enjoy. This can be seen in some Board of Trade correspondence of September 1898, where the BoT observed that it had heard of some "tentative agreement" between the SER and LCDR which it would not oppose on the assumption that it would be placed before Parliament. In fact in July 1898 Bonsor had stated his clear belief that no Parliamentary sanction was needed as both companies already had the powers to "make any arrangement they please for the more efficient and economical working of their competitive traffic." The two companies certainly did have powers to "pool" their competitive traffic by the Act of 1893, but discerning critics pointed out that this did not include services where they did not compete. The result of this was that the Joint Committee decided that it would promote a Bill in the next Parliamentary session; there was perhaps some fear that any other attempts at legislation would be blocked otherwise.

This plan to go to Parliament resulted in the first signs of friction. It was agreed that a Bill should be drafted that included the working union, but "excluding for the present the proposal to amalgamate the two Boards." The SER Board was in favour of complete amalgamation, perhaps because of its relatively weak financial prospects. In February 1902 Forbes was able to boast to the LCDR shareholders that, "...the Chatham Company was handed over to the Managing Committee in something like a reasonable condition, and in a much better condition than the South Eastern Company." However this was something of a distortion, for the LCDR had accumulated a number of capital-intensive problems such as poor passenger stock and a main-line that required heavy investment to bring it up to modern standards.

The new "united" companies began to run some integrated services from 1 January 1899, though they published their own separate timetables. Some of the services were intended to convince the public of the improvements that would result. An express service from Victoria to Hastings via Tunbridge Wells was introduced whilst ex-SER trains from Farringdon Street via the Blackfriars spur could now call at Ludgate Hill - though this dingy stop can hardly have seemed an advantage to some!

However, the major cause of opposition to the Bill was the fear among the Kent people that the new arrangement would hand monopoly powers to an organisation in which they had no reason to feel confident. This view was shared by the Board of Trade, who in February 1899 expressed fears about clauses in the Bill dealing with passenger fares - suspecting that the plan was to remove many of the reduced fares that had resulted from competition. Bonsor and Forbes assured the public that no fare would increase, but the directors were busy making speeches in the Kent towns, such as Colonel Mellor's at Folkestone on 6 September.

The SECR responded to this by agreeing to replace clause ten in the Bill with a new scale of maximum charges per mile, ranging from 3d for first class down to 1d for third; the lowest fares on the Reading branch were already fixed by a statute and would remain the same. Deputations from Folkestone, Ramsgate and Gravesend were soothed, and the Bill won its second reading in the Commons by 287 votes to 82. It was then referred to a Committee chaired by Lord Stanley, which ensured a tight interpretation of the fares clauses.

Further opposition came from Kent fruit growers and the fruiterers at Covent Garden, who sent a large petition to the London County Council. In March a Maidstone farmers' meeting decided to argue for a clause in the Bill preventing raised rates and Canterbury Farmers' Club insisted on something similar. The SECR bought off the farmers by allowing fruit to be sent by passenger trains from 1 May 1899. Dover Chamber of Commerce wanted 3rd class carriages on all trains and a reduction of fares.

Another tactic was to make some well-timed contributions to ease local feelings; in March 1899 it was agreed to contribute to the cost of widening Nunnery Fields bridge in Canterbury, but a year later there were complaints that the agreement had not been honoured. In July 1899 an agreement was signed to widen a bridge over the SER at Margate.

Stanley had to consider petitions against the Bill from railway companies like the Great Northern and also from London County Council. However most opposition was eventually bribed or cajoled into withdrawing, and the Bill gained its Royal Assent on 1 August 1899 thus giving the Managing Committee a legal status. There remained some anomalies, though; the London & Greenwich Railway remained in a separate existence, while subsidiaries like the Bexley Heath Railway was vested in the SER and not the SECR. Even the Mid Kent Railway (Bromley to St Mary Cray) maintained an independent existence, its directors waking from their slumbers in 1908 to ask the SECR for free passes. However, the buying off of opposition continued after this date - an agreement was reached with the City of Rochester on 18 August that the SECR would not close any station without its consent and would maintain the level of fast trains; this sort of step reduced the Committee's capacity to make effective economies.

The negotiations of 1899 left the SECR in a weakened position. By agreement of 5 August 1899 it had accepted limits on its passenger fares per mile, reducing its ability to fund later investment by retained profits. However attempts were made to get around this restriction, notably with higher fares on boat trains.

Bonsor promised great improvements in efficient working, but there was soon disillusionment. On 31 October 1900 the Board received a deputation from many Kent towns complaining that "the management of the lines generally had been worse since the working union." Bonsor accepted the truth of this, blaming the rebuilding of Bricklayers Arms, the running of extra trains, and the late delivery of new locomotives. Then *The Times* complained of the "tyranny" of the SECR

The Kent towns may have complained about SECR services but some isolated communities must have been glad to have a station; there is little obvious traffic potential in this view of Grove Ferry station.

and the MP for Gravesend criticised its "ill-kept, dirty compartments and worn-out, jolting carriages." During November 1900 Kent County Council adopted a motion complaining about the "gross irregularity" of the service - despite having two SECR Board members sitting on its benches!

There were occasional moments when it seemed that the Kent towns' dislike of the SECR might lead to real opposition. In September 1902 there was much publicity for the Southern Counties Mono-Rail Syndicate, who planned a 110mph line from London to Dover with a station to serve the Medway towns.

Relations between the two partners were not always sound. In January 1901 there was some panic among the SER shareholders that the LCDR would be able to take control of the whole enterprise, and attempts were made to change the composition of the Joint Board. This resulted in a price collapse for the LCDR "A" stock from 119 to 67.

In January 1903 the LCDR disputed a decision over legal ownership of the new electricity works at Victoria which had to be sorted out by the two Chairmen. A few months later there was another dispute over the land cost - payable to the LCDR - for a new siding at Catford Bridge. This was typical of the sort of problem that could arise from a pooling arrangement that covered only traffic receipts.

In February 1905 there was a campaign by some LCDR shareholders to have the "arrangements" altered in favour of their company. In October 1906 Nathaniel Spens, an active member of the LCDR Board, proposed a plan to allow either company to buy the other but this was dropped within a fortnight. In October 1908 the LCDR was still pressing for a proper amalgamation, but it was felt that Parliament's reluctance to see the amalgamation of northern railway companies would prevent this.

Thus the first decade of marriage did not entirely solve the problems of the two companies, though the 1909 Act at least provided for the two to have joint general meetings in future - which at least reduced the wear and tear on the directors. However, it was clear by this stage that the joint working had not produced the efficiencies or the improvements that had been expected, and Bonsor roundly blamed Parliament and its interference with the 1899 Bill for this. In February 1909 the SECR received a deputation led by Lord Brassey and the mayors of various Kent towns, complaining about the lack of improvement in services.

In 1911 some shareholders demanded that the SECR should revise its arrangements so that only one Board of directors was needed instead of two Boards and one Managing Committee. Occasional tensions were still surfacing at this time, as in the example of the SER's scheme to build an hotel on some of its land at Boulogne; the LCDR felt this was "too speculative".

Probably the first connection to be opened was the spur at Otford, as this involved relaying the south to east spur that had previously existed. This plan was reported in *The Times* on 27 September 1898, amidst some confusion, for it was claimed that the spur would allow trains to "run from Victoria to Maidstone." It would seem that, in fact, the two companies were considering a direct link from the SER main-line between Halstead and Dunton Green to the LCDR line at Otford as part of a scheme to make the LCDR's Maidstone line "a main through route to the coast" with improved access to the east at Ashford. The Otford spur was reported as being "in existence" by *The Times* on 2 January 1899, reporting that 15 minutes would be saved on a journey from Sevenoaks to Maidstone; LCDR trains had previously not run beyond their own station at Bat & Ball. Work was reported as being completed before 6 December 1899.

Even this minor change, though, provoked some discord. There were complaints of a poorer local service, especially for passengers travelling between Sevenoaks and Bromley who had to change at Otford and Swanley in advance of the new Chislehurst junctions being completed.

The new "main through route to the coast" reflected changes introduced at Ashford, where the LCDR's station (West) was closed from 1 January 1899 with all passenger services running through to the SER station - something for which Maidstone had lobbied for many years. At the time there were already plans to rebuild Ashford station, but this was continuously delayed. In November 1904 a reduced £47,000 scheme was agreed, with extra platforms and sidings as well as widening the bridges over the river. It was also decided to remove a cattle dock so that trains from the Maidstone line could run into the ex-SER station without having to use the main Charing Cross lines. Rebuilding did not actually start until 1907, by which time parts of the old West station were in use for housing and parcels traffic.

One of the best known results of the working union was the construction of the junctions at Chislehurst which provided services from both SER and LCDR routes with a wide choice of London destinations. These were recommended by Willis in September 1898, but had already been called for by a shareholder, H Brocklebank, in August; he observed that the junctions would allow a reduction in marshalling at Herne Hill. The scheme was included in the "working union" Bill and purchase of land had begun by November 1899. In June 1901 the cost was estimated at £58,000. The loop between Bickley and Orpington was opened to goods on 8 September 1902 and to passengers on 14 September. The loops to allow through running between Charing Cross and Swanley were opened on 19 June 1904.

Connection between the lines at Margate was an early priority and included in the initial Bill, so that by January 1899 the SECR was buying nineteen acres of land. The plan was to close the SER station to passengers and enlarge the LCDR one. However once the 1899 Act had been obtained, activity more or less ceased until 1912 when the SECR decided to build an extra platform for ordinary and excursion traffic, widen the other two platforms, provide a subway and add some carriage sidings at Margate West. A double track connection onto the SER Margate Sands line was also proposed so that that station could be closed. Work on the station was done by the contractor Rigby and "partially ready" in time for the 1913 excursion season in June. In the event the through connection was not completed at the time and Margate Sands survived until the Southern Railway Ramsgate area rebuilding scheme of 1926 - a good example of how the SECR working union failed to deliver real economies, though Margate West was improved at a cost of £58,000 by 1916. However the link was finished during the war and was available

for traffic from 25 October 1917, whilst it had been used "for emergency purposes" by August 1918.

There were also possible economies to be made at Dover. After complaints
about handling local goods traffic, it was decided in December 1898 to run all SER
route passenger trains to Dover Priory (which some already served anyway) and to
convert the old SER station at Dover Town into a carriage shed and bonded store.
In fact this station remained open until 14 October 1914, though its use was much
reduced and the buildings on the spur to Dover Priory were demolished in 1903.
Dover Town was closed permantley from 11 August 1919.

In Ramsgate the two systems were quite separate, and any link between them
involved costly work. Despite this, the town of Ramsgate was alarmed in October
1898 to hear of rumours that one of their stations was to be closed and sent a
deputation to visit the Joint Committee, though they were right in that a link to St
Lawrence as suggested by Willis would have allowed a station to be closed. Plans
for a link from the LCDR at St Peter's, Broadstairs to the SER at St Lawrence,
Ramsgate, were included in the Bill of 1898-9.

The Medway towns had seen a costly attempt by the South Eastern to infil-
trate Chatham territory. One legacy of this, the omnibus service from Chatham
Central to New Brompton, had been withdrawn by July 1899. From 1 January
1899 the new SECR showed its existence in the Medway towns by introducing a
stopping service between Charing Cross and New Brompton. This new arrangement would clearly put pressure on the limited facilities at the latter, so on 15
March 1899 the SECR decided to buy 2.25 acres of land there for stock facilities.

The Medway towns rearrangement also increased traffic at the ex-LCDR
Chatham station, where extra offices were needed because of this in late 1904. The
survival of Chatham Central was an anomaly by this time, and in June 1903 the
SECR had begun an investigation as to how to get rid of it. The two problems,
though, were that closure of the line would put extra pressure on the LCDR route
and the two ex-SER stations on the branch could only be closed with the authority
of Rochester Corporation.

The whole scheme was estimated in July 1905 as likely to cost £100,000 as
a proper connection between the systems would be needed instead of the "Toomer
loop" and two extra lines would have to be provided through the ex-LCDR Rochester
station. To secure the support of Rochester, the station at Rochester Bridge would
have to be rebuilt and there were road and bridge widenings proposed for Rochester
High Street and Gas House Road.

Rochester City Council guarded its interests very carefully throughout this
period and was especially anxious that Rochester Bridge station - the LCDR's
equivalent of Strood - should remain open. In February 1906 the SECR had to
concede to the rebuilding of it, therefore, and an imposing building was finished in
1908. Similar pressure was brought by Gillingham Borough Council, which threatened to oppose the SECR Bill in March 1907 unless improvements were made -
they wanted covered ways, a new booking office on the up side, waiting rooms and
the station name changed from New Brompton & Gillingham to Gillingham.

By January 1906 the SECR had secured the agreement of Rochester Corpo-

The Managing Committee favoured closing Rochester Bridge station, but political pressure led to an impressive rebuilding after destruction by fire. The 1908 buildings are seen here in 1933, long after the station had closed - supposedly as a wartime economy - in 1917. (L T Catchpole)

ration to close the Toomer Loop and part of the Chatham Central branch, but within a few months there was something of a ratepayers' revolt in the city. Local people wanted extra footbridges, the opening of the gates across Blue Boar Lane which were often blocked by shunting trains, and lower passenger fares.

The Blue Boar Lane issue reflected the concern of Rochester people that the expanding Chatham goods depot was blocking access to the wharves. In May 1909 the SECR agreed to spend £1340 on a new iron footbridge across the sidings and the following month had reached a decision on a programme of works to satisfy Rochester and allow closure of the Chatham Central branch.

The scheme included a partial rebuilding of Rochester Bridge station (£7500), the new footbridge which was 218ft long, filling in of Blue Boar Creek (£1460), raising the headway of the Five Bells roadbridge in Rochester High Street (£10,670), reconstruction of "Rochester Banks" station (£20,540) and widening of the ex-LCDR route through it to four tracks (£37,310), providing a new connection instead of the Toomer loop and strengthening the Medway bridge of the LCDR (£25,710), and demolition of timber viaducts and two stations on the ex-SER branch (£2200).

This was a major project and shows the costs that the SECR had to bear in order to enforce the economies of working that the working union was meant to make possible. The Five Bells bridge was reported by *The Times* as having already been "recently widened" by ten feet and the rails raised, but was now to be given an extra six inches headway, while the Furnell's Wharf bridge was also to be raised.

The rebuilt Rochester station was to have two island platforms of 600ft each.

The Chatham Central branch and its two stations was closed on 1 October 1911, after less than twenty years service. The new lines through Rochester and the new junctions were opened on 28 January 1912 together with the new Chatham goods depot, marking also the closure of the Toomer loop.

One weakness of the new arrangement was that all the trains from Victoria continued to run over the LCDR bridge, the older and weaker of the two, as the lines connected east of the Medway. In June 1915 the SECR considered putting in a new connection west of the Medway, so that all trains could use the ex-SER bridge, but this would have cost £50,000. However, on 29 June 1919 the ex-SER

The Chatham Central branch closed in 1911 and the timber parts of its viaduct were demolished rapidly as they made access to the Rochester waterfront - and Chatham goods depot - difficult. In this view, Rochester Common is being obliterated. (E Course collection)

bridge caught fire, probably due to sparks from a river boat igniting the timber decking. It burnt for eighteen hours and Port of London Authority fireboats had to be used. Because of this the old "Toomer loop" had to be restored so that trains from Strood could once more gain access to the ex-LCDR main-line on the west side of the Medway. The bridge was renovated at a cost of £19,000 in 1920-21 and reopened on 8 January 1922. There was a less well-known fire on the LCDR bridge on 27 August 1919, which encouraged the SECR to consider fitting both bridges with a sprinkler system.

At Whitstable the SER's Canterbury & Whitstable line passed over the LCDR's Kent Coast route with no joint station. Plans for a west to south spur to join the systems were included in the first Bill, land was bought by the SER in 1899 and in 1901 a signalbox was actually built to control the junction which in

May 1901 was expected to cost £5000. The signalbox must have remained strangely useless until 1907, when the signalling on the Harbour line was reorganised and the box brought into use to reduce blockage by shunting of Tankerton Road. In 1908 the cost of the link was estimated at £12,000 - a paltry sum - but, despite this, was deferred.

The Whitstable connection was never built, for in March 1909 the SECR decided instead to rebuild its station on the LCDR line closer to where the lines crossed, and provide a new halt at Rayham Crossing (for a minimal £210!) on the Harbour line with a road link between the two. A new halt was opened further south at South Street Halt on 1 June 1911, but the overall plan stalled in November 1911 as the General Manager argued against rebuilding the main station further east. He suggested improving the old station with wider platforms and a new roof, but this made Whitstable Council most irate. Another policy change then occurred, so that by July 1912 Whitstable was confident that it would get a new station and that it would be connected by covered way to Tankerton Halt - costing £28,500. Tankerton Halt, on the Canterbury line, opened on 1 July 1914.

The new station opened as Whitstable & Tankerton on 1 January 1915, Whitstable Town closing the same day. Parts of the old station were left standing to be rented out.

At Gravesend the two systems crossed each other and the 1900 Act included a scheme, called "railway number four", to link the two together. This was not pursued with any alacrity, the survey not being started until at least October 1903. Powers to make the connection expired in August 1904 and in July 1905 the SECR decided not to do the work.

The knitting together of the two systems was thus still very much unfinished business by the start of the 1920s. Though the Chislehurst loops were a major improvement, connections at Gravesend, Margate and Ramsgate had not been completed and the link at Canterbury was really due to pressure of wartime traffic and was open only briefly from 1918 to 1920. The Railways Act of 1921 provided that both companies would become part of the new Southern Railway group, although the Act curiously named the SER, LCDR and SECR individually. This allowed a scheme to fully amalgamate the SER and LCDR first, creating a new SECR Company with a combined value of £59,281,158 - of which the LCDR was valued at 42.5%. The scheme envisaged that the new SECR would be formed on 1 January 1923, as delays were anticipated in creating the Southern Railway. The SER also had to swallow up in preliminary amalgamations the Victoria Station & Pimlico Railway, the London & Greenwich, and the Mid-Kent (Bromley-St Mary Cray), but the actual union of the SER and LCDR was not brought to a conclusion.

On 1 January 1923 the SECR Managing Committee became the SR (SE & C) Committee, continuing to meet until July 1923 due to delays in setting up the management of the new united company.

Chapter Three:

Main Line & Country

Outside of the London area, the SECR system comprised an interesting mixture of busy main-lines, pastoral secondary routes like that through Rye, and country branches often of a surprisingly remote nature - of which the Hundred of Hoo line was the classic example. During the era of the SECR, parts of this system hardly evolved at all, but there were some significant changes though they were not always glamorous enough to attract the praise of jaundiced newspaper editors. The reconstruction of many bridges on the main lines went on throughout the period but even in 1923 the weight limit per axle on the ex-LCDR line remained at 17.5tons - a problematic inheritance that the SECR never really conquered.

The most glamorous trains on the SECR were the Continental expresses, but their relative short-hauls meant that they were less celebrated than the expresses of the northern railways. Here a "D" class 4-4-0 approaches Dover at Shakespeare Cliff.

The Kingsferry Bridge and Sheerness

The first railway bridge across the Swale linking Sittingbourne with Sheerness was constructed by the LCDR with a movable central span due to the influence of the Admiralty. This was an annoyance to the railway for operational reasons, but also because several staff were required to control and signal it. By 1899 the bridge was showing its age and had to be closed from 2 February until 11 February, following which the SECR began to discuss its replacement with the Admiralty.

The old bridge was reopened to rail traffic as a "fixed" bridge with strengthened shore spans, causing some complaints from the Admiralty in November 1899. However, a month later the SECR felt confident that the Admiralty would not force the restitution of a movable span. In fact the Admiralty made little use of the Swale at this time, though merchant boats and barges did; by 1900 the SECR was facing possible legal action from the Conservators of Milton Creek, who rightfully insisted that the SECR was legally obliged to maintain an opening span. The railway companies decided to face this challenge headlong, by applying for Parliamentary powers for a fixed bridge.

This ruse ran into a double problem. By April 1901 it had become clear that the Admiralty would not allow a fixed bridge to be built, and a few days later the SECR learnt that the Milton Creek Conservators would take legal action if an opening bridge was not restored within a fortnight. The SECR again responded with an aggressive move - deciding to "open" the bridge, close the rail link, and serve Sheerness by ferry from Port Victoria. No doubt this move was intended to divide local opinion. The SECR was also irritated by the Conservators' attitude that vessels should not have to lower their masts if the bridge could be opened - the SECR saw the issue in quite the opposite fashion! However it had no legal defence and in September 1901 was forced to pay £14 compensation for delaying the ketch *Laura*.

At this point the SECR found a strong bargaining point. In May 1900 Sheerness Urban District Council had approached it with a request to extend the railway near the Dockyard to a proposed new wharf and also into the Royal Dockyard itself. On 11 July 1900 the SECR agreed to prepare a Light Railway Order application to extend across a road to the Dockyard gates. The importance the Admiralty attached to its Sheerness Dockyard meant that a secure rail service was needed, and Vincent Hill tried to exploit this when he wrote to the Admiralty on 30 July 1901. Hill pointed out that the bridge was "broken down" but that the Conservators' action meant it needed to be fixed in an "open" position, "cutting off Sheerness and the Isle of Sheppey from any connection with the mainland, except by water." By September the Admiralty had conceded that the bridge should be allowed to be "closed", and strongly rejected the Conservators' idea that the bridge should normally be open to river traffic rather than rail. As a result of this concession the SECR agreed to the Dockyard extension, which cost £6843 and opened in 1902.

The start of 1902 saw a SECR Bill in progress to permit a fixed bridge, and an action by the Attorney General to enforce the opening of the old bridge. The Milton Creek Conservators maintianed their opposition and it was clear by June that the Bill was in trouble; Sir Benjamin Baker was asked to get information from America about reinstalling an opening bridge and the Bill was dropped. In return, injunctions on the SECR were suspended for fifteen months to allow proper repairs. By October 1902 Baker had begun trial drilling for a new bridge and agreement had been reached with the Scherzer Rolling Lift Company of Chicago to design a new bridge: the SECR had lost.

Sir William Arrol was contracted to start work on widening and lengthening the piers, which was done on a "costs plus" basis due to the risky nature of the work. However the Conservators then insisted on restricting the amount of staging that could be erected for the workmen, slowing progress and ensuring that the new bridge could not be completed within the 15 months. By January 1904 an extension to August had been negotiated, but only on the condition that the SECR provided a tug to help boats through; the SECR tried to restrict this to only providing a tug "if compelled".

By July it was clear that the bridge would not be fully ready in time, but it was decided to operate it by hand power from September. The new span was lowered into place on 6 November and the bridge reopened that day, a temporary ferry service being provided, but the rolling lift operated only by hand.

The new span did not affect facilities for road traffic, which paid a toll at a toll-house in the middle. This soon gave rise to more trouble, for by June 1907 Kent County Council and Sheerness UDC were campaigning for the abolition of the tolls. They were also angry that the heaviest vehicles that could be taken were five tons, wanting the load increased to allow 15 ton traction engines which the SECR estimated to cost £2225. The road tolls yielded about £380 a year.

Typically in matters to do with the Kingsferry Bridge, tempers soon rose. The SECR had long been uncertain about the safety of the bridge for heavy traction engines and so had allowed them to use the bridge for free so as not to be liable in the event of an accident. Now it had banned all traffic over five tons, so Mr Elgar of the Wingham Agricultural Implement Company "thought they had better force the matter by running their locos over the bridge whenever they wished and see what happened." It is not clear how many drivers volunteered for this task, but the SECR had to consider an injunction.

In March 1908 the SECR supported a suggestion that the local authorities should pay it £1000 to abandon the tolls, and also pay for strengthening the bridge. This did not win support with Kent CC, so the SECR tried to negotiate on the basis that KCC might adopt the approach roads and so save it £143 per year. By October this scheme had met with the Council's agreement, the approach roads to be maintained by the Council for ten years.

The Bill for 1909 included powers for a new carriage road to the bridge which the Council would maintain, with the road part of the bridge being strengthened. The new road facilities were completed by 1 June 1910.

Construction of Ridham Dock began in 1913 and this meant an increase in the river traffic especially during wartime, causing delays to trains and road vehicles. Extra timber fenders and "dolphins" were provided to protect the bridge from the larger than usual vessels negotiating the Swale. In November 1917 Kent CC suggested rebuilding the Kingsferry bridge further east, which the SECR agreed to - on the condition that the County pay. However there were some problems opening the bridge at this time, and further work on it had to be done in January 1918.

After the War it was decided to remove the extra timber defences in 1921. This was inviting disaster, of course, which duly happened on 17 December 1922 when the steamer *Gyp* from Preston hit the main pier of the bridge, closing it completely for both road and rail traffic. From 27 December a temporary service to Sheerness was re-established via Port Victoria, though some local passengers could use a motor boat via Sittingbourne and temporary halts either side of the bridge. The Southern Railway thus received the Kingsferry bridge into its keeping as a liability and a worry, being unable to reopen it until November 1923.

The temporary service made use of the new halt which was then being constructed for Ridham Dock, for which an agreement with the developers had been reached in August 1922. However a service had been operated to a temporary halt for the workers who actually built the Dock; this was in use in December 1913, with men being charged 4d for the return trip from Sittingbourne. A halt on the northern side, known as King's Ferry Bridge North Halt, remained in service only until 1 November 1923.

A more useful improvement was made at Sheerness in the last days of the SECR. On 2 January 1922 a new loop was opened, costing less than £9000, that provided a direct route to Sheerness-on-Sea, so that trains did not need to reverse at Sheerness Dockyard - the original station, which closed the same day. One of the conditions of this improvement was that the SECR had to turf over the old Drill Ground.

Improved Stations

When the Managing Committee began its operations, the SER was already contemplating major changes to Tonbridge and Ashford stations. In April 1899 plans for Tonbridge were estimated at £40,000, but this had risen to £67,000 five months later. Ashford was to be improved on a site closer to London with six through roads, allowing for traffic from the Maidstone line, new subways and lifts - the works alone were expected to cost nearly £88,000, with the old LCDR station being converted to goods use. Extra land to rebuild the station on a more westerly site would have added a further £60,000 to this. Work was also proceeding at Paddock Wood, where extensive new sidings and a footbridge were being added.

The cost of the Ashford scheme impeded its progress, so that in January 1907 the SECR vowed once more to start work on the rebuilding having bought some land from Ashford cattle market in the previous few months. There was a clear operational need to alter the station layout to improve working of Maidstone trains without impeding the main line. The cost of property was a major problem with these schemes - in Tonbridge in 1911 the SECR had to buy land in Hectorage Road to rehouse the working classes without the landowner knowing the identity of the purchaser. The SECR also considered a new route to avoid the slow curves at Tonbridge altogether, with a start "soon" predicted by the press in March 1914 - not a good time for major improvements. Neither of these ambitious plans were brought to fruition, though there was some track remodelling and resignalling at Ashford in 1907-8.

Both the Maidstone stations received rather more efficient improvements. Alterations to both were already ongoing when the SECR was formed in order to accommodate extra traffic for the Agricultural Show, held there in 1899. £30,000 was spent on Maidstone West, including a new "back" platform, extensions to the up platform, and resignalling.

Another station much affected by the alteration of services was New

Brompton, which replaced Chatham Central as the terminal station for local services via Gravesend. The area, better known as Gillingham, was the most rapidly expanding part of the Medway towns in 1900 so that in March of that year the SECR was buying land for new goods sidings. There were also requests in October 1900 to serve part of Gillingham and Chatham with a new station at Luton Arch, at the foot of Chatham Hill, but the SECR thought a light railway or tramway along the Luton valley was more appropriate. In 1905 Sir Douglas Fox suggested that the 1897 scheme for a high level loop line through Chatham be revived, but this would have been hugely costly.

Plans to expand at Gillingham ran into legal problems when it was discovered that the LCDR did not own the mineral rights of the land there, but by August 1901 the SECR was committed to buying extra land in order to improve the passenger station. Significant rebuilding work had begun by April 1907, starting with the approach roads and then excavating for the station and sidings; excavated material from New Brompton was being tipped at Rochester for the widenings there. In May 1911 it was decided to renew the waiting rooms, signalboxes and install a new turntable, but there was typically not a complete reconstruction.

The Borough of Gillingham had been created in 1903, and it was somewhat irksome to this corporation not to have its identity prominently recognised in the name of the local station. In July 1912 the SECR agreed to a request to rename New Brompton & Gillingham station, altering it to plain "Gillingham" from 1 October.

On 14 January 1914 the SECR decided to make Gillingham the terminus for many North Kent services, thus requiring a new carriage depot costing £20,000.

All this rebuilding at Gillingham should have left the ex-LCDR main-line with four major stations within three miles, but the SECR was keen to rid itself of Rochester Bridge - a station built by the LCDR to compete for Strood and Rochester traffic. On the night of 1 March 1901 the station was damaged by "a disastrous fire" and had to be closed, the SECR being reluctant to reopen it despite being able to claim insurance of £5000. The City of Rochester pressed for rebuilding but it was not until April 1902 that the SECR decided to provide temporary stairs to both platforms and a wooden booking office; this was only because 1900 figures showed that the station produced an excess of receipts over expenses of £2832. The contract for a proper renewal was let in May 1907 and it was rebuilt on a grand scale over the next year, but closed as a convenient economy during the War.

At the end of the War, Rochester Bridge did not reopen, and requests from Rochester Corporation were rebuffed in May 1919. However the fire on the bridge over the Medway on 29 June 1919 meant that Rochester Bridge station returned to brief life, for *The Times* reported that "passengers from Chatham to London via the South Eastern have to alight at Rochester Bridge station and walk to Strood, and vice versa with travellers from London;" this arrangement lasted until Toomer's Loop was reactivated, then Rochester Bridge station closed for good.

On 11 July 1900 Fawkham station, on the ex-LCDR main-line, caught fire and all the down side buildings were badly damaged. The SECR had to reimburse the Horton Kirby fire brigade £9-18-6d for their services. The buildings cost £3200

The improved station at Rochester Bridge was one of Arthur Blomfield's solid designs, but although rebuilt in 1908 it closed in 1917. Here it is shown, bereft of track, in 1933 following alterations to the lines across the Medway. (L T Catchpole)

to replace.

Hythe station caused rather a different problem - it had a tendency to sink. This had been a problem in 1891 and the station showed renewed downward mobility in 1900.

Merstham station, north of Redhill, was in a tired state by January 1905. At first the SECR planned to spend £14,000 on major improvements to passenger and goods facilities, but then limited the budget to half this. Deal was improved in 1906 ready for the Great Western Railway through service, with extra sidings and standpipes for carriages, a rebuilt signalbox and extra signalling. The same year Hastings platforms were improved so that it could handle London and Ashford trains simultaneously. The platforms at Wellington College, built partially out of old sleepers, were improved in 1907.

In 1909 Higham was reported as being a poor station, "for a long time past the station buildings have been in a very dilapidated and insanitary condition." In fact the station building was the old canal toll-house that had been taken over for railway use, and this was to be replaced with a new building "of the plainest description." In June 1909 Penshurst, also "very dilapidated", had improvements authorised.

At Tunbridge Wells the road bridge beside the station had been widened in 1907 but this was also a prestigious station so in June 1910 the SECR decided to rebuild it on the down side to commercial advantage, by including six new shops facing into Mount Pleasant. It was estimated these ought to earn a 5% return on their cost of £12,500. Also included was a new turret to hold the clock, which had been paid for by public subscription. By December the SECR had arranged lettings of two units to an automobile dealer and one to an antiques shop, but the arrange-

The improvement to Tunbridge Wells was an early example of a railway station being rebuilt with an eye to commercial development. The new buildings were on the down side, but given the street pattern of the town were much more conveniently located than the up side buildings. This view also shows part of the widened road bridge, for which the Council was largely responsible. (D Cullum)

ments fell through due to slow completion of the work. In fact the tender was not let until August 1911, and the next letting to be arranged was to a dentist in July 1913. Work at the station included a ticket hall, electric luggage lift and offices, continuing until 1914.

Some stations also lacked basic safety features. A passenger was run over and killed at Wateringbury while crossing the line on 27 October 1909, the inquest Jury recommending a footbridge should be provided.

An unusual scheme affected Edenbridge, when in August 1922 the SECR agreed to rent out a strip of land 190ft long and 10ft wide for £7 a year; the tenant was the Air Ministry, who wanted to display an "Edenbridge" sign in large white letters. The name was angled for the benefit of London to Paris pilots, who flew along the SE main line, and names may have been painted on station roofs at earlier dates.

New Stations

In November 1899 the SECR learnt that the British Uralite Company was to buy land at Shorne to establish a new building materials factory, close to Hoo Junction. On 14 November 1900 the SECR decided to spend £160 erecting a wooden platform for Uralite use, suggesting the possibility that a private works "station" existed here prior to the public halt being opened in 1906.

Another new station was required on the Hastings main-line when the branch to Bexhill was being developed. In December 1899 the SECR decided to spend £15,000 on a junction station at Crowhurst although this did not open until 1 June

1902.

The most extensive programme of "new stations" was linked to the introduction of the Kitson railmotors, ordered in January 1906 to develop traffic on lightly-used branches. The lines identified for these were the Sheppey Light, Westerham, Hayes, Port Victoria and Dungeness branches as well as the Otford to Sevenoaks service. In March 1906 the SECR agreed to invest a minimalist £50 in a new halt at Chevening (opened 16 April 1906); there were also to be six halts between Gravesend and Port Victoria, at Milton Road, Denton Crossing, High Halstow, Beluncle, Stoke Crossing and Grain Crossing - costing a total of £338. The omission of Uralite Halt from this list would tend to confirm its prior existence as a private halt. All the halts opened to the public in July 1906. Also not mentioned was Milton Range Halt, which gave access to the firing range on the marshes; this was a simple wooden platform positioned between the running lines and track access was guarded by stiles not gates. In February 1914 the SECR decided to build two separate platforms, and slew the tracks, at a cost of £837.

The SECR was sufficiently encouraged to try the same scheme on the Ashford to Hastings line, deciding in April 1907 to spend £295 on halts at Three Oaks Bridge, Guestling and Snailham. The actual result was Snailham, Doleham and Three Oaks & Guestling Halts (1 July 1907).

1908 saw a further rush of activity. Blean & Tyler Hill was opened on the Canterbury & Whitstable line (£115), the gateman being instructed to issue tickets and use his "lodge" as a booking office; Cheriton Halt (£270) was served by Elham Valley trains after its opening on 1 May. In February 1908 the SECR also considered halts at Cliffsend and Ebbsfleet near Ramsgate, as well as reopening the old halt at Folkestone Warren which could be served by the Elham Valley trains and the Dover to Sandgate railmotor. Ebbsfleet & Cliffsend Halt opened on 1 May 1908 to serve a nearby new golf course and Warren Halt probably on the same day. Swanscombe Halt opened on 2 November 1908 which, with nearby Stone Crossing Halt (opened 11 October 1905) justified some railmotors between Dartford and Gravesend. However 1909 ideas for a halt at Graveney were rejected - though it is hard to imagine what Beluncle had that Graveney did not! A golf club also persuaded the SECR to open South Street Halt near Whitstable on 1 June 1911.

Attention then shifted to the western side of SECR territory, when in May 1909 it was decided to build a new halt for Sandhurst to be served by trains between Reading and Ash. This was opened soon afterwards, bringing trains back to a settlement that had lost them in 1852! In November 1909 the people of Hurst and Sindlesham, between Wokingham and Reading, requested a halt which opened as Sindlesham & Hurst on 1 January 1910 - changing to Winnersh in 1930; it was provided with platform shelters at a mere £12 each.

Another lightly used line in need of local traffic was between Tonbridge and Redhill. In May 1911 the SECR decided to open a halt at Leigh (spelt as "Lyghe") and this entered the public domain on 1 September 1911, but a halt at Bough Beech was rejected. A halt was opened at East Malling after a decision in October 1912; this would suggest that the halt would have been ready in the early part of 1913. Traffic there was showing "a very satisfactory increase" by 1921.

A report in *The Times* on 29 September 1913 that the SECR had decided to "make an extension of their line in order to open a new station at the Cliftonville end of Margate" is supported by a comment in the *Railway Magazine* of June 1913 that a Cliftonville station was "under construction". Possibly there was a suggestion of opening a new halt to secure local traffic.

The Way and the Works

It has been noted above that major bridge reconstruction was a feature of the SECR. In February 1901 there were 1,958 bridges on the system of which 158 were rail overbridges of cast iron - no longer permitted by the Board of Trade. To replace these would cost £150,000 and would include the swing bridges near Minster and Rye. This did not only affect main lines, for in 1901 the bridge over Janes' Creek on the Strood to Maidstone West line was rebuilt for heavier trains. By 1902 bridges in the Ramsgate area and on the Hastings line were being strengthened. By 1906 the programme on the ex-LCDR line was progressing, with renewal work between Selling and Newington and at Camberwell.

Another bridge requiring replacement was over the Rother at Rye, originally built as a single-track swing span to allow navigation. This needed replacing by 1902 and a double-track fixed bridge was decided upon, though the SECR selected an iron rather than steel structure due to its proximity to the sea. The new bridge was finished in 1903 and the nearby bridge over the Royal Military Canal was done at about the same time.

After the War the SECR returned to its programme of bridge improvements on the ex-LCDR routes, estimating a bill of £275,000 which would have been only £93,000 before wartime inflation. In 1922 it also decided to renew the old swing

A SECR country station: Blackwater on the Reading branch. Even small stations like this employed up to a dozen men. (Wakeman Collection, Ashford Library)

bridge over the Stour between Minster and Sandwich; there was a serious defect on the old cast iron bridge, but plans to replace it had been dropped in 1901 as there had been opposition to a fixed span. This opposition had now faded away.

Bridges were not always replaced for railway purposes. In 1901 the Borough of Reigate made major changes to five bridges across its main roads, costing over £30,000 to which the SECR contributed £10,280. Similarly, in March 1903 the SECR agreed to rebuild Tunbridge Wells High Street bridge in conjunction with the local authority - at a cost of over £15,000 with the Council paying two-thirds.

The tunnels on the Hastings line had caused problems for the SER that were becoming increasingly vexatious by the turn of the century. Clearances at Bo-Peep Tunnel were limited, and in August 1877 the guard on a LBSCR train had been killed by the projecting "observatory" on a passing brake van. Since then no trains had been allowed to pass in the tunnel, causing major delays in summer especially. The tunnel had been relined but by September 1900 was reported as being "out of line" and in need of relining again.

In January 1905 the Board of Trade said that it would not object to resumed "two line working" in Bo-Peep Tunnel if bars were placed across carriage windows and notices displayed in guards' rooms. Double line working resumed on 1 June 1906 but without window bars or notices as the lines had been further slewed to improve clearances.

There were some similar problems with the nearby Ore Tunnel; in November 1909 a passenger was killed in this tunnel while leaning out, and the Jury at the inquest called for window bars to be fitted.

The SECR also had problems with other people's tunnels. Lord Darnley had forced the SER to grant powers for him to tunnel beneath the canal at Higham - the canal was the Railway's property. He had never exercised these powers, but in May 1906 decided that he would like to tunnel beneath it at Denton instead. A similar case then arose with APCM, the cement company, near Gravesend; during 1909 the SECR fought a furious legal battle to stop them tunnelling beneath the North Kent line, but lost the court case and the subsequent appeal. Tunnelling beneath the line was not unusual - APCM eventually had nine such tunnels.

Another cause of congestion was the level crossings on the Dover waterfront such as Hawkesbury Street; in November 1900 the SECR decided to seek powers to close them and divert the streets. By December 1902 this policy had evolved into a decision to try and replace all the level crossings with a new road bridge. Some level crossings were replaced elsewhere - in 1904 four crossings between Teynham and Sittingbourne were replaced with two bridges.

However it was Dover Corporation that really pressed with a major new viaduct to cross all the lines in the area and give better road access to the harbour. In May 1906 this was estimated to cost £106,000 - the Council hoped that the SECR would contribute £41,000. The Corporation obtained Parliamentary powers for the viaduct in 1906; the SECR agreed to pay the interest on the capital sum, amounting to £1700 per year, and the Dover Harbour Board contributed £25,000. However, closure of the crossings would save the SECR £733 a year for watchmen at Council House Street and Great Street.

Work on the viaduct began towards the end of 1913. Altogether the SECR paid over £40,000 to Dover Corporation, but then the War broke out and work on the viaduct was suspended by order of the Ministry of Munitions with the SECR unable to close the crossings. A compromise was reached, so the Corporation allowed the SECR to close the crossings to traffic in 1917 although pedestrians could use the wicket gates. In January 1920 the Minstry of Health, which was involved as it regulated local government, ordered that the viaduct must be completed by June 1920 although all parties were keen to drop the original plan for a tramway along it.

Occupational crossings were also a nuisance and a danger. A crossing between Rainham and Otterham Quay Lane had been provided in 1856, but by 1920 had been unused for fourteen years; the SECR decided to close it quickly before anyone began to use it again, and paid the landowner £100 to extinguish his rights.

The Dover-Folkestone Landslips

There were many difficulties with the stability of the ground through which the railway passed so spectacularly between the two Kent Channel ports. Problems at Folkestone Warren in June 1905 were such that the SECR considered buying a portable narrow-gauge railway to help with repairs and in February 1906 there was a major slip at the Dover end of Shakespeare Cliff Tunnel, involving 45,000 cubic yards of rock. During 1908 large quantities of shingle were being brought from Dungeness to protect the sea wall at Folkestone Warren, work there continuing until 1911.

In 1896 a retaining wall had been built to protect Abbotscliff and Martello tunnels from the sea, but by 1912 the Abbotscliff portion was in need of further

The famous landslip at Folkestone Warren in December 1915. Fortunately for Britain, it occurred on a section of track that was not vital to the war effort. (R W Kidner collection)

work.

The most famous slip occurred on 19 December 1915, between Abbotscliff and Martello tunnels. Three men of the Lancashire Regiment were on guard duty and showed decisive conduct in warning the driver of the 6.10pm Ashford to Dover passenger train; the sergeant was rewarded with £5 and the two privates with £2, but another man in the "Devon Cyclists" took a long time to trace. One and half miles of line were described as "completely wrecked", and the passenger train marooned though its passengers were escorted safely back to Folkestone. Warren Halt was dislocated severely.

Suggestions that the slip was a national disaster were always erroneous. At the time, SECR sources accepted that traffic between Folkestone and Dover was "extremely light" since Dover was a closed port, and the operational problems were dealt with by installing a 65ft turntable at Folkestone. Two months after the slip, Sir Francis Dent told Folkestone Town Council that the line could not be reopened, "the Government being opposed to the expenditure of either money or labour for the purpose." He also said that a new connection at Canterbury could not be constructed.

The slip added 1,200 light engine miles per week to the SECR's costs, but the real concern was what to do in the long term. In May 1916 the SECR thought the restoration of the line would cost £289,000 and might involve an inland deviation, but Government compensation awarded in July was only £136,500; this was set aside for later use, Bonsor telling the SECR general meeting that the terms were "exceedingly good.".

Meanwhile the engineers were considering what could be done. One suggestion was to re-establish a single line through the Warren to Shakespeare Intermediate signalbox, with a speed limit of 25mph. This would have needed a new signalbox at the east end of Martello Tunnel, and the trimming of the cliff - costing about £17,500 in all. The SECR decided only to pursue this option if the Army or Navy ordered it, which they did not.

By June 1918 there was mounting public pressure to reopen the link. The SECR engineer said that there had been no further movement at the site so that a light railway connection could be installed, which would have cost £30,000 and taken three months. However, the Admiralty then declared its wish to use Abbotscliff Tunnel "for a national purpose" - actually the storage of explosive materials - and the matter was left in abeyance with an inland deviation under consideration again.

On 13 November 1918, two days after the Armistice, the SECR again considered its options; however it still could not get Admiralty agreement for a single line to be installed. However, in January 1919 the SECR was at last able to proceed and agreed with the contractor William Rigby to do the work on a "costs plus 10%" basis. There were three suggested schemes:

(1) A single track of 3 miles from the east end of Martello Tunnel to Shakespeare Intermediate signalbox, with a new signalbox at the west end of Martello Tunnel: £29,500.

(2) A single track of one mile from Martello Tunnel to the site of Abbotscliff Intermediate box, and rebuild the box: £36,750.

(3) Restore double track throughout Abbotscliff and a new signalbox at Martello in case of further problems: £45,750.

The Government paid the SECR £310,288 for the repair work and compensation, scheme three was chosen and the line was able to reopen on 11 August 1919, but there was another slip at Warren cutting within the next year. Rigby had to do further work at the Warren to protect the beach from being denuded.

A number of other places were regular scenes of landslips. There had to be occasional single-line working between Herne Bay and Birchington due to slips near the former, so in February 1910 it was decided to install a new crossover near Eddington, about a mile from Herne Bay, and move the "Intermediate" signalbox there. There were a number of slips between Weald Siding and Sevenoaks Tunnel, as well as at Hildenborough nearby.

Chapter Four:

London and Suburban

The SECR took over a dense and complex system of railways running right into the heart of London, with numerous central stations but also with huge problems - the cost of improving its London facilities was a significant burden to the SECR. During this time the managing committee faced the steady loss of its inner suburban passenger traffic, though some voices argued that this was good as it created space for more profitable outer suburban and long distance trade. There was also a reorganisation of London goods traffic following the development of Hither Green, which also freed some capacity.

SECR changes in the London were hastened by public criticism. The foggy morning of 6 January 1900 brought chaos, with a collision at Charing Cross at about 7.20am and another at 7.30am near Spa Road, when a Reading goods train was shunted across the lines causing an accident which blocked all tracks into London Bridge and caused a queue of 1,000 passengers at Spa Road station alone. Over the next few weeks the press was full of letters of complaint and suggestions, of which an end to the "shunting in and out" of Cannon Street was the most common. One letter even suggested the abandonment of Cannon Street altogether. However, although the SECR took steps to improve line capacity it was to be several more years before the archaic practice of working in and out of Cannon Street was dropped.

However, the complexity and scale of the SECR's London network was one factor in its reluctance to embrace electrification as a solution to the problem of how to handle dense suburban traffic; in the event, tram and tube competition took away many of the short distance passengers and inner London stations closed as wartime economies never reopened. Motor buses were a significant competition for inner London traffic after about 1910.

The South Eastern System

At the formation of the SECR, the South Eastern was already working on an expensive plan to improve its system from London Bridge station out as far as Chislehurst, parts of which had been authorised in 1892. This included a cherished scheme to end the use of right-hand running between London Bridge and Charlton, which was achieved from 27 May 1901.

There was great congestion between London Bridge, Cannon Street and Charing Cross. Slow and costly progress was made in widening the lines west of London Bridge, it costing £27,000 just to widen Southwark Street bridge from three tracks to four in 1900-03 and the new down line between Belvedere Road and Metropolitan Junction was brought into use on 2 June 1901. Waterloo Junction, where an extra up platform was added in 1898, was rebuilt by January 1901 with substantial extra roofing and a footbridge to improve conditions for passengers

Charing Cross station and the impressive hotel frontage; it remains a part of the London scene despite repeated attempts during the SECR years to clear it away.

joining or leaving the London & South Western Railway; a covered way between the stations seems to have been finished in 1904. In October 1910 the SECR discussed the closure of the through line between the SECR and LSWR at Waterloo Junction, which the LSWR wished to close in order to ease the rebuilding of its own station. The SECR sold some of its Waterloo property to the LSWR for £18,998. The connecting line was last used in early March 1911 and severed at the LSWR end on 26 March.

The completion of the Southwark Street bridge in March 1903 finished the widenings between Charing Cross and London Bridge.

An extra down line was provided between Metropolitan Junction and Cannon Street in 1901-2, though the practice of reversing in and out of Cannon Street was falling out of favour but was still common until 31 December 1916. Track improvements did not totally impress Greenwich Council, who in October 1913 complained to the Board of Trade about the "crossover roads" being dangerous and slowing down services.

At Charing Cross the SECR decided to widen the bridge and station on the east side. However, in July 1901 the Managing Committee discussed a plan by London County Council to buy the station and bridge as part of an improvement scheme; according to *The Times* of 30 November 1899 the SER itself had contemplated abandoning the station "at times in the past." This delayed SECR work at Charing Cross although in April 1903 widening the bridge was estimated to cost £225,000 and improving the station £125,000; Barry and Tempest were reckoning on a total cost of £355,000 in January 1904 and planning to start on the east side. In July 1904 the LCC revived its own plans for Charing Cross, involving taking over the station, hotel and bridge. On 23 November the SECR discussed a letter from the LCC, proposing their purchase of the station and Hungerford Bridge, with a scheme to build a new station on the south bank; the LCC declared their opposition to the SECR rebuilding the Charing Cross station, but the Managing Committee retorted that they were not planning to do this. Plans for the station and bridge to be rebuilt on the east side were again discussed in October 1905, the LCC having dropped its plans in February of that year due largely to the cost of buying a new terminal site on the south bank. The collapse of the station roof on 5 December 1905 then forced a more immediate intervention, with both Charing Cross and Waterloo Junction having to close. By January 1906 the SECR had decided that Charing Cross should have a new roof of the "Euston type", but parts of the station buildings and signalbox also needed replacing. Because of this, train services recommenced as far as Waterloo Junction only from 1 January.

These closures prevented passengers from the London & South Western Railway changing at Waterloo for Charing Cross. Between 5 and 31 December travellers were allowed to use the Waterloo & City line instead, but only 4,138 single tickets were used in this way showing the lack of interest in this route. In contrast, season holders made an additional 478,733 journeys on the Metropolitan District line between Charing Cross and Cannon Street up to the reopening. Charing Cross reopened on 19 March 1906, to all services except Continentals and a few others which continued to be diverted to Cannon Street or Victoria; the Continentals returned to Charing Cross on 1 July 1906.

The collapse caused some dispute between the SER and the LCDR as the former had a financial interest in the Charing Cross Hotel, whose takings suffered especially from the transfer of the Continental services.

After all this, no progress had been made on the bridge apart from some minor strengthening work in 1906 and inner suburban traffic had fallen sufficiently by 1909 to make the SECR consider whether a widening was really necessary - though there was contrary pressure from growing Continental traffic. In 1911 a Mr G Middleton proposed a "high level road" to replace the railway between Charing Cross and Cannon Street with a new railway terminus near Guy's Hospital.

In February 1912 the SECR proposed a scheme to improve the facilities at Charing Cross. This included a central booking office, new waiting rooms and an underground ladies' toilet. Train indicators were added in 1913. Two extra baths were added to the ladies' dressing room in 1914.

By March 1915 the Hungerford Bridge situation was becoming critical, due to increasing weight of trains which meant that restrictions had to be imposed on the number of trains using it at any one time; it was estimated that the older eastern side needed to be replaced at a cost of £125,000. Powers to do the work had lapsed since the 1900 Act, and a fresh Bill was proposed - to come into effect after the end of the War. However SECR plans to strengthen the bridge with new brick piers and masonry blocks between the old columns provoked an outraged response, condemning the scheme as "unsightly"; opposition was led by Ernest Newton, President of the Royal Institute of British Architects, and another architect Aston Webb, who was Chairman of the London Society. The Bill came under attack in the House of Lords, where Viscount Chilston argued that the SECR could not be expected to build a new and attractive bridge "merely to meet the views of people with aesthetic tastes." He also argued that a new bridge would interefere more with river traffic.

Although the Bill had passed the Lords by 25 May 1916, opposition had not ended. Sir Lionel Earle, Secretary to the Office of Works, thought that the strengthening plans would make the bridge uglier. He supported the idea that the Charing Cross site should be used for a national war memorial, "a really beautiful bridge for ordinary traffic" built, and a large new station provided on the south bank "capable of handling Channel Tunnel traffic."

The Bill was lost by 42 votes (67 to 25) on its second reading in the House of Commons, though the majority of Kent MPs for once supported their railway. This was despite estimates of £1,000,000 for the LCC's bridge scheme, and Board of Trade support for the immediate strengthening of the SECR's. Public sentiment was against the SECR, especially when the war memorial idea was aired; "a fine bridge at this spot would almost be a small part of a European policy of peace, union and good will" one letter to *The Times* argued. Another writer believed that "in no centre of population on God's earth is there any spot comparable in beauty and accumulated history and sentiment..." G Swinton got even more excited when reviewing the development of the scheme: "though its genesis was architectural, it has now gone far beyond artistic conceptions, even than the convenience of the people of London, and has become a trumpet call to the spirit of the British race..." What chance did the humble SECR have against pan-European peace, accumulated history, beauty and the spirit of British national feeling?

It did have the Board of Trade on its side, which granted a one year extension to the SECR's powers for widening the bridge. In the light of this, the SECR gave its engineer authority to start strengthening the old bridge at an estimated cost of £170,000 - starting on 30 October 1916. To do this, he needed possession of four lines (there were six altogether) from 12.30am each night until 8.30am the next morning, and to allow for this the workmen's services were reduced. By December 1916 travellers were starting to argue that the war memorial scheme would force them to walk an extra half mile across a windy bridge, while others argued as to who would be responsible if the old bridge collapsed in the meantime - the House of Commons? It was noted that 18 million people crossed it every year. Bonsor defended the SECR by arguing that it had to exist in the real world, unlike the opponents who were "people absorbed in aesthetic and artistic ideas," among whom he included the LCC's Improvements Committee.

At the end of 1916 the SECR re-submitted a Bill to permit a time extension on its bridge works, further legislation being needed as the Wandsworth Gas Company - who used the river - had objected. Bonsor observed that the SECR had rebuilt 398 bridges since 1900 including 127 on the SER route to Dover, leaving only Hungerford Bridge to be strengthened. He thought that the LCC schemes would cost £20,000,000, but the LCC continued to oppose the Bill.

In the House of Commons in March 1917 Sir W Essex referred to "the abomination already caused by the use of the bridge as a lay-by for locomotives." The MP for Stafford attacked the SER, saying that "for fifty years the railway had been a blight on Kent. It was ill-planned, equipped and managed. In the railway world it was a jest." The SECR wanted a Bill to allow the strengthening of the bridge, legislation being needed due to the opposition and the effect on the river, but agreed to a clause that would allow it to be compensated if the bridge was subsequently "taken over". With the Board of Trade again in favour, the Bill passed its readings in the Commons and the Lords. In the Lords Committee Percy Tempest explained that an average locomotive had weighed 52.5 tons in 1864, but was 97.5 tons in 1917; the Committee approved the Bill on condition that the SECR spent no more money on Charing Cross station - a novel imposition on the SECR which excited some hilarity. The Act was passed on 2 August 1917 though no work was done for three more years, by which time estimates of the cost for strengthening had risen to £390,000.

A fine picture of Cannon Street, one of the SECR's cramped and restricted London termini. (Wakeman Collection, Ashford Library)

Cannon Street station mainly relied on "business" traffic and in October 1900 the SECR considered closing it after 10pm as an economy, but concluded that the savings would be too little. The practice of working trains in and out of Cannon Street on their way to Charing Cross continued, though it was challenged by a radical scheme of 1901. This was for a Behr monorail to be installed above the SECR tracks, starting at London Bridge. From there it was to run on one side of the bridge over the Thames, sweep round Cannon Street station, and leave back across the river on the other side of the bridge, returning to London Bridge in a continuous loop with a service every two minutes. The cost was estimated at £100,000, but the scheme came to nothing. This would have allowed the SECR to cease using Cannon Street as "a wayside station". A letter in *The Times* in February 1901 complained that the detour in and out of Cannon Street meant that it was quicker for Charing Cross passengers to get a cab from London Bridge!

The Cannon Street bridge was reported as needing strengthening in 1907, especially at the "fan end", and by 1910 an £80,000 contract had been arranged - but then the firm went bankrupt. The work was eventually completed by 1913. Overall, though, the station was largely neglected throughout the SECR period; somehow the decision in April 1920 to move its wooden offices away from the buffers on roads nos. 5 and 6 seemed the maximum glamour it could expect. The War had been cruel to Cannon Street, seeing the end of regular Continental services from 15 November 1914, loss of the Charing Cross reversals, and increasingly severe restrictions on its opening hours. It was never again to be the equal of Charing Cross.

London Bridge had lost importance as a terminal station due to the SER's investment in Charing Cross and Cannon Street, but street arrangements in connection with the opening of Tower Bridge improved its role. The old "low level" station had been in use as a continental goods station, but the SER had decided to rebuild it with a new central and two side platforms, and a footbridge to improve access to the "high level" through station. This work cost about £38,000 and provided a terminus for Caterham, Redhill and North Kent trains, opening on 2 June 1902. The continental goods was moved to a new depot at Ewer Street, on the down side near Metropolitan Junction.

Outside London Bridge station there was a need here to rearrange the tracks of the Greenwich line, which limited the capacity of the route into London Bridge. The ambitious plan to add three extra tracks between London Bridge and North Kent East Junction was already in progress by 1899 but had run into problems due to the location of the Peek Frean biscuit factory close to the railway on its northern side, forcing consideration of a new high-level route to accomodate more tracks; the biscuit firm held out for exorbitant terms, forcing the SECR to include in its proposed Bill (October 1899) a loop line which Bonsor called "a circular widening" from London Bridge to Rotherhithe. In July 1900 it was suggested that the SECR add only two extra tracks, the remaining space being used to improve the safety of track workers.

During 1900 terms were eventually agreed with Peek Frean's - the SECR was to pay £178,500, showing the huge cost of urban improvements. For this money the SECR acquired a strip of land 1100ft long and 50ft wide. This allowed work on "reversing" the Greenwich lines to proceed and it was finished on 25 May 1901, Whit Sunday, with the new arrangement starting the next day. This enabled improvements to be made to Spa Road station in 1901-2 and the opening of a new station at Southwark Park on 1 October 1902. However the two stations suffered from tramway competition and from October 1904 both were supervised by the Spa Road stationmaster. Both stations closed as a wartime measure from 15 March 1915 - they never reopened although saw some staff use.

The widening of the Peek Frean's section was contracted to Messrs Firbank for £39,592, but did not start until at least April 1903 and eventually cost £68,416 including "signal bridges" at St James and Blue Anchor. On 5 January 1905 the third down line between London Bridge "C" signalbox and Southwark Park Junction was completed, with new platforms being opened at Spa Road and Southwark Park; this completed the widening scheme between London Bridge and New Cross. The scheme had resulted in two extra tracks from London Bridge to Spa Road and three beyond there.

East of London Bridge the widening railway passed through the densely populated parish of Bermondsey. The Rector of the parish, Henry Lewis, was not impressed by the fate of those "struggling poor" dispossessed by the railway scheme. He reported that "We see the South Eastern taking forcible possession of a considerable number of poor, struggling people's homes and turning the occupants out to find fresh abodes in an already crowded neighbourhood." New houses erected for them two to five miles away were uslesss for "casual" workers.

The SER defended itself, saying that no house had been removed until provision had been made for its residents. It had spent £80,000 on building seven blocks in Trundley's Road, just over a mile away, although a site bought for £25,000 in Tooley Street had been vetoed by the Government; altogether it estimated it would spend £250,000 replacing 900 houses. However, the Rector later wrote that the situation had been much helped by the Home Office.

Widening from Corbett's Lane, south-east of Southwark Park station, to New Cross was contracted to William Rigby in June 1900 for £130,000. This section was ready for ballasting in April 1903. The two new lines between New Cross and North Kent East Junction, near Southwark Park, opened on 13 December 1903; they passed over the Bricklayers Arms branch and by-passed North Kent East Junction on a separate viaduct.

In September 1899 the Engineer, Tempest, was doing the plans for the quadrupling from St John's to Orpington. He estimated £279,000 for the section to Elmstead Lane, to be done by William Rigby, and £219,600 for the second stage to Orpington which was placed in the hands of Aird & Sons. Lewisham Borough Council took the opportunity to campaign for a station to be placed at Lewisham High Street, south of Park's Bridge Junction, which would have given the town a station on the ex-SER main-line.

South of St John's the work of quadrupling to Chislehurst was completed in sections, so that the whole quadrupling was not complete until 18 June 1905. In May 1905 the section was reported as ready for opening; new signalboxes at Hither Green had opened on 30 April, the new Hither Green Junction was being laid in and only Grove Park signalbox remained to be done. Total cost of the scheme at this stage was reckoned as being £716,579 - including the Chislehurst loops. After the widenings had been completed the chance was taken to transfer much of the Loughborough Junction goods traffic to new sidings at Hither Green via the Blackfriars spur.

Messrs Sykes took longer than expected to complete Grove Park signalbox, eventually setting 17 June as the date.

Beyond Grove Park the widening to four tracks was made easier by the semi-rural landscape, though the tunnels at Chislehurst were an extra cost. Land was being purchased in 1900 though individual landowners clearly saw the chance to

The improved layout at St John's after quadrupling, photographed in July 1913. (H Patterson Rutherford)

Elmstead Woods, which was significantly improved by the quadrupling of the main line and the opening of a new station on 1 July 1904. (Ashford Library, Wakeman Collection)

enhance property values; the Scott Trustees agreed to sell land to the SECR on condition that a station with two platforms was provided at Elmstead Lane by 1 May 1903 or a penalty of £1 a day paid. Unfortunately for the SECR, the station (renamed Elmstead Woods from 1 October 1908) did not open until 1 July 1904!

A two platform station at Elmstead Woods would have been possible with the original scheme for track arrangements, but in 1901 the SECR decided to have an "in and out running" arrangement so that four platforms were built at all the improved stations.

In the middle of the work, there was a crisis when cracks were discovered in the brickwork of the old tunnel north of Chislehurst at about 4pm on 17 July 1902. All traffic had to be suspended and then diverted, the tunnel being shored up. Repair work was expected to cost at least £13,000 but, more seriously, take three months though rapid work at Bickley meant that the new loops there were opened in September. In the meanwhile, Chislehurst was provided with a road service to Bickley but the hired carriages were unpopular as they were "filthy, with black greasy handles outside....miserable, dangerous old vehicles;" Orpington was served from Sundridge Park with "antiquated omnibuses." Extra land had to be purchased at Elmstead cutting for the spoil, but the opportunity was taken to open up the end of Chislehurst Tunnel and start building Elmstead station. The land was sold to the SECR on condition that it was never re-used for houses unless they were to cost over £1,500.

The new Chislehurst Tunnel opened to goods traffic on 1 November 1902 and to passengers on 3 November 1902. The quadrupling from Elmstead to Orpington was opened on 6 June 1904.

The "Chatham" Lines in London

The LCDR suffered less from chronic overcrowding than the SER had as its suburban traffic was less intensive, but there were several places in which improvements were needed. Regarding the approaches to Victoria, in November 1899 *The Times* reported that the SECR planned to widen the ex-LCDR line between Battersea Park Road and Clapham.

Victoria itself was shambles in 1899, the wooden buildings a disgrace for an international terminus. In November 1900 the SECR decided to spend £35,000 on improvements but did nothing. In January 1903 Victoria was a cause of a dispute between SER and LCDR when the latter wanted to rent out the old electrical works as an automobile store - the revenue not accruing to the traffic account. The SER challenged this, claiming that there was already a lack of space for the legitimate horse and carriage traffic at the station.

The continued existence of wooden buildings caused a threat to the the licence of the station in January 1905, it being granted only on condition that improvements were made and so plans were submitted in March; Percy Tempest was instructed to organise the building of new refreshment rooms. However, rebuilding of the station was complicated by the fact that it was actually a joint station with the Great Western Railway, who still owned a 2130 of a total of 32,000 shares.

In April 1906 a major contract for the rebuilding of Victoria was at last let to Higgs & Hill, for £83,000. The ramshackle wooden huts at the front were replaced with a four-storey block of which the main feature was a graceful archway.

Extra space was created by filling in the old Grosvenor Dock by 12 October 1904, and two years later the carriage sidings were extended over the site. It was

The frontage of Victoria was rebuilt in 1906-7, removing an ugly collection of ramshackle wooden huts that had been one of London's most conspicuous railway embarrassments. (Lens of Sutton)

then suggested that the arrival platform could be extended by removing a turntable. The turntable at the down end of platforms 5 and 6 seems to have survived until 1920, when it was removed to make more space for passengers to "circulate". At about the same time the wartime military buffet was converted into cloakrooms.

The tracks on the approach to Victoria had been roofed over as a concession to local sensitivities at the time of construction, the line here still belonging to the technically-independent Victoria Station & Pimlico Railway. Decayed parts of the roof had been removed by late 1905 and the SECR Bill of that year planned to get authorisation this, but an action was brought against it and the Managing Committee decided to restore walls over Elizabeth Bridge. The 1906 SECR Act allowed removal of roofing west of Eccleston Bridge as it was in a decayed state. However, by June 1906 much of the section north-east of Eccleston Bridge was also dangerous and the roof girders had to be removed.

The LCDR also had had a direct line through the City in its "Metropolitan Extension." Improvements of this were also being considered in November 1899 at Loughborough Junction, though this would mean the removal of Loughborough Hall which was let to the Salvation Army. However the key factor proved to be tramway competition, which reduced the number of suburban trains on the Metropolitan Extension so that in February 1906 it was decided to alter the track arrangement at Loughborough Junction to make all four "running lines" rather than have two stopping lines. At about the same time the goods sidings saw most of their traffic transferred to Hither Green, and the down side became carriage sidings instead.

Both trams and tubes contributed to the decline of the LCDR's "Metropoli-

SECR trains were a common sight north of King's Cross until the First World War. The War caused the cutback of services already weakened by tram and tube competition. A Q1 class 0-4-4T heads north on the Great Northern at Belle Isle. (R W Kidner collection)

tan Extension", so called as it joined on to the Metropolitan Railway. Services from Great Northern stations Muswell Hill and Enfield to Woolwich, via the spur at Blackfriars bridge, ceased on 30 April 1907 and through services to Victoria from Barnet or Enfield five months later; the end of the Midland Railway's service from Kentish Town or Hendon on 30 June 1908 left this costly section devoid of through suburban passenger services, although the SECR continued its own service into Moorgate Street. In the midst of this decline, the City & South London tube provided a through line between Euston, King's Cross and London Bridge from 12 May 1907. South of the Thames, it was largely the tram that undercut the inner suburban services. There was some small benefit - in 1908 the SECR won a rates revaluation case against Southwark on the basis that its property had lost value due to trams, tubes and motor buses.

The platforms on the Brixton spur at Loughborough Junction closed on 1 April 1916 as a wartime restriction, but they had already outlived their usefulness and never reopened. The same date saw an end of the SECR trains into Moorgate Street.

Borough Road station, a victim of tramway competition, closed on 31 March 1907. Grosvenor Road, the first station out of Victoria on the run to the City stations, closed on 30 September 1911. Walworth Road survived until 1 April 1916 when it closed as a wartime measure - but it did not reopen, to the disgust of Southwark Council who complained to the Minister of Transport in 1921; Wandsworth Road lost its SECR services at the same date.

The line crossed the Thames at Blackfriars, where the bridge needed strengthening work in 1904. By March 1909 it had been decided to remove the platforms, but this caused problems with tenants in the arches beneath.

The "City" stations on this line also received well-merited criticism, especially Ludgate Hill which was a cramped and dingy station with narrow platforms and bad staircases. Snow Hill was better lit and also, according to the SECR at least, had clean toilets. However concern was such that the City of London initiated discussions with the Board of Trade in January 1899. The LCDR then applied for permission in August 1900 to put up fourteen shops in the forecourt at Ludgate Hill, which the City Corporation refused.

The Central London railway, a tube scheme that numbered Sir Benjamin Baker the engineer and Henry Oakley of the Great Northern among its backers, saw this as an opportunity to force the SECR to agree to the interchange it wanted at Ludgate Hill. In March 1901 it offered to provide £20,000 to help improve the station. Ever quick to exploit a chance when it came to other people's money, the SECR managed to force the CLR offer up to £40,000. In May 1902 the CLR Bill fell foul of the House of Lords, but two other tube schemes immediately asked for similar terms for an interchange at Ludgate Hill. The SECR dithered, unsure of its attitude to tube railways in general.

Ludgate Hill was improved by the removal of its old wooden roofs and the installation of a new "umbrella roof" over the one island platform serving Metropolitan line trains for £41,000 in a rebuilding scheme lasting from 1907 to 1912, main-line traffic being removed altogether to St Paul's. This was forced on the SECR by two factors - the MP for the City of London threatened to put a clause in its Bill in 1906 to insist on the rebuilding, and the state of the roof had become so bad that closure of the station was a possibility. This allowed the LCDR to revive its shops plan, which it hoped would yield a rental of £1,500 per year, but Ludgate Hill was already a dying station with its Metropolitan line services (including those to the GNR) already in terminal decline. The *Railway Magazine* described it as "the most inconvenient and unsatisfactory station" in London and complained of the way it was "swept from end to end by the cold winds of winter."

North of Snow Hill, SECR trains ran to the Moorgate Street station of the Metropolitan Railway. The LCDR had kept its own staff there, but from 1 May 1909 the SECR withdrew its men in order to save £183 per year.

In February 1908 the closure of Holborn Viaduct altogether was suggested by LCDR shareholders, who thought the land was of more value than the station. The SECR complained that the issue had been "frequently discussed." One economy was the closure of Ludgate Hill on Sundays from the start of 1910; from 11 April a number of suburban trains used St Pauls instead of Ludgate Hill and from 24 April Sunday SECR services ceased at Snow Hill, Aldersgate Street and Moorgate Street. Snow Hill was renamed Holborn Viaduct Low Level from 1 May 1912; traffic continued to decline, due to both tube trains and trams, so this station was an obvious candidate for wartime closure, on 31 May 1916, an event from which it did not recover.

Penge Tunnel and the political power of Dulwich College always meant that the SECR had no prospect of quadrupling the route via Beckenham, though the Catford loop meant that there were effectively four tracks. However in November

Former LCDR class "A" tank engine prepares to leave Herne Hill with a set of Midland Railway carriages. This service was killed off as a wartime economy. (R W Kidner collection)

1898 plans to widen from Penge to Shortlands were already advanced though by May 1899 this had been abbreviated to Beckenham to Shortlands. A minor improvement in this area was the extension of the platforms at Sydenham Hill in late 1906, which obviated trains stopping with some vehicles in the tunnel; in late 1911 the SECR also decided to alter the station and build a new signalbox so that up trains could start from the down platform though the idea of a new through road was not carried out.

Shortlands to Bickley had already been quadrupled by the LCDR in 1894 so in August 1913 the SECR decided to quadruple the line between Bickley station and Bickley Junction, a relatively minor improvement of about half a mile completed the following year, though plans also included moving Bickley Junction signalbox to a new position in the fork.

The South East Suburbs and Kent

In 1900 the SECR was considering several improvement schemes including at Ladywell and Catford Bridge on the Mid-Kent line, noting that houses needed to be bought to improve the former.

Major improvements were needed at Woolwich Arsenal, one of the busiest stations in the Kent suburban area although really a traffic centre in its own right. A major improvement scheme, costing £42,000, was postponed in September 1899. Minor modifications failed to soothe local animosity, so in March 1900 the SECR decided to invest £38,500 largely due to the pressure from the Woolwich Local Board - who wanted total rebuilding and especially a booking office at street level. Lack of progress by June 1901 meant that Woolwich Chamber of Commerce joined the protests and the SECR decided, once again, to proceed; over a year later, nothing had been done, and then matters became entangled in a property dispute with the Borough Council.

In November 1905 the SECR vowed to make an immediate start at Woolwich, planning to remove locomotive coaling and watering facilities to Plumstead to create space. Woolwich Council, having at last secured a victory, then requested the covering over of the line between New Road bridge and Green's End; the SECR feared this would cause the new station to fill with smoke, but it was prepared to remove the "ugly brick parapets" above its cutting.

Another station in need of refurbishment was Deptford, over which London County Council began a legal action before the Railway Commissioners to force repairs in 1902. Deptford was within the radius of tramway competition and the SECR doubted the value of a major investment. In December 1902 the SECR met LCC representatives to discuss the situation and agreed a plan to widen the platforms, move the signalbox and provide better stairs. The problem for the SECR was that annual receipts at the station were only £8760 and the improvements would cost nearly £5000.

Further east, Dartford station was confined by the goods yard to the immediate south of the passenger facilities. In 1899 it was considered that improvements could be made if the goods facilities were put elsewhere, but this was not done.

In December 1905 it was decided to rebuild Bromley North but no extensive work was done.

Several of the outer suburbs in Kent were developed by large estate companies, often in arrangement with the SER or LCDR. The SECR thus took on some complex agreements, such as the 1897 deal between the SER and the Cator Estate to build a new station and bridges at New Beckenham and Lower Sydenham as compensation for blocking two roads in the district. However the work was not completed by the agreed date of June 1901, though the public subway to the south of New Beckenham seems to have been ready by 1902. The bridges on Bridge Road, and possibly the work on New Beckenham station, were also complete by July 1904 though the Cator Estate refused to pay for them as Lower Sydenham station was unsatisfactory; this station was rebuilt during late 1905 slightly further south, replacing its predecessor during 1906.

Another active developer was Cameron Corbett MP, who in June 1899 began to press the SECR to move Well Hall station nearer to Welling in order to encourage housing development. The SECR rejected the idea at first, but changed its mind. The move was expected to cost £15,000 and the SECR agreed on 13 October 1900 that Corbett would guarantee receipts of £10,000 per annum within five years; survey work had begun by November 1900. By January 1901 the building of Corbett's Eltham Park estate was in progress and the existing sidings at Well Hall were proving inadequate, so extra facilities had to be laid in.

It was then realised that the agreement with Corbett to replace Well Hall station conflicted with the Bexley Heath Railway Acts of 1886 and 1887, meaning that the existing station could not be closed. In 1903 it was agreed to build a new station in any case, with Corbett to give land and guarantee 3% per annum for ten years on the £37,000 cost unless season ticket sales were over £4,000, but by July 1904 the relationship between railway and developer had descended into acrimony with Corbett issuing a writ for breach of the 1900 agreement and demanding £50,000 damages. The SECR lost the case and thus was forced to accept it would have to have two stations close to each other, so it appealed and in May 1906 won two votes to one, plus costs. Corbett then took the case to the Lords but lost, so he had to agree to pay interest on the new station until season sales reached £3500 per year. A new agreement was reached on 12 December 1906.

A contract to build the station buildings, to be known as Shooter's Hill & Eltham Park, was let in 1907 but the buildings infringed the LCC's building line and had to be set back in 1908. The station opened on 1 July 1908, two months later than planned. The SECR Minutes give season ticket sales for 1907 as £4,043 from all Corbett Estate commuters, but much of this traffic would have been likely to simply switch to the new station. Season ticket sales in 1919 were £7343, which the SECR felt was sufficient to justify building a new booking office.

The embryonic commuter station of Eltham Park just after its completion in 1908 - stylistic similarities to Rochester Bridge will be noted. (Edwin Course collection)

Sometimes the SECR's own activities created the need for a station. The SER had begun construction of a new locomotive depot at Slades Green and in January 1899 had considered whether a station should be provided there. One was opened on 1 July 1900.

After the Great War, new housing tended to be more associated with Council developments in 1920-22. This led to big increases of traffic at stations like Kidbrooke, which served a Woolwich housing scheme.

Pressure for a new station also came from the managers of the City of London Mental Hospital east of Dartford, who asked for a new station at Cotton Lane Crossing between Dartford and Greenhithe in July 1900. This idea was rejected by the SECR as the site was too close to a cement work and traffic was expected to be low. A station was opened slightly further east at Stone Crossing Halt on 2 November 1908. More colourfully, during 1899 the SECR was lobbied to provide a new station near Crayford for the Wagner Opera House Association.

The Crystal Palace once created large amounts of leisure traffic for the LCDR in particular, which had its own branch to the High Level station with intensive services of up to a hundred trains a day to stations in the City and West End. However fashions change, and by November 1907 the Crystal Palace itself was in financial difficulties and would not have avoided immediate bankruptcy if the SECR had not paid inclusive ticket fees in advance. The operating company planned to close it in the winter months, though it was hoped that a Mexican exhibition would save it. However the SECR refused to support the Company indefinitely and it went into receivership in 1909. Attempts were made to revive it as a going concern, but even the 1911 Festival of Empire failed to secure the finances. Meanwhile, trams were eating away at the branch-line traffic, although a 1911 monorail scheme for the Strand to Crystal Palace did not get off the ground.

Another Cystal Palace highlight of 1911 was the King's Fete, held to celebrate the Coronation. The SECR ran 47 special trains - 40 for children, three for attendants, three for performers and choirs, and one for LCC officials. Most were from the SE suburbs, but some ran from northern stations like West Hampstead and Holloway. To accomodate them, the SEC cancelled 31 down and 30 up services on the branch. The GWR ran a dozen connecting services via Victoria. Ninety extra railway staff were employed at Crystal Palace High Level, with the officer in charge being located - megaphone in hand - at the north end balcony overlooking the platforms. Each train had a LCC "train load commander".

The Crystal Palace line was a noted casualty of the war but reopened on 1 March 1919; it did not regain its Sunday service afterwards - to the disgust of Camberwell Borough Council, who complained to the Minister of Transport, and trains ran only to City stations. The Palace itself reopened in 1920.

The Hayes branch saw little excitement, except for a brief period early in 1909 when the 8.37am Hayes to Charing Cross was formed regularly of "Continental" carriages! This luxurious train proceeded the 14.5 miles to Charing Cross in a stately 51 minutes, then departed as the 10am to Folkestone in - it is hoped - rather less leisurely fashion.

Eden Park was the subject of an attempted suffragette outrage in June 1913, when a bomb was found hidden in a leather-covered bench although its clock had failed. *The Times* commented that "the station is not much used..."

The Surrey Suburbs

The Caterham branch benefitted from the growth of outer suburban commuting so that, at the inception of the SECR, it was being widened to double track. The new track opened on 1 January 1900 and other improvements were made including a new goods shed at the terminus. Whyteleafe station was opened at the same time though a private platform at Burntwood Bridge, generally used by school groups, was removed; this was known as Halliloo.

The Chipstead Valley line was one that Cosmo Bonsor took an especial interest in, since his house - *Kingswood Warren*- was located close to it. He had many other interests in the area such as forming a committee in 1899 to develop Banstead Heath with a golf club and cricket ground. The line had been opened in stages - from Purley to Kingswood on 2 November 1897, then on to Tadworth on 1 July 1900, finally to Tattenham Corner on 4 June 1901. The final part of this line was promoted as the Epsom Downs Extension Railway and was intended to capture the Race traffic from the LBSCR; thus the SECR schemed to get the line ready for Derby Day - it did indeed open on that day. In December 1900 it had been worried that the terminal buildings would not be ready for the great event. The Chipstead Valley company was vested in the SER on 13 July 1899.

Cosmo Bonsor's local station - Kingswood, on the Chipstead Valley line. The very substantial up buildings will be noted, complete with tearooms and verandah. (Ashford Library, Wakeman Collection)

On the day that Tattenham Corner opened *The Times* complained that the SECR should not be advertising special services when the line was already overcrowded. Presumably this referred back to the previous year's Derby Day, when the line had still been largely single track though widening was completed by November 1900.

For its second season, the SECR decided that Tattenham Corner needed extra toilets and refreshment accomodation, suggesting that it had been inconveniently sparse in its initial facilities. However attempts to develop traffic to Tattenham Corner failed and after 1907 the station lost any regular service.

Of course the staple diet of the Chipstead Valley line was the commuter traffic, which was enabled to grow by the improvements to London Bridge completed in 1902. The SECR though was less charitable to estate developers than it had been and in 1905 refused to extend the special season rates offered to residents on the Hooley House estate at Coulsdon. In May 1902 the subject of opening a station at Smitham was raised, this being forced on the SECR due to a clause in the 1893 Act - it opened on 1 January 1904. The designs of the station were paid for by Colonel Baring, a member of the banking family and a SECR director. SECR Minutes indicate that the station was partially built in June 1903 (in fact it seems to have been largely built in 1900), when it was agreed to add new buildings and provide a down side shelter made out of "uralite"; this state of affairs is perhaps explained by it opening to goods earlier than for passengers, on 20 July 1903. At Kingswood, the unusual down side passenger shelter seems to have been added in 1902.

By November 1910 the SECR was able to report pleasing traffic increases at Tadworth and Kingswood, so was able to view favourably an "extensively signed testimonial" for a halt at Old Lodge Lane between Purley and Smitham especially as there was a fear of road competition. This opened as Reedham Halt on 1 March 1911. However trains normally did not run beyond Tadworth to Tattenham Corner except on race days, although in the summer they could be extended "as required" until September 1914.

One of the far outposts of SECR suburban growth was Merstham, which received attention in October 1905 when a plan to rebuild it was agreed. Both platforms were to be extended and widened, the goods yard and shed were to be enlarged, the stationmaster's house repaired, a new footbridge built and the signalling to be replaced.

Chapter Five:

Continental Services & Other Maritime Matters

The Continental traffic was highly important to the SECR both in terms of profitability and also because of the prestige it brought - the SECR could boast little else that attracted press attention. The working union gave it a strong position in the cross-Channel trade where the only competitor on the Paris route was the LBSCR via Newhaven, which involved a lengthy detour on the French leg until 1913; competition was reduced by agreements over fare levels. To Belgium it was also well placed, but faced increasing competition for the Netherlands and Germany from the Great Eastern Railway via Parkeston Quay.

However the SECR can be accused of adopting a short-sighted approach to some aspects of the cross-Channel traffic. It continued to hope for a Channel Tunnel, but in the interim refused to consider the idea of train ferries despite their proven success elsewhere in the world and later at Richborough; an opportunity was lost to the rival Harwich route. More progressive was the real opening up of continental travel for 3rd class passengers.

Folkestone Harbour belonged to the SECR though there was a possibility it could have been abandoned; instead the pier was extended in 1900-05, as shown in this picture of about 1907.

Continental Passenger Facilities

Both the SECR and LCDR had the right to nominate representatives on the Dover Harbour Board, though this was still an independent organisation fiercely protective of Dover's interests against upstart rivals like Folkestone. In October 1899 the SECR met the Harbour Board to review plans, including the ongoing extension of the "eastern" pier - which became the Prince of Wales Pier - and which was handed over to the Harbour Board on 1 January 1902 and used for the first time by Princess Beatrice in July 1902. At the same time they discussed the proposals for improving the main ferry station on Admiralty Pier and the construction of a commercial harbour east of Admiralty Pier. All these works were to be funded by a poll tax of 6d on each passenger. The Admiralty was to take charge of building an outer wall.

The financial power of the Harbour Board was quite stretched by this expansion. The completion of the Prince of Wales Pier cost £568,000 and seemed likely to leave it with only £232,000 to build the commercial harbour, the Marine station, build a new lock for the inner harbour, convert that to a wet dock, and provide a rail link to the new pier. This was likely to amount to £1.4m - a huge sum given that the Board had an annual surplus of £288. Its main revenue came from a one shilling poll tax levied under powers of 1891 but it hoped to charge five shillings for each Atlantic passenger. The Harbour Board was obliged by an agreement of 1896 to start work on land reclamation for the Marine station.

In January 1902 the SECR agreed to guarantee up to £800,000 so the DHB could start reclaiming the land for the Marine station, but said that the Board should "look elsewhere" for the cost of the branch line to Prince of Wales Pier. It suggested the Board charge an extra 6d poll tax to fund the reclamation - but the DHB wanted a further shilling to total 2s6d altogether. Agreement between the SECR and the DHB was reached in May 1902, so that the latter's Bill could proceed without such significant opposition - though the price was an increase in the railways' representation on the DHB.

The slow progress in negotiating with the Admiralty over the improvement of its pier made the construction of the Prince of Wales Pier by the Harbour Board more significant. Though it has been alleged that Bonsor opposed connecting this to the SECR £10,000 was provided to help in its construction; a single track connection was laid in with a swing bridge over the commercial harbour entrance and the first trial train with two decorated engines ran to the Pier on 25 June 1904; a "relatively tiny and quite unpretentious" station was provided. The line had a short stretch of 1 in 30 but was clearly regarded as a temporary connection only, the actual cost of the original work apparently being only about £2500 apart from the swing bridge. Bonsor was unhappy that the cost of a permanent link was in the region of £32,000.

This facility was important as it was intended to be Dover's chance to gain a hold on the Atlantic trade. The Hamburg-Amerika Line's *Prinz Waldemar* called at the pier on 1 July 1904 and the Red Star Line began to use it from August. The Admiralty was never happy about this and was objecting to commercial use of the east side of the pier in October 1904. During the next year five companies were

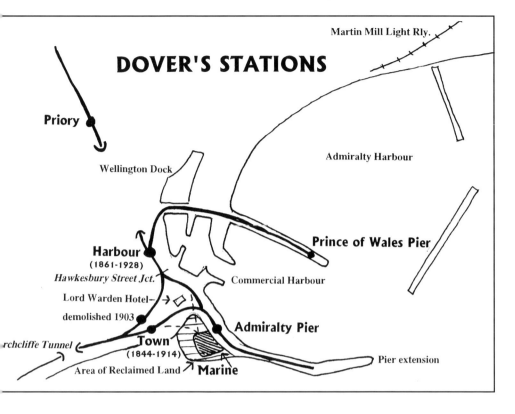

DOVER'S STATIONS

Martin Mill Light Rly.

Priory

Wellington Dock

Admiralty Harbour

Harbour
(1861-1928)

Prince of Wales Pier

Hawkesbury Street Jct.

Commercial Harbour

Lord Warden Hotel—

demolished 1903

Admiralty Pier

rchcliffe Tunnel

Town
(1844-1914)

Pier extension

Area of Reclaimed Land

Marine

making regular calls and on 11 May 1906 the largest liner in the world made a stop - the *Kaiserin Victoria Auguste*. The HAL tried to negotiate reduced passenger fares over the SECR from and to London - the 1st class fare was 19s which included Dover poll tax. At first the poll tax was 3s a head, but this was planned to rise to 5s from 1 July 1908. During the first year of operation HAL ships called about five times a week and the SECR provided a train alongside, although in October 1905 the Committee decided to buy a £70 omnibus for when a train was not needed - it had a capacity of eight passengers.

The intention was that the Admiralty would take over the use of the Prince of Wales Pier when work on the Admiralty Pier and the "Harbour of Refuge" was finished, but in the interim period the Admiralty also had the right to restrict use of the neighbouring facility. However work at the Admiralty Pier caused dangerous currents in the harbour and began to make docking at the Prince of Wales Pier hazardous - on 21 June 1906 the *Prinz Joachim* hit some contractor's staging and HAL captains began to complain about the difficulty of getting into Dover against the tide. On 13 July the *Deutschland* struck the Prince of Wales Pier and had to abandon a voyage to America. The Admiralty then declared the harbour unsafe for large vessels, though it was felt that this was in line with their lordships' desire to keep foreign vessels out of Dover altogether. The HAL withdrew "temporarily" but although there were occasional visits by liners in 1908, the experiment had failed; the call of "Victoria for New York" was not to be heard again.

The "station" at the end of the Prince of Wales Pier became sad and forgotten. In May 1921 it was decided to sweep it away to make room for commercial development on the pier.

Of course the SECR received most of the blame for the antiquated nature of the Admiralty Pier facilities, yet it had to force improvements through against the wishes of the Admiralty. One example of this was the erection of electric cranes, which were tried for the first time on 26 June 1903.

Dover's Admiralty Pier was an exposed position, limited by its access being via two single tracks controlled from the "turret" box; "harbour of refuge" work had already begun when this picture was taken, in about 1907. (R W Kidner collection)

Coode, Sons & Matthews prepared three plans in 1903; two of these involved a new "Marine" station at the root end of Admiralty Pier and a station on Prince of Wales Pier was featured in one. Coode also suggested a widened Admiralty Pier could handle Channel traffic on the west and Atlantic on the east. In August 1903 the SECR was expecting the new station to cost £700,000 excluding buildings. The Dover Harbour Board prepared a Bill to widen the Pier and build a Marine station, under the powers of which the east side of the Prince of Wales Pier was to be leased to the Admiralty in exchange for the Admiralty Pier. The Act was passed 29 November 1906, but there was some unhappiness about the proposal to finance it by raising the Dover poll tax to 2s6d. The Board of Trade permitted only an increase to 2s, after a public inquiry.

The DHB's net income in 1909 was only £36,845, so paying for the scheme out of retained profit was impossible; it decided to issue £1m in new debenture stock. The War caused a drop in this income, so that the DHB's overdraft limit had to be extended from £10,000 to £25,000 in order to meet its interest repayments of

£18,000 per year. The railways and the Treasury had to pay to keep the Harbour Board afloat, with the Treasury paying the interest on the debentures.

Work on reclaiming land was due to start at the end of 1907 when Percy Tempest, the SECR engineer, was instructed to prepare plans for a station. He prepared two schemes with a maximum cost of £125,000 which would allow for the abolition of the old SER Dover Town station and combine the Pier and Harbour stations. The eventual plan was for two 700ft platforms of 60ft width with a contract for £92,052.

A contract with Pearson's was let in May 1909 for £374,255. As the works got under way, a temporary station was needed at the end of the pier and some resignalling required in late 1910. This was ready about 1 November 1910 but there were immediate complaints about poor track.

Extensive work on widening the Admiralty Pier in order to create the Dover Marine station has begun and a temporary passenger station erected, suggesting a date of about 1913 for this view. (Wakeman Collection, Ashford Library)

Work at Admiralty Pier made a bad place even worse. In December 1910 *The Times* printed a vituperative letter complaining of conditions on a winter night - the writer had to wait at the Pier from 10pm until 1.30am with no food or shelter, having crossed the Channel on a "tug": "the law would have compelled the Company to provide food and water at Dover for cattle and pigs." The SECR defended itself by saying that the "tug" was, in fact, the *Canterbury*, and that the lengthy delay was due to the need to load over 2,000 Christmas mail bags. *The Times* thought nothing would improve until someone important died of exposure.

After Christmas, *The Times* received some more angry letters. "I have never failed to feel disgusted at the inadequate and scandalous way with which passengers are received at Dover," wrote W C Edwards. He thought that the SECR "are the worst managed and the very worst in almost every way that we have in England." The facilities at Dover consisted of "just a small shed where you can get some tea if you wait long enough, and where there is always a crowd of hungry and despairing passengers trying to get some kind of warmth and refreshment into their shivering bodies." The newspaper's Dover correspondent tried to defend the SECR, pointing out that the Marine station was a temporary affair and that the main problem was with the late night India Mails service.

S Pearson & Co continued to work on reclaiming and filling in at the Admiralty Pier. Materials for filling came from Dover's Eastcliff roadworks and there was to be a minimum draught of 16ft. Pearson expected to complete the works by February 1913 so that the SECR could then prepare for trackwork and buildings. The last section of the sea wall was laid on 8 January 1913, enclosing an area of 11 acres at a cost of £600,000. Sir William Crundall, chairman of DHB, laid the final stone of the new pier on 2 April.

The licence for Dover Town station was moved to the Pier in January 1914 and a 60ft turntable ordered. Work on the pier was sufficiently advanced for a start to be made on the Marine station in May 1914, but Dover's civilian services were suspended on 4 August 1914. The last arrivals were *Engadine* from Calais with only 20 passengers, but *Rapide* from Ostend arrived with nearly 1,000. In the middle of all the carnage Marine station was thrust into unscheduled use, but not for any service trains; it was used briefly for refugee and wounded soldier traffic until its incomplete state forced a realisation that it had to be properly completed. The contract for its buildings was judged complete in April 1917. Ambulance trains used the new station from 2 January 1915 but public use did not begin until 18 January 1919 when a Dover to Ostend service resumed. The station did not actually revert to the SECR's control until April 1919.

Work on the new Marine station is almost complete except for some of the trackwork. (E Course collection)

After the opening of Marine, the SECR concentrated its passenger services there. A shortage of services via Folkestone was exacerbated by a shortage of ships, so in March and April 1920 Folkestone had no passenger services at all except for the Flushing steamers.

There was also a debate in the SECR as to which London stations should be used - in 1920 Victoria was gaining the lead. This mattered, as the SER and LCDR each gained profits from hotel takings, bookstall rentals etc at their own stations. Sir Francis Dent investigated and found Victoria limited by weight restrictions while Charing Cross was overcrowded and its use restricted by the need to work empty stock trains to Rotherhithe Road. He suggested completing bridge strengthening on the LCDR route and recommended the alteration of the arrangement at Rochester so that boat trains could use the ex-SER Medway bridge; however, he also thought that continental passengers would prefer the North Kent line - "from a spectacular point of view it is much more interesting."

The impressive interior of Dover Marine station. (E Course collection)

For the Belgian service the SECR was in partnership with the Belgian government. The Belgians objected to the charge of a poll tax at Dover and also felt the SECR had too large a share of the receipts - 2/3rds of the Brussels to London fares. One tactic of exerting pressure to get this changed was to threaten to transfer services to Canvey Island.

Folkestone's harbour belonged to the SER, so was not neglected. In 1900 the SECR was planning the completion of 900ft extensions to the new pier, which would allow the creation of five berths. In October 1903 the contract was let for new station buildings and a house for the stationmaster. The pier extension was finished in late 1903 and the "Knuckle Station" on it was used from 18 October for the winter traffic. By this stage Folkestone improvements had cost £436,000 - hardly suggesting that the SECR had any plans to concentrate at Dover. "Folkestone Pier" station buildings were contracted to builders to be ready for June 1904. The station was on a more gentle curve than its predecessor, to allow for the new bogie carriages. Much work was also done to the Harbour station, slightly further north, and the adjacent swing bridge was replaced in 1903.

The extended facilities at Folkestone Pier, with one of the "old generation" of paddle-steamers departing. (R W Kidner collection)

The ceremonial final stone was laid at Folkestone by the French Ambassador on 12 July 1904, the Prince of Wales being unavailable. Part of the Old Block Yard to the west was converted to sidings and the remainder became a tennis court for the Pavilion Hotel. The station and stationmaster's house were completed by November 1904.

The third principal port used by the SECR was the Pier at Queenborough, from where services ran to Flushing in the Netherlands. On 19 July 1900 there was

Queenborough Pier was rebuilt in 1901, but was a continental port whose role steadily declined during SECR years and never recovered from World War I. (R W Kidner collection)

a serious fire which caused the buildings to "disappear" despite the efforts of detachments from the Bluejackets and Royal Marines. The station was insured for £60,000 although only £33,800 was claimed. Services were transferred to Port Victoria, though the goods traffic went via Tilbury and later Folkestone.

The SECR would perhaps have liked to have abandoned Queenborough, but the Zealand Company made it clear that they hated Port Victoria and refused to use Dover in winter - thus in October the SECR accepted that they would need to rebuild Queenborough and provide at least one berth as soon as possible. Late in November the Zealand Company repeated their objections to the arrangements - which at that point meant they had to unload passengers at Port Victoria and then goods at Queenborough! Again the SECR resolved to provide a berth at the latter.

From 26 January 1901 the day service began to use Queenborough Pier again after a traffic analysis had shown the value of this route. The 1898 traffic had amounted to £65,730 - but costs were a mere £24,192 thus revealing the profitability of the Continental trade. Queenborough also handled coal traffic for Canterbury, which was worth £2176 per year. All this made an investment of £78,000 in rebuilding the pier seem worthwhile and interim work was finished by July 1901. In October it was decided to spend a further £50,000 on the Pier and to include electric lights with completion due in September 1902. In fact the formal reopening of Queenborough Pier was on 3 June 1904, which also marked the end of the use of Port Victoria. The total cost for restoring Queenborough Pier was £103,000. However it lost some services to Folkestone in 1911.

In May 1913 an organisation known as the Queenborough Syndicate approached the SECR about developing the area for industrial use so that by October the SECR was planning to install new sidings. In October 1913 the SECR gave permission for Short Brothers, aircraft engineers who had a base at Eastchurch, to

Some of the Flushing services were transferred to Folkestone in 1911.

moor three seaplanes at the Pier.

Queenborough did not win back its services after the War and in July 1921 was considered by a Sheffield firm as a base for ship-breaking, using power from the SECR's own power station. From 1 June 1922 the Zealand Company transferred its principal services from Folkestone - but not to Queenborough, for the Great Eastern's port at Parkeston Quay was selected. In December 1922 it was agreed to let half the pier to a different firm, Cox & Danks, for £2500 per year.

Continental Passenger Services

Early patterns of service for the SECR showed attempts to adjust to traffic patterns with dated services. Analysis of the services for 1899 showed that some trains ran much heavier than others, and that seasonal loads varied enormously. The "afternoon" service via Folkestone and Boulogne ran between 1 June and 30 September only, but in 1900 was extended for an extra month for the Paris Exhibition traffic - this event added about £40,000 to SECR revenues. Regular excursions were also run. On 23 December 1901 a 1st and 2nd class train was run through from Boulogne to Nice and Monte Carlo for £9-11s 1st class return.

One of the first acts of the Committee in November 1898 was to fit four locomotives with Westinghouse brakes so that LCDR stock could be worked down the Folkestone Harbour branch.

Third class passengers had received a poor treatment from both SER and LCDR - at the turn of the century they usually had to travel at night. Vincent Hill saw this traffic as an opportunity for growth and opened the 10am and 2.20pm Paris services to third class in 1902. The 2.20pm became an all year service at the

A view of Dover Admiralty Pier early in the SECR period shows the *Lord Warden Hotel* and, just to the left of it, an area of goods storage beside the former SER Dover Town station which closed to passengers on 14 October 1914. (R W Kidner collection)

same time - it provided good Paris connections for overnight trains to the south. Cheap "night" tickets were offered for the Brussels exhibition in 1910, using the 9pm Charing Cross/9.05pm Cannon Street. However the 3rd class were not treated equally - in 1914 1st and 2nd class passengers travelled down on the 9am from Charing Cross to Admiralty Pier for the 11am sailing, but 3rd class had to leave at 7am, change at Ashford, and walk a quarter of a mile from Dover Town station.

The Paris traffic was always the core of the SECR business; in 1906 there were 300,000 passengers to Paris via Boulogne alone. This was encouraged by Hill's initiatives like the Paris cheap weekend tickets, introduced in November 1909. A comparison can be made of all the SECR routes in 1911:

Table 1: 1911 Passenger Figures	
Route	
Dover/Folkestone-Calais	360,759
Dover/Folkestone-Boulogne	394,355
Dover-Ostend	181,568
Queenborough-Flushing	154,999

Better steamers (crossings could be made in 90mins from Boulogne by 1910) and railways made for gradual improvements in the service. For May 1910 a faster 8.20am from Paris to Charing Cross via Boulogne was offered, arriving at 3.25pm; in the opposite direction, the 10am from Charing Cross reached Paris at 5.20pm. At popular times the 11am from Victoria to Paris had to run in three portions as did the 5.10pm up from Dover; it was also common for baggage to run in a separate train.

The practice of serving both Charing Cross and Cannon Street began to crumble from 1 May 1911 as the 9am and 9pm mail trains ceased to provide passenger facilities from the latter. The 11am down and 5.20pm up Dover services lost their City portions in May 1912.

From 1 July 1913 the 4.30pm London to Paris service was accelerated to 6hrs55mins and from 1 December was timed at 6hrs30mins - the fastest attained at that date. Between 1 July 1913 and 31 October a sleeping car service operated from Paris, arriving at Calais at 6.20am; the balancing working left Charing Cross at 4.30pm but these trains failed to meet their costs which were £22,000 a year.

In June 1913 *The Times* and the *Railway Gazette* reviewed the state of the Paris services. The former reckoned that the fastest outward journey was seven hours by the via Folkestone and Boulogne, with the fastest return being the 4pm from Paris in 15 minutes less; the LBSCR's service via Dieppe was only an hour slower, much helped by the opening of a more direct route from Dieppe to Paris via Pontoise on 25 June 1913. *The Times* complained that SECR trains were too slow. The *Railway Gazette* blamed a 30 minute delay for customs examination but thought that it should be possible to reach Dover in 90 minutes by train. The SECR response was a new afternoon train to Paris which took only 6hrs 55mins , and was cut to 6hrs 30mins on 1 December. Early in 1914 the SECR ordered 20 new engines to haul the Boat Trains.

An unusual higher level view of the railway on Folkestone Pier; in the foreground can be seen a few of the SECR's continental baggage containers. (Wakeman Collection, Ashford Library)

The Belgian service improved less impressively. During 1904 the SECR became increasingly frustrated at the failure of the Belgians to accelerate their own boat trains, and because of this decided to stop running the 10am London to Dover service from 1 October. Instead they put on the 11am via Calais and Courtrai to Brussels, thus reducing the extent of the slow passage over Belgian metals compared to the Ostend route; this annoyed the Belgians, who refused to let the service use Brussels Nord station.

On the Flushing route the SECR faced growing competition from the Great Eastern Railway via Parkeston Quay and Hook of Holland. In April 1911 the SECR learnt that the GER's night service to Berlin would become two hours faster than their own, so they decided to transfer the Flushing night sailing to Folkestone after 30 April though this meant some dredging work was needed at the Kent port; trains continued to operate from Victoria. The day service continued to use Queenborough, which had a sea voyage 16 miles longer. The night service was more important, carrying 106,276 passengers in 1910 compared to 42,799 by day.

By mid-August 1914 the SECR continental service was down to three a day due to the outbreak of war. At the end of the month there was a service to Paris via Folkestone and Dieppe on three days a week, returning on three subsequent days. Initially this left London at 9am and reached Paris at 9.42pm.; after 4 September there were two daily services to Boulogne only. By November the 10am service from Victoria was able to reach Paris at 8.33pm. Not surprisingly traffic fell and leisure journeys almost ceased, so the job of Continental Traffic Manager was abolished in January 1915. The Flushing service, which continued to run to neutral

Holland, was transferred first to Tilbury and in late 1916 to Gravesend Pier, which cost £450 to adapt.

From 18 December 1918 civilians could cross via Dover and Boulogne again using the 11am service only and a Belgian service resumed three times a week from 18 January 1919. The Folkestone-Boulogne route regained a normal service from 3 February. A 9.25am service started on 2 February 1919, reaching Paris at 6.40pm. An extra Victoria departure was added in October, leaving at 12.20pm and an 11.15pm from Paris resumed with a sleeping car to Boulogne and a Victoria arrival at 3pm. There were no services via Dover and Calais until 8 January 1920, with the period also marking the final triumph of Victoria over Charing Cross as the London terminal; the new Dover service ran from Victoria at 11am reaching Paris at 8.15pm and the 8am via Folkestone also ran from Victoria. By the Spring of 1920 the SECR was operating four Paris services via Dover and had also begun to market "battlefield tours".

The winter service that began on 24 October 1920 included three daily Paris services, one via Boulogne; a fourth service, the 10am via Boulogne, was added from Easter 1921.

Flushing services were delayed in restarting due to the need for dredging at Queenborough. In June 1919 the SECR was supporting a thrice a week Flushing service via Folkestone; this left Charing Cross at 9pm and gave an Amsterdam arrival at 5.38pm. Belgium was served by the 8.45am from Charing Cross, arriving at Brussels at 7.10pm. By April 1920 there were six services a week.

Then, in April 1922, the SECR heard the devastating news that the Zealand Steamship Company was going to tranfer its services to the GER's Parkeston Quay from 1 June. This was a complete surprise to the SECR, but was prompted by Zealand's financial difficulties caused by the cost of its new *Mecklenburg* and the collapse of the German traffic. This was a significant loss to the SECR, whose share of the trade had been £124,388 in 1913 - of which about £60,000 had been profit; even in 1921 it had made a profit of £49,000 on trade of £103,000. The SECR's panic response was to plan a service using its own *Empress* and *Invicta*, which operated by day and started at the same time as the GER's service. In fact the Zealand Company ran the service, but was paid £3000 by the SECR. From 15 June there was also a service to Rotterdam offered by the Batavier Line, calling at Gravesend West Street Pier about five times a week; this had called at Tilbury before the War and was served by the 5.45pm fast from Victoria.

During the coal strike of 18 October to 8 November 1920 the Dover and Calais route was reduced to one service.

Beyond the French coast, the SECR tried to widen the range of through destinations. On 11 October 1901 a through carriage began running from Calais to Cannes and Ventimiglia and twice a week there was a carriage to San Remo. From July 1904 it was possible to travel by through carriage from Calais to Vienna on the 9pm from Charing Cross. For the summer of 1908 a through service to Basel was offered by the 11am from Victoria - taking 17 hours for the journey.

There were also through carriages from Calais to Marseilles which connected with the P&O liners to Bombay. This service ran over the Paris Petite Ceinture railway to the Gare de Lyon; it left Calais at 3pm and reached the Paris station at 6.40pm in 1909. On the Flushing route at this time it was possible to take a through carriage to Trieste; in 1911 this was covered by the 8.45pm from Victoria, arriving at Amsterdam at 7.58am and Trieste at 8.52am the following day. From 1 October 1911 the *Simplon Express* provided a daily service via Calais and Venice to Trieste.

Through services were important in encouraging the holiday trade which, from about 1910, did especially well from Sir Henry Lunn's Swiss excursions. This form of traffic ceased during the War, but was encouraged again by the introduction in December 1919 of a 1.30pm express from Boulogne to St Moritz, arriving at 8pm the next day. However by February 1920 there was no reliable service to eastern Europe except for occupied areas of Germany; SECR director Mr Brant thought that traffic here could be encouraged as "the feeling towards the British is decidedly friendly but the French are cordially disliked." From April 1920 it was possible to catch the 8.45am from Victoria via Ostend, reaching Vienna at 10.55pm the next day.

In October 1905 two new sets of boat train stock were ordered with steam heat throughout. The SECR contracted the work to the Metropolitan Amalgamated Railway Carriage & Wagon Company for £40,000. Another ten carriage set was ordered from the same source in November 1907 to allow for extra traffic for the Franco-British Exhibition at the White City in 1908, at which the SECR exhibited a locomotive, carriage (no.915) and some ship models. The models and some paintings were destroyed in a fire at the exhibition.

In October 1913 the SECR decided that 1st class boat train stock should have light switches! A new set of eight corridor coaches, all with tables, came into use on the 7.05pm from Victoria on 21 March 1921. They broke new ground with Pullman gangways and inward-opening doors.

In 1904 the SECR discussed with its partner, the Nord, and the Wagons-Lits Company whether a "Palace Train de Luxe" should be introduced with the aim of a 6hr15min time to Paris. One of the ways of achieving such a time would have been with customs examination on the train, but this could not be agreed and the scheme lapsed. In April 1907 the International Sleeping Car Company suggested that the SECR should run a "train de luxe" with "drawing room cars" to Dover and Folkestone. By June 1907 this proposal had become a firm request to run one of the Company's cars on the 11am boat train and return. The problem was that fares on boat trains were restricted by law, though the SECR thought it might be possible to charge 2s6d extra if a normal 1st class carriage was available - but a separate luxury train may infringe the rules. In contrast, the LBSCR had been running an "American car" on its Newhaven service since 1891.

By February 1908 the SECR was negotiating with the Pullman Car Company, who wanted a 15 year contract for their cars to be included in the 11.30am service from Charing Cross to Folkestone; the SECR seems to have been undecided, liking the principle but also considering whether it would be better to run a separate "train de luxe" with its own steamer service. In the event weight and length of the cars was felt to be a severe problem.

In May 1909 the idea resurfaced, this time as a suggestion that a Pullman buffet and parlour car should be included in selected trains with a 2s6d surcharge. By October it had been decided that a service should start in February 1910 with one parlour and one buffet included on the 9am and 11am down trains, and 3.20pm and 5.20pm up trains. In fact a demonstration run took place on 15 March led by Davison Dalziel MP, the chairman of the Pullman Company. Birmingham Railway Carriage & Wagon Company supplied six cars - three buffet and three parlour, although only four were needed for the service. The cars were named *Corunna*, *Florence*, *Savona*, *Valencia*, *Sorrento* and *Clementina*; internal design varied between them, with styles ranging from Louis XVI to Georgian. Davison Dalziel reckoned that they formed "the most luxurious train in the world" and even the *Railway Magazine* was pleased with "the delicious and daintily served tea...." The first public run commenced on 21 March 1910. The Pullman conductors travelled across the Channel so that they could "book" seats for the return journey.

In July 1910 Bonsor told SECR shareholders that the Pullmans were "a conspicuous success" and that one would be introduced on the Flushing route. Not everyone agreed, as a few weeks later *The Times* printed a letter complaining that 2s6d was charged for "entrance" to the buffet car and 1s for tea; there was no corridor connection for passengers to escape, and using the Pullman raised the 1st class fare from 2.1d a mile to 3.41d - but the 47mph average speed remained a "miserable gait".

From 14 November Pullman cars were added to the 2.20pm down and 9.05pm up Folkestone boat trains, with new cars *Regina*, *Emerald*, *Sapphire* and *Palermo* in service. From 1 April 1911 a Pullman, the *Shamrock*, was attached to the 8.35pm Victoria to Queenborough and the 6.25am return working with an intial supplement planned at 1s, rising to 2s6d; however this sailing transferred to Folkestone a few weeks later. From 7 May 1911 a new SECR Pullman, the *Cosmo Bonsor*, was used on the 2.20pm Charing Cross to Folkestone; this was built by Cravens and had 19 seats. By this stage four of the five daily Paris boat trains had Pullman facilities.

The Pullmans were then hit by the legal challenge that had always seemed likely, and that were an effect of the decision to authorise the joint working through an Act of Parliament: in June 1911 a solicitor challenged the legality of the Pullman supplement on the grounds that it was part of the 1st class fare and exceeded the legal maximum. At the same time a letter to the press alleged that the SECR was the only railway in Britain that still charged extra for "express" services - a Continental fare to Dover being 6s more than a normal service one. It was suggested that fares were set at 3d a mile in the case of Nicholson v. LCDR and that there should be a campaign of refusing to pay anything over 17s, but another solicitor argued that the Pullmans were an "extra" and therefore the supplement was legitimate.

In 1913 more Pullman cars were delivered. These included *Seville*, *Alicante* and *Leghorn*, all built by Cravens, and used on the 11am Victoria to Dover and Calais.

Pullman services were suspended during the War although some of the carriages were used on the specials from Charing Cross, but in January 1917 the SECR learnt that the Pullman Company was to build six extra carriages for when peace returned. In October 1918 it was decided to sell 15 vehicles from the SECR Hastings and Folkestone Car Trains to the Pullman Company for £15,000; they had cost £28,000 new but were in need of refitting. Pullmans were restored on the Folkestone route on 16 June 1919. Supplements were raised to 3s6d in 1920.

In February 1921 six new Pullman cars were introduced with electric table lamps. A demonstration run was made on 1 February 1921 but the cars did not enter full service until June.

Royalty made regular use of the cross-Channel services. In March 1904 the SECR decided to order a "continental royal saloon" from the International Sleeping Car Company. This seems to have been a speculative venture, as it was only in October 1905 that the King offered to hire it for two years at £500 per year, though this was forced up to £600. The SECR itself was hiring the saloon from the International Sleeping Car Co. for £465 p.a. and had really hoped to get £650 p.a. from the King.

By 1912 three saloons were being kept at Calais for the King's use, costing the SECR £1650 a year of which only £950 was refunded; the Committee therefore decided to withdraw saloons nos 1 and 3, offering no.1 for Queen Alexandra, and charging the King £480 for no.2. During the War saloons nos. 1 and 2 were stabled at St Denis, Paris and also at Le Landy. In March 1919 the principal saloon returned to Ashford for repair, using the Richborough train ferry.

One of the greatest royal occasions for the SECR was the funeral of Edward VII in 1910. From 8 May onwards the SECR brought over fifty kings and princes to London and on 18 May ran seven royal trains. These were:

Table 2: May 1910 Royal Specials

Day	Timing & Route	Personnel
18 May	1.25pm Folkestone-Victoria	Duke of Aosta
	3pm Admiralty Pier-Victoria	Crown Prince of Romania and German Grand Dukes
	3.10pm Prince of Wales Pier-Victoria	King of Portugal, Crown Prince of Serbia
	3.30pm Admiralty Pier-Victoria	Diplomats from France, Turkey and China
	5.15pm Port Victoria-Victoria	Prince Henry of Netherlands
	5.20pm Admiralty Pier-Victoria	Prince Fushimi of Japan
19 May	Port Victoria-Victoria	Kaiser Wilhelm of Germany
	Queenborough-Victoria	Prince John of Saxony, Princess Ellen of Greece
	3pm Prince of Wales Pier-Victoria	King of Bulgaria
	3.30pm Prince of Wales Pier-Victoria	Archduke Ferdinand of Austria, Persian diplomats

On 18 May the Swedish Queen Mother made do with a compartment on the 9pm to Charing Cross while the following day Prince Bovarady of Siam had a saloon on the 1.40pm from Folkestone. The Kaiser returned on 23 May, again via

Port Victoria, though others did not go home until 30 May. The SECR's own domestic royal train saw intensive service; in was formed of five teak carriages painted in the standard crimson lake.

The SECR soon realised that the motor car was becoming a useful source of revenue, describing them in 1900 as an "important traffic". It was decided to erect "stages" at Folkestone and Boulogne in order to handle them more easily. This did not solve all problems since, on 5 July 1907, Lord Compton's car was dropped off a derrick while being loaded onto the *Queen* - this cost the SECR £157. Another one was smashed at Boulogne in May 1908. To facilitate this market, the *Riviera* and *Engadine* were introduced in 1911 with strengthened decks to carry cars. In February 1912 the SECR ruled that the petrol tanks of cars should be emptied before they were loaded aboard. In 1921 the SECR provided a lock-up for the cars at Folkestone.

A perpetual problem was the hazardous business of loading and unloading the ships. Passengers regularly sued for damages, such as Mrs Ada French who won £43 after a box of "wearing apparel" fell into Boulogne harbour. In December 1905 the SECR paid out £102 after some ostrich feathers fell into the sea at Dover. The SECR also used "baggage boxes" which were sealed by customs and loaded onto flat wagons that ran in the continental train formations.

6   FOLKESTONE. — On the Pier. — LL.

Baggage boxes are being loaded onto *Onward* at Folkestone Pier in about 1912. There seems to have been little concern for health and safety issues! (R W Kidner collection)

Another complaint was about the unpleasant waits at Dover, notably for customs examination. From July 1901 passengers on the night mail from France could get their baggage examined at the London terminus instead, which saved much "tedious waiting...in the early morning."

Apart from the main business of the Channel ferries, the SECR also ran a number of excursions. For example, in summer 1906 the *Calais* did trips from Folkestone or Margate to Dunkirk or Calais. Towns like Boulogne also did their best to encourage a weekend trade - they offered to subsidise the 9am steamer to Folkestone in 1907 to develop this market; in fact the arrival of the new steamer *Invicta* made it possible to offer a 8.50am from Boulogne, arriving in Cannon Street at noon.

An unusual excursion was to the Rheims air show in August 1909; this left Charing Cross at 9pm and arrived at Rheims at 5am, using a special platform constructed for the air show traffic.

Finally, it should be realised that the SECR operated on the continent although it did not run trains there except to manage affairs in the port of Boulogne in wartime. There was an office in Paris and the SECR ran the buffet at Gare Maritime, Boulogne.

Continental Freight Traffic

The traffic in high-value, mostly perishable goods was known as *Grande Vitesse*, and was handled by the SER at the old low level part of its London Bridge station. This was inadequate and also needed for expanding passenger traffic, so when the SECR was formed the process of creating a new depot at Ewer Street was under way with total costs expected to reach £50,000, and requiring an expensive approach road from Gambia Street. It seems to have been the original intention for the site to be used as carriage sidings as there was so little space west of Rotherhithe. The goods depot opened in 1901. Goods travelling by *Grande Vitesse* were charged between 50% and 120% above normal rates and included fruit, pork, French rabbits and fashion hats. Growth of the traffic was notable:

Table 3: Growth of Freight Traffic (tons per annum)

Route:	1885	1898
Flushing-Queenborough	13,677	44,612
Calais-Dover	37,435	44,149
Boulogne-Folkestone	12,500	24,966

The SECR was still badly placed to handle this traffic due to a poor record of investing in suitable vans. In 1899 the SECR possessed a total of only 81 vans for the traffic and was unable to borrow any from the Midland Railway, who had helped out the LCDR in the past. As an indicator of the pressure, 71 of these arrived full at London Bridge on 28 July 1899. This was causing traffic to desert to the LBSCR, so the Managing Committee decided to spend over £400,000 on a new fleet of *Grande Vitesse* vans; 50 vans were ordered in March 1900. In January 1902 a fleet of new trucks for handling registered baggage in boxes was ordered - this counted as a *Grande Vitesse* traffic. Certain types of traffic grew, such as French flowers for Covent Garden which came across the Channel on the night cargo sailings.

At about the same time it was decided to concentrate the whole cross-Channel goods operation at Folkestone. This required some changes, such as a new engine shed, goods shed and sidings at Folkestone Junction and the old goods shed

Maidstone, built in 1898, was one of a small number of dedicated cargo boats in the SECR fleet.

there was converted into a stables. However, it was estimated that this concentration would save £3000 per year. After the destruction by fire of Queenborough in 1900, the Zealand goods traffic was eventually routed via Folkestone after a period of running via Tilbury. In June 1913 Folkestone received a new travelling crane and an electric capstan system to cope with increasing goods traffic. Another improvement was made at Folkestone in 1920 when "gravity rollers" were installed to deliver champagne imports to the customs warehouse.

One of the most important types of traffic was the mails. In 1909 the SECR was negotiating terms for a new French mails contract with the Post Office, revealing some interesting details of this business. The 1907 traffic amounted to 399,296 bags of mail, of which nearly 276,000 were sent from Britain to France and 90,000 returned - the latter including the Night Mails and India Mails; the balance came from France on day steamers. There were also 55,100 "parcels receptacles" of 100lbs each, but other parcels were dealt with under a separate French Post Office contract. The GPO wanted to reduce rates, especially for parcels, so that SECR income would have been £20,900 per year. This was not good enough for the SECR, who forced up the price to £29,721 by January 1910. The GPO offered to pay £28,500 until all new steamers were in operation, when the price would increase to £32,000 - but the SECR really wanted £42,000 and a 15 year contract. The GPO refused this, so the SECR retorted by running the mail steamers at convenient passenger times and reducing the winter service.

By this stage the Postmaster General, Herbert Samuel MP, was at the end of his patience. He ordered that the SECR should reinstate the 11.05am Dover to Calais and 1.40pm return, and wanted the problem sorted by the Railway Commissioners. The SECR defended itself with a claim about having to withdraw services due to safety concerns with old paddle steamers and by January 1911 was asking for £52,000 a year. On 1 June 1911 the Railway Commissioners ruled that the GPO should pay £27,000 a year up to 30 September 1910, and then £30,000 after that with an extra £10,000 for the India Mails.

The contract with the French Post Office covered only the rail section and produced much smaller sums, falling from £1878 in 1909 to £1594 two years later; most of it was contracted to the Nord, which had its own steamers. In 1920 the Nord decided to stop running its own steamers and the service was contracted out, causing the SECR to fear a transfer to the Dieppe-Newhaven route or even an air service. The night mail from Paris was retimed to 11pm and the return left from Victoria at 4.55pm, reaching Paris at 5am; this was inconvenient for passenger use, but much better for the Post Office in France.

A highly prestigious traffic was the transport of gold bullion. The Hamburg-Amerika Line ships handled this at Dover, so in 1905 the SECR was handling between £100,000 and £530,000 of bullion between Cannon Street and Dover every fortnight. This was charged at 90s a ton and needed the strengthening of the bullion room at Cannon Street. During March 1918 Barings Bank in London sent several very large consignments of silver bullion to Argentina via Paris in at least six consignments of 150,000 sovereigns each.

The SECR Fleet

The merging of two fleets meant that some old vessels could be disposed of. In October 1898 the Joint Committee reviewed the state of the fleet and decided to dispose of the *Calais-Douvres* as it needed new boilers and to get rid of *Roubaix*, a cargo boat. *Foam* was to be retained only for the Indian Mails service although a new mail steamer was being built at Birkenhead. The Committee then decided to dispose of the mail steamers *Mary Beatrice, Albert Victor, Louise Dagmar, Invicta, Petrel, Maid of Kent, Ware, Breeze, Samphire, Prince* and *France*. Also no longer required was the life vessel *Jubilee*. This large disposal brought a great increase in efficiency but also was the prelude to the wholesale re-equipping of the cross-Channel fleet with modern turbine steamers - one of the most notable achievements of the SECR. However the SECR was not altogether progressive - in December 1905 it decided against wireless telegraphy for its fleet as "too expensive" although the Marconi telegraph was installed on two vessels in 1910.

On 9 April the *Maidstone* arrived new from Denny at Dumbarton, but immediately disgraced itself by colliding with a pier at Dover and three weeks later sustaining damage at Calais. In the meantime, the SECR had a problem with the Birkenhead vessel, *Mabel Grace*. In September 1899 the SECR refused to formally accept the vessel, but decided to keep it and see whether its performance improved. It was sold in January 1909 for a mere £4750, showing how the value of paddle steamers had depreciated.

Next to go was *Foam* in 1901, built in 1863 and only used for the Indian Mails traffic. The first new ship to be ordered was the *Canterbury*, from the Denny shipyard at Dumbarton as a replacement for the *Calais-Douvres*. It was delivered in January 1901 and was successful, so that by July the SECR had already decided to get a similar vessel to replace the *Folkestone*, built in 1878. The cost of the new ship was £83,000 and it was designed for a load of 1000 passengers; the *Queen* made her first trial voyages in June 1903 and proved a highly successful ship. The old *Folkestone* was sold to the British Central Africa Company in 1903 for £3500 and the name was re-used for a new cargo vessel that arrived at Dover in December 1903.

In August 1901 the SECR learnt that the LBSCR was to sell *Prince Arthur*, *Trouville* and *Calvados* from its Dieppe service - all these were of the *Canterbury* type. The LBSCR agreed to sell them for cargo use at £35,000, and to pay the SECR £10,000 for *Paris* and *Roubaix* in return. The deal took place on 2 October 1901, with the SECR reselling the *Calvados* for £13,750; *Prince Arthur* became *Deal* and *Trouville* became *Walmer*.

In August 1903 it was decided to sell the *Duchess of York* as she had developed serious faults. The *Mabel Grace*, *Empress* and *Chatham* were sold in 1904-5 and the SECR ordered one cargo boat of the *Folkestone* type (called *Hythe*, launched January 1905) and two passenger vessels like the *Queen* instead (*Invicta* and *Onward*). The *Victoria* was sold for scrap in 1905, but the *Empress* escaped this fate for a season as she was put to work on summer excursions to Dunkirk and sold when winter arrived. *Chatham* was sold at about the same time.

Onward leaving Folkestone, where it was later to catch fire and sink during World War I. (Wakeman Collection, Ashford Library)

In August 1906 two more turbine steamers were ordered from Denny at £75,500 each - the first was the *Victoria* (launched February 1907). Thus by June 1907 the principal steamers were *Empress*, *Invicta*, *Onward*, *Queen* and *Victoria*. The latter achieved a cross-Channel record of 51mins from Dover to Calais on 1 May 1907. This virtually completed the transformation of the fleet, though other services lagged behind; the Zealand Company, operating on the Queenborough to Flushing route, did not replace their paddle steamers until the end of 1909.

The *Princess of Wales* was sold to Argentina in 1910 for £12,000. A few weeks later the *Lord Warden* was disposed of to Holland as she needed new boilers and, with old paddle steamers *Calais* and *Dover* very tired, another new turbine steamer was ordered for £81,000.

In November 1910 the *Dover* broke down before its replacement had arrived, so the *Mellifont* was chartered from the Lancashire & Yorkshire Railway until April 1911. This was at a time when traffic was increasing rapidly, but the *Riviera* arrived at Dover in June 1911 and the *Engadine* was "taken over" in November; the latter cost £82,000. *Dover* was then sold to Norway and *Calais* went in November.

In 1912 the whole of Britain was stunned by the loss of the *Titanic*, where a factor in the high number of deaths had been an inadequate supply of lifeboats. A letter to *The Times* in April alleged that SECR ships could carry up to 1,300 passengers but had lifeboats for only a quarter that number.

A new steamer was ordered for £110,000 in November 1913, the *Biarritz*. This was being built as the War broke out, at which point the Admiralty requisitioned most of the SECR fleet. This left it with an inadequate stock to operate the remaining services, and so two more ships were ordered. *Biarritz* was launched in December 1914 but a month later the Admiralty declared that they wanted it - the SECR offered to sell it, incomplete, for £84,000. In March 1915 the SECR was annoyed as it had neither the ship nor the Admiralty's money! In the end the SECR agreed to rent it to the Admiralty for 24s per ton per month.

To fill the gaps in the service the SECR chartered other vessels including a French trawler, *L'Alsace*, for the fruit traffic in 1915, the *Alprecht* and *City of Charleroy* for goods. *Alprecht* was promptly requisitioned for minesweeping. The Admiralty lent the *Deal* back to help. In 1916 *Galacum* was brought in, but *Canterbury* and *Victoria* were both damaged in collisions.

The ultimate in SECR passenger steamers, *Maid of Orleans*, delivered in 1918.

Fortunately the new steamer *Maid of Orleans* arrived in 1918 at a cost of £108,000, and was fitted with wireless. The *Lochside* was chartered in May 1919 to help with the goods service until *Folkestone* returned although in June the best the SECR knew was that it was "supposed to be on the way home." A review of the passenger fleet at that date revealed that *Maid of Orleans*, *Biarritz*, *Victoria* and

Invicta all needed reconditioning whilst *Riviera* was at Denny's being repaired. *Engadine* was supposedly en route for home, but *Empress* had just set out for the Black Sea. On loan the SECR had *Princess Victoria* (Larne-Stranraer), *Arundel* (LBSCR), *Golden Eagle* (GSR of Ireland) and three Belgian steamers - *PS Leopold II*, *Princess Henrietta* and *Princess Clementine*.

At the end of the war *Onward* was rescued from its watery rest at Folkestone and sold to the Isle of Man Steam Packet Company in 1920. *C W Eborall* was sold at about the same time. However in February 1920 the SECR was feeling the shortage of decent ships, and especially wanted the return of the *Riviera*.

The SECR owned a number of other vessels which could hardly be described as part of its "fleet". This included the *Poste*, a hulk kept at Calais as a floating store and accommodation for workmen. It was disposed of in 1901.

The various SECR ships were involved in a number of accidents, but there were no major losses. For example, on 9 December 1899 the *Mabel Grace* collided with a Swedish steamer near the Varne lightship. Able Seaman Thomas Ford was killed, and the SECR ship cost £4030 to repair. Less than a year later the same ship hit the rocks near Folkestone Pier.

On 22 January 1901 the *Achille Adam* ran down and sank a schooner near Folkestone. 18 April 1903 was a day of heavy seas, causing the *Canterbury* to collide with Calais Pier and the French authorities to threaten arrest of the vessel unless damages were paid for. *Canterbury* was towed to Poplar for repair, but was then hit by a barge causing damage to a propeller. The *Chatham* ran aground in fog off Calais on 19 October 1904. *Queen* struck Calais pier on 30 December 1904.

On 30 May 1908 the *Onward* and *Queen* collided in fog; a seaman acting as look-out was killed. As a result of this the captain of the *Onward* lost his Master's Certificate for six months and a woman sued the SECR, claiming that she had lost

Invicta at Boulogne, scene of the accidental drownings in 1914.

all her hair because of the shock. *Queen* cost £2600 to repair.

During a gale on 1 September 1908 the crew of the *Dover* manned their own lifeboat to rescue men from the Norwegian *SS Pilen*; the sea was so strong that it broke most of the oars of the lifeboat.

Accidents were also caused by dangerous work practices. Greaser White on the *Queen* lost an arm in February 1904 when a cleaning rag caught in coupling bolts - this type of practice was forbidden. Two stewards on the *Invicta* were drowned at Boulogne in April 1914 as they did not use the gangway onto the ship.

The SECR fleet and its men were under the control of the Marine Superintendent, Captain Dixon. He had some difficulty with unrest among the engine-room crews in 1900, with the men timing their unrest to coincide with the peak traffic for the Paris Exhibition. In June 1900 Dixon wrote to the Managing Committee:

"I feel very strongly that they are taking a mean advantage of the position, and I should like to fight them but am afraid that the company's interests would suffer more than theirs. At the same time I shall not forget their action, and when we have tided over the difficulty will deal out to them the same measures that they have dealt to us."

Dixon also had charge of the Marine Repairs Dept at Dover, but this was replaced by contractors in 1899.

The captains of the SECR fleet also came under Dixon's control. In July 1905 he reduced the salary of the *Maidstone's* captain by £10 a year after he collided with the Admiralty Pier. Captain Goodburn was removed from command of the *Lord Warden* after it collided in 1907 with a Belgian vessel, the *Princess Henrietta*.

In 1919 Captain J Blake became Marine Superintendent and was given the first known SECR "company car" to help him shuttle between the various ports.

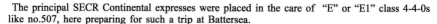

The principal SECR Continental expresses were placed in the care of "E" or "E1" class 4-4-0s like no.507, here preparing for such a trip at Battersea.

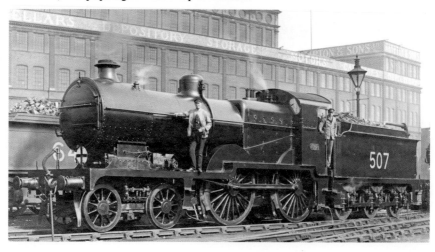

Finally, we should consider what crossing the Channel was really like - even after massive improvements in the SECR fleet. On 19 March 1921 a lady died on the up boat train near Tonbridge - "due to the exertion of vomiting acting upon a weak and lymphatic heart" - after an unpleasant voyage from France.

Port Victoria

Port Victoria had been built by the SER to rival the LCDR's establishment at Queenborough, but never secured any secure hold on the market for ferries to Holland; the SECR thus controlled 579 fairly useless acres of empty land. It saw some use for summer pleasure traffic but the SECR invited an independent report on the Port Victoria to Margate service in 1899 - so clearly it had its doubts! By 1899 the jetty was in need of repair and the SECR was considering spending £28,000 to overhaul it. Seeing little future use for it, on 18 July 1900 the SECR discussed a proposal to lease (or even to sell completely) the whole line from Sharnal Street to Port Victoria to the Admiralty - hoping for a return of 4.5%. As the Admiralty wanted to use it to land explosives for storage at Lodge Hill, the SECR would have had to abandon its tenuous plans for a dock at Port Victoria.

An unexpected boost to Port Victoria's fortunes came when Queenborough Pier caught fire on 19 July 1900. £80 was spent extending the platform and the hulk *Gannet* chartered to accommodate the extra staff but by September the SECR had decided that the service for Flushing would be better handled via Dover or Folkestone. Queenborough services continued to make some use of Port Victoria until 3 June 1904.

Perhaps this realisation that Port Victoria could be useful prompted the SECR's next suggestion to the Admiralty - that the line east of Sharnal Street could be doubled, with the SECR and the Admiralty having one track each. The idea was dropped in 1900 but revived in November 1901, when the SECR considered leasing the line east of Sharnal Street and selling Port Victoria. The pier itself was suffering from marine worms, and the wooden pillars needed to be encased in concrete at a cost of £21,000 in 1900-01.

However, in October 1902 the SECR learnt that the Admiralty had decided to build their own line from Sharnal Street to Teapot Hard on the banks of the Medway. This was an extension of the Chattenden Naval Tramway, which received a Light Railway Order in 1901. In the event the Tramway was completed only as far as exchange sidings at Sharnal Street, though the route was largely matched by the 1915 extension to Kingsnorth that became, in 1927, the Kingsnorth Light Railway. In June 1904 discussions about an Admiralty coaling station at Port Victoria were begun, and in July 1905 using it for Admiralty stores of coal and oil was suggested - with a portable platform being kept for "royal occasions". The Admiralty refused terms as "excessive".

In February 1901 the funeral of Queen Victoria attracted many foreign dignitaries. Kaiser Wilhelm returned to his yacht at Sheerness via Port Victoria. However the SECR found a more useful role for some of its property there by letting it to the Royal Corinthian Yacht Club from 1 May 1901 though their use of the creek meant that the *Gannet*, in use as staff accommodation, had to be replaced by two galvanised iron buildings. Four old 3rd class carriages were brought in for sleeping accommodation - possibly these were the same carriages being used for workmen's accommodation in 1910. Another party interested in renting land during 1902 was American Produce Importers Ltd.

The summer use of Port Victoria for pleasure cruises from Gravesend to Sheerness and other coastal locations was dropped for 1901. This left the *Myleta* and *Edward William* for disposal, but the SECR decided to keep them - they were sold in late 1908. There were occasionally other pleasure users, such as in 1909 when a private company ran cruises to inspect the fleet at the Nore using LBSCR and LSWR steamers.

The failure to sell the whole area to the Admiralty benefitted the Royal Corinthian Yacht Club, who were able to lease the hotel building in May 1906.

The Admiralty showed renewed interest in the Isle of Grain when planning to set up an "Aviation Establishment" in July 1913, for which the SECR offered to let land. In 1917 the Admiralty opened a gunnery testing range just to the north, at Yantlet Creek, and this was served by a short branch.

In January 1919 the Trinidad Central Oilfields Company, run by Alexander Duckham, became interested in renting part of the pier to unload crude oil to a proposed refinery nearby but this scheme failed to develop - though it was a foretaste of what was to happen at Port Victoria in the 1950s.

Other Docks and Wharves

Grosvenor Dock, on the north side of the line at Grosvenor Road, was the property of the railway and thus the SECR had to contribute £62 in 1900 to clear it of mud. In 1905 the SECR had to pay £700 to the owners of the *Vistula* after it was "lost" in the Basin. However the dock was filled in soon afterwards to make space for extra carriage sidings serving Victoria - a waste contractor paying the SECR 100 guineas for the privilege of filling it!

Charing Cross Pier was another fluvial outpost of the SECR which required investment. In May 1900 it needed dredging and repair. The Pier had been rented out to the Thames Steamboat Company since 1897, but their use was cancelled in 1903 after a year without payment. The pier was sold to London County Council in 1905 for £4241.

Further down the river was Angerstein's Wharf, an important industrial centre. In July 1910 it was decided to rebuild this so that steamers could unload more directly into trucks.

At Gravesend the SECR controlled a wealth of facilities. One of these was the Pier, which was struck and damaged by the *S S Bolderaa* in June 1900. In January 1906 the pier managed to find a use as a mooring for a hulk used to house immigrants under the powers of the Aliens Act. It also owned the canal basin, which was connected to the tidal Thames by lock gates. This was an expense, so in September 1900 the SECR proposed demolishing the gates although opposition made them decide the gates would have to be renewed. In 1905 there was an accident with the gates and the barge *Vistula*, which blocked the basin so that owners of other barges trapped inside sued the SECR. The SECR also had to pay £703 for damages to the *Vistula*, but at least the dock basin was earning over £3000 a year in dues.

At the other end of the Thames & Medway Canal, though not connected by water for a long time, was Strood Dock. This was in regular use so in July 1900 the SECR paid out £1750 to have it dredged although it 1904 it needed extensive re-building of the dock walls as well; it was hoped that the improvements would attract new users. A new coal wharf was completed and rented out in 1906. By 1919 it was badly silted again and William Rigby cleared it. Adjacent to the dock was Strood Pier which had once been a useful means of SER access by steamer into the Sun Pier at Chatham; however by 1903 it saw only occasional use by the *Belle* steamer and had annual receipts of £62-19-2d against expenses of £83-17-2d. The SECR thought it would be nice if the Medway Conservators took it over.

In 1902 a Bill was brought to Parliament for a new ship canal to connect the Thames and the Medway, to be known as the Medway & Thames Canal. The pro-moters persevered for several years, but withdrew their Bill in March 1905. The promoters had agreed to lease the Thames & Medway Canal for £1350 per year if their Bill was successful. The Canal was a liability for the SECR, especially as it overflowed regularly causing a local farmer to lose sheep; he sued, and won £300 in 1904. It still saw some use for commercial traffic and earned dues of £1306 in 1905.

The Canal was equipped with five cottages, used mainly by gangers and platelayers whose wives turned the bridges for the barges in exchange for paying no rent.

Another far flung "station" of the SECR maritime empire was Rye Harbour, which still saw some use for coastal traffic and had its own short branch. A new landing stage had to be provided in 1903 at a cost of £2200 after the old one had rotted and silted up - its traffic having migrated to Newhaven.

Tunnel and Train Ferry - Schemes that Failed

Passengers could at least walk from train to ferry but goods required slow and expensive handling from ship to shore or the reverse. In America, Russia and the Baltic such movements were being replaced by train ferries where goods wag-ons - and passenger carriages - could be hauled on and off of special ferries. The Intercontinental Railway Company was formed to bring such modernity to Dover with an emphasis on goods traffic; it was led P Stanhope MP and by the famous engineer Sir Benjamin Baker, with ferry designs prepared by Armstrong Whitworth. In June 1903 the Company offered to guarantee SECR losses on its goods boats.

The SECR employed Jabez Light to report on the Channel Ferry scheme and he argued that the SECR should not co-operate with its promoters; this was a spec-tacular error, as the train ferry idea offered vast improvements in the cost and time involved with handling goods. The IRC was upset about Light's report but pro-ceeded with its Bill, the Channel Ferry Railway & Quay Bill. In May 1905 the SECR had discussions with Sir Henry Oakley, one of the IRC directors, over new proposals, and the Channel Ferry Bill was postponed soon afterwards.

By 1906 it had acquired the Channel Ferry Railway & Quay Act of 20 July and an impressive board of directors - chaired by Lord Weardale, it included two Admirals, two "Sirs" and two "Hons." However Benjamin Baker died and was replaced as engineer by Sir John Wolfe Barry. Not to be downcast, the Channel Ferry Company was in negotiation with the Nord Railway of France by July 1907 and also discussing the vexed questions of berths at Dover harbour. In order to pacify the SECR it set itself a restricted market - the goods traffic to Calais, with a particular emphasis on refrigerated wagons, and the night passenger services. Under these terms the SECR thought it might be possible to accommodate the Train Ferry at the new Marine station or at the Prince of Wales Pier.

Despite the possibility of compromise, in July 1907 the SECR decided that its own engineer, Percy Tempest, should not co-operate with the Ferry Company. This short-sighted decision became an obvious error, especially when the War placed great pressure on cross-Channel facilities. The Nord, however, seems to have been more positive about the idea and this prompted the SECR into considering whether it should propose its own scheme - suggesting that its real objection was a fear that it would lose its control of the Channel. *The Times* reported that the SECR opposed the scheme "for practical reasons", which evolved into a dispute over the site of the ferry terminal south-east of the Lord Warden Hotel.

The SECR sent a group to look at the Baltic train ferries. The Danish ferries they found largely used for goods traffic with poor passenger accommodation, but the Warnemunde route carried through carriages for Berlin and Hamburg; the ships had two lines of rails taking seven 60ft carriages. However the group reported against the ferry idea for practical reasons - citing lack of shunting space at Dover and the present goods traffic being "small". The SECR even decided that if the DHB sided with the Ferry Company, then they would take some of their services to Folkestone and this would, of course, jeopardise the finances of the Marine station project.

The Ferry Company tried to negotiate a deal with the Dover Graving Docks Co. and also suggested a joint Marine station, but in March 1909 was rebuffed by the DHB on the grounds that it had "no space". Lord Weardale wanted berths in the Marine station adjacent to Prince of Wales Pier, and complained of "two years wearisome negotiations." He could not understand the SECR's attitude that there were technical problems when eighty similar ferries were in use in North America alone; the SECR argued that a trade in perishable goods could not be developed as there was "no space for the establishment of such a service". Nonetheless it was happy to accept plum traffic from Perigueux to England in 1913.

By March 1909 the SECR's stance was clearly one of "rivalry not co-operation". In May the Ferry Company visited the Board of Trade, but the Nord questioned whether the sea voyage would damage rolling stock. However Board of Trade pressure secured a "Conference of Engineers" to meet to discuss terms. According to the *Daily Mail* the main problem was the SECR's refusal to grant running powers and a German newspaper blamed the "short-sightedness of the Railway Company." By the middle of 1910 the scheme had effectively foundered, yet a new train ferry built for Swedish State Railways in 1909 was produced in Britain!

In 1911 the LBSCR promoted a scheme for a train ferry between Newhaven and Dieppe. This was in association with the Channel Ferry Company, again led by Lord Weardale, but had made no progress when war broke out.

As can be seen in the chapter on the SECR in wartime, the Great War gifted the SECR a fully developed train ferry at Richborough which began operating to Dunkirk on 6 February 1918. For a short time from 28 February 1919 the SECR controlled this facility itself and there were rumours that the ferries would be bought for a Calais service, but in November 1920 decided to cease running it as the traffic was small. From 1 February 1921 it reverted to control by the Ministry of Munitions although the SECR loaned six staff. However, some commercial experiments were made.

On 11 October 1921 the Richborough ferry was used for the first time by a commercial service, bringing 125 tons of fruit in sealed trucks so that no customs inspection was needed until London. This reached Ewer Street at 2.26pm. The load included eight decorated baskets of grapes and pears from the Garonne, as a present for the King; there were also 17,517lbs of nuts and 4526lbs of fruit. Each truck was decorated with bouquets and rosettes. A week later it was suggested that a regular service could be run from Rome for fruit and flowers.

Later that month the French Minister of Agriculture, M. Bouat, discussed the service. He said that new trucks were needed as the French ones were too broad for the English loading gauge and the SECR "possess no trucks really suitable for the transport of fruit and vegetables." He also thought it possible that English lorries could collect French produce from the ports, especially as there was little traffic to send back to France! Thus a brave experiment failed, and the train ferries were sold to the London & North Eastern Railway who operated them from Harwich from 1924.

A Bill for the Channel Tunnel, under the guiding influence of Baron d'Erlanger and with the Nord Railway's engineer, M. Sartiaux, was deposited in late 1906; it was estimated to cost £16million and was to have electric traction. In January 1907 the War Office decided to oppose it - being joined by the Prime Minister and Foreign Secretary. Some SECR shareholders objected to it as being "unpatriotic". The DHB also opposed and the Bill was withdrawn in April.

On 24 April 1913 Asquith announced a government inquiry into the Channel Tunnel, so on 11 June 1913 Arthur Fell MP founded a House of Commons Channel Tunnel Committee; Fell argued that a Channel Tunnel was needed to safeguard Britain's food supplies in the event of war - an interesting claim in the light of the subsequent U-boat campaign. Some military personnel felt that the Tunnel would be a strategic advantage in helping Britain to support its ally, France. During summer 1913 there were rumours that a new line would be built to serve the Channel Tunnel. The Bill was lost in February 1914, largely because of Campbell-Bannerman's arguments over the security issue. On 15 July 1914 the Committee of Imperial Defence decided against the Tunnel; no doubt their sense of personal wisdom was confirmed by the events of the following few weeks.

Even during the War, though, there was hope. A report on the planned changes to Charing Cross in May 1916 mentioned the need to accommodate Channel Tunnel traffic while in November the Channel Tunnel Company was seeking to engage Tempest as engineer to replace Francis Brady. In 1922 the Company was still active with Baron d'Erlanger still in command, and hopeful that the new Southern Railway would support it.

There were other schemes for new ports that failed. One of these was for a huge wharf, 1   miles long, at Greenhithe that was intended for the Atlantic trade. Its promoters predicted annual tonnage of goods at 4-6 million tons (the whole Port of London handled only 6m at the time) and a large meat traffic; the SECR promised to provide a connection. This scheme was still active in 1916 but in 1917 Gravesend Corporation attempted to get backing for their own deep water scheme, though the Port of London Authority did not support them - the SECR subscribed £200, suspecting that the PLA cared only to protect its own investment at Tilbury.

Chapter Six:

Problems with the Neighbours

The SECR had few geographical neighbours and only one of any significance; it also had a shared interest in only a small number of joint lines. The principal neighbour was the London, Brighton & South Coast Railway; this Company had its own territory at Victoria and London Bridge and shared the route from the latter to Redhill, which was owned by the old South Eastern between Coulsdon and Redhill. The Companies owned jointly the line between South Croydon and Crowhurst North Junction, which had been authorised as the Croydon, Oxted and East Grinstead Railway in 1878. This meant there was some tension over services further south, including to Tunbridge Wells.

Relations with the LBSCR tended to be difficult as the two companies shared a route between Redhill and London Bridge. The busy section at Redhill itself, shown here in about 1910, was owned by the SECR although the situation was improved by the opening of the LBSCR's avoiding line in 1900. (Wakeman Collection, Ashford Library)

Connecting to this was the Woodside & South Croydon, a jointly owned line, which gave access from the SER's Mid-Kent line. This connection opened in 1885 but had proved a financial disaster.

The two companies also had a share in the East London Railway, together with several other railway companies.

In the 1890s the SER had shown growing interest in the area south of Croydon, seeking to expand its interests with the Chipstead Valley line while the LBSCR planned to duplicate the SER's main line between Purley and Redhill with its own

"Quarry line" (opened 1899-1900) between Coulsdon and Earlswood, by-passing Redhill.

Relationships between the two were hedged around by various formal agreements, such as those of July 1848 and March 1864 covering much of the disputed territory in Surrey and Sussex. The SER received what it felt to be "a very large sum of money" for not providing a service to Eastbourne under terms of 1877. Purley station remained an issue because of the method used to divide the traffic receipts after the LBSCR had invested heavily in rebuilding it. Traffic receipts between Croydon and Redhill were covered by a series of agreements whereby takings were pooled and divided on an agreed percentage. The LBSCR took the view that these expired at the end of 1908 and wanted them renewed with the division based on actual takings over the previous ten years, perhaps with Chipstead Valley traffic being added to the pool. Bonsor disliked this idea and favoured arbitration.

The LBSCR had two main issues. Firstly, it contended that the SECR made great use of the Brighton's Purley station for little cost - SECR trains were stabled in the sidings there on race days and made no contribution to the costs estimated at £600 except for a few staff; secondly, it contended that the SECR had gradually increased competition.

The Managing Committee's response was aggressive: on 2 December 1908 they instructed the Superintendent to prepare a new timetable that would involve intense competition for the Croydon traffic. Within a few days the LBSCR had discovered this plan and had forced a meeting between its own Chairman, Lord

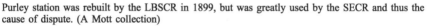

Purley station was rebuilt by the LBSCR in 1899, but was greatly used by the SECR and thus the cause of dispute. (A Mott collection)

Bessborough, and Bonsor. Bessborough wanted an agreement to share the costs of Purley fairly (with SECR arrears to be paid!) and wanted the traffic agreements based on the percentage of traffic actually carried, as well as Chipstead Valley traffic added to the "pool". In compensation, Bessborough offered to continue an allowance for the cost of Charing Cross in the calculations and to continue to "compensate" the SECR for not competing to some destinations.

Bonsor proved evasive, so that Bessborough was forced into sending him long explanatory letters - to which Bonsor replied with retorts such as, "I was greatly disappointed to receive another long letter from you..." Although the LBSCR had completed drafting the "Heads of Agreement" by January 1909, the SECR decided to escalate the situation by running extra trains on the Oxted route.

At first it planned an extra train from Sanderstead to London Bridge, from 1 May 1909; when the LBSCR objected, it put on two extra services from Edenbridge, via Sanderstead which conflicted with a LBSCR plan to run a train from Purley to London Bridge in a timing "they had long desired". The SECR erred here in that Edenbridge was already covered by a traffic agreement.

July 1909 brought a softening of attitudes, with the SECR agreeing to refer the Purley situation to arbitration and to make a contribution to LBSCR staff costs at Redhill and Croydon. However, when the LBSCR opened its South London line electrification later in 1909 it inaugurated a cheap fares policy ostensibly "to meet tramway competition." This forced the SECR to reduce its own fares between Victoria and Peckham Rye, also affecting off-peak traffic to areas such as Penge; the SECR reckoned it lost £2300 through the LBSCR's actions.

Relations worsened in February 1910 when the traffic agreements concluded and terms reverted to those agreed in 1848! The SECR decided to lower its Croydon fares, though the LBSCR responded by withdrawing interchange facilities between the two companies at Croydon, disputing tolls payable to Hastings and, two months later, interrupting access to the Caterham branch although Race traffic was handled in June. One of these issues were resolved later in 1910 when the SECR agreed to pay £1300 per year for the use of Purley station.

In February 1911 the SECR heard that the LBSCR was planning cheap season tickets from Croydon, though in fact this was the abolition of the five shilling deposit. The Brighton company offered to drop this idea if the SECR would allow changes to the Croydon fares and to third class fares south of there - which it would not.

Eventually William Forbes of the LBSCR and Francis Dent of the SECR reached an agreement, dated 4 December 1912 but backdated to 1 January 1909. This divided the revenues to various stations from London, though it was initially planned to last until 1915 only. Fare structures were liberalised and the LBSCR was permitted to issue 3rd class seasons on the Oxted line. In 1916 there were further disputes over money owed from the Croydon & Oxted accounts, although this was settled in February 1917.

During the War years, SECR and LBSCR tickets were interchangeable, but after it the SECR would have preferred the old divided system - causing reported problems with season tickets at Croydon in 1920. As late as January 1922 these bad-tempered neighbours were still arguing - the LBSCR complaining that it had to run all the Oxted services except two up and one down - whereas the SECR used to run eleven. It calculated that the SECR would receive an excess payment of £10,500 in 1922.

The Woodside & South Croydon

This short joint line was of strategic significance to the SECR since it gave access to the Oxted line without having to rely on the LBSCR's route through East Croydon. However, the line was a very poor financial performer and consistently lost money on working - which did not allow for the line's capital cost:

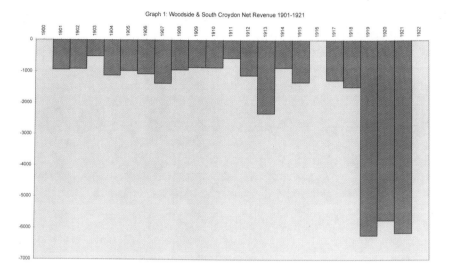

Graph 1: Woodside & South Croydon Net Revenue 1901-1921

However, in 1899 the SECR was in an expansionist mood in this part of Surrey since it was opening up and doubling the Chipstead Valley line and also doubling its Caterham branch. Both of these lines connected into the LBSCR at Purley, whereas the SECR would have preferred to connect onto its own Mid-Kent line.Thus it prepared a Bill for its own line from Selsdon Road to Coulsdon or Purley Junction, with connections onto the two branches which it justified by arguing that profitability on the Woodside line would be improved. Less charitably, the LBSCR saw it as an excuse to grab the Purley traffic and clearly felt threatened that it could be used to provide more competition over the Oxted route.

The SER Bill went forwards and was passed on 6 August 1900, authorising a line from Sanderstead to a junction with the Caterham branch between Purley and Kenley, with a spur to the Chipstead Valley line. There would have been a 580 yard tunnel and a new Purley Junction station, but the lines were never built - because the two companies were already taking steps to avert a costly "war". The two met in January 1900 and then employed Sir Charles Scotter to mediate on a new traffic award which gave the LBSCR a firmer share of Purley takings. A few months later the SECR made assurances about not reducing its Caterham fares and in May 1902 an agreement was also reached on pooling the Bexhill receipts.

The collapse of hostilities meant that the Woodside joint line reverted to its normal insignificance. Coombe Lane lost its own stationmaster from 1 October 1904, coming under the supervision of Selsdon Road. In a bid to foster suburban traffic, new halts were opened at Spencer Road and Bingham Road on 1 September 1906, with a railmotor service from a down bay platform at Woodside. They closed again on 15 March 1915 and only Bingham Road was ever reopened - but not until 30 September 1935. At the end of 1916 it was decided to close Selsdon Road's SECR platforms for passengers, so that local passenger services over the line ceased after 31 December, and to terminate the SECR Oxted goods there with a connection into the LBSCR's service; the former ceased running any Oxted line services for the duration of the war.

The Oxted Line

The Oxted line was the joint property of the two rival concerns as far south as Crowhurst but received far more attention than the Woodside line. Regular improvements were made, such as the decision to build a new elevated signalbox at Riddlesdown Viaduct in December 1898. A similar type of box was installed at Oxted Lime Siding in 1900 and a new crossover installed there on 20 June 1900.

The period saw gradual growth of goods traffic. New sidings were installed at Upper Warlingham in 1902, although there were complaints here at this time about manure being unloaded too close to the public road.

At Oxted there was expansion of facilities for the gas works in 1899-1902, including improvements to the coal chute. In 1902 two new sidings, a weighbridge and crane were installed with a goods shed following the next year. An extra timber siding was provided in 1914.

The fact that Oxted station was owned and served jointly by both the LBSCR and SECR had clearly not registered with the manufacturer of this commercial postcard! (Lens of Sutton)

Oxted Station. L. B. & S. C. Rly.

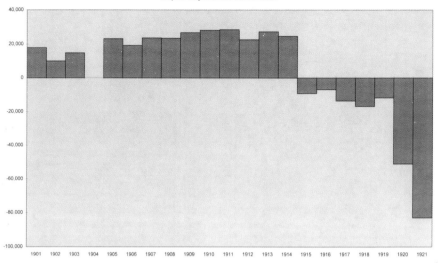

Graph 2: Croydon & Oxted Net Revenue

The main problem on the Oxted line was the state of its tunnels. A scheme of relining Oxted Tunnel began in December 1898, continuing until 1901 and being matched by work at Limpsfield. An extra ring of brickwork at the north end was added in 1903. On 15 June 1917 a ten foot section of the Oxted Tunnel roof collapsed, with a further 50ft being declared unsafe. It was about two weeks before one track was restored to use and a further three weeks for normal service to resume. However, there was a further fall of bricks in no.7 shaft of the same tunnel on 29 April 1919 just after the passage of the 2.45pm up Oxted train, closing it until 7 May.

Proper investigation revealed a serious state of affairs; in February 1920 an estimate of £25,000 was given with single-line working being necessary. It was decided to instal electric train staff signalling between Woldingham and Oxted Lime Siding to facilitate this. However the lowest quote that the Croydon & Oxted could get for the task was £53,000 - and an insistence on no penal clause due to the hazards of the work. Work on providing an extra lining in the middle section of 1,100 yards continued until 1921; concerns about the south end as well prompted the C & O to buy its own compressor and cement gun. The total cost came to about £88,000 and normal traffic did not resume until November 1921.

The line's viaducts gave periodic trouble; in the case of the Riddlesdown viaduct, which needed alterations in 1908, this meant that permission was needed from the owners of the quarry it passed over.

Six railway cottages were built at Oxted in 1899 and a stationmaster's house in 1900-01.

An attempt to foster local traffic on the outer reaches of the line was made with the introduction of a steam railmotor service on 1 June 1907, running between Oxted and Groombridge. To make this worthwhile, new halts were opened at Hurst

Green and Monks Lane.

Further traffic might have accrued nearer to Croydon if the Arkwright Estate had been successful in persuading the line's joint owners to open a new station between Sanderstead and Upper Warlingham in 1908-12; extensive building in this area did not start until the 1920s and Riddlesdown station was opened to serve it in1927. From about 1914 until 1927 Purley Downs Golf Club had its own halt adjacent to Purley Downs Road.

In April 1913 an attempt was made to blow up the gentlemen's toilet at Oxted station as part of the campaign for women's suffrage. A clock timed to go off at 3am, a nickel-plated pistol with one cartridge and a two gallon can of Shell petrol were left by two men, though the gun was picked up by a postman; it went off in his hand, but injured no-one. At about 4.30am two men were seen in Caterham trying to get to Croydon, one of whom left his hat behind, but it has only recently emerged that one of the two was Harold Laski, later to become a noted political philosopher. After the attempted "bombing" he was driven by a friend to Dover and then went into hiding in Paris - but was never suspected. On 14 September 1913 the stationmaster's office at Woldingham was ransacked and "Votes for Women" daubed around.

The effect of the costly tunnel repairs on the finances of the Oxted line can be seen from the following chart of net traffic receipts - the tunnel repairs being charged to the traffic account. It can also be seen that the start of the War brought an end to a period of relative prosperity for this line.

Chapter Seven:

New Lines and Light Railways

The Bexhill Branch

The principal new line opened under SECR influence was the short branch from Crowhurst to Bexhill on 1 June 1902, following a private ceremony the previous day. This was the nominal responsibility of an independent company, the Crowhurst, Sidley & Bexhill; however its directors included Sir George Russell, J J Mellor and Cosmo Bonsor and it received much capital from the SER. The fine

Two views of the impressive SECR station at Bexhill, designed by Blomfield in anticipation of significant traffic levels and with an eye on Edwardian standards of gracious elegance. (Author's collection)

terminus was designed by Arthur Blomfield, with whom Bonsor had a long association. Bonsor resigned in 1899 to allow Earl de la Warr to become a director - he wrote in from Bexhill Manor House and requested a seat on the Board. The company struggled to raise independent capital and as late as August 1900 the SECR was subscribing an additional £200,000. The SECR guaranteed a return of 3% on capital; total cost of the line was £472,700 though initial capital powers had only been for £180,000. The Bexhill company was absorbed into the SER on 1 January 1907.

The principal feature of the line was the seventeen arch Coombe Haven Viaduct, from where water was piped to Bexhill for the locomotives. An attractive terminus was built at Bexhill to the designs of Barry & Mercer, although houses were not provided for stationmasters until after the line had opened. Refreshment rooms were built at Bexhill, and let to Spiers & Pond. An intermediate station opened at Sidley on the same day as the rest of the line but the other large station was the junction at Crowhurst. This was a substantial creation, with two through lines and two loops for stopping trains.

The opening of the line strengthened the SECR's position on the Sussex coast and it campaigned for an adjustment of the revenue agreement with the LBSCR. A pooling agreement was reached in February 1902 for the Bexhill traffic with the SECR getting 25% and improved to 29% in June 1912; this was in the face of a determined effort to win traffic by the SECR, which provided at least one through Bexhill train daily from the outset until 1913. The War brought closure for the branch, after which it had no real chance to recover its competitive edge before the arrival of the Southern Railway rendered a competitive line superfluous.

After the line opened there was a lengthy debate in the town about improving pedestrian access from the new station to the seafront, which was blocked by the LBSCR line. In 1906 the town wanted to build a new subway beneath the rival line, but the SECR would not contribute, though there was a change of heart in 1909.

The Sheppey Light Railway

The Sheppey Light is another example of a nominally independent line that was closely involved with the SECR from the outset although its engineer was the light railway "king", Holman F Stephens. Willis of the SECR was a guiding light in it and in January 1899 was able to report to his SECR bosses that it promised to develop a traffic in market gardening produce, to encourage housing development at Leysdown and Minster, and to encourage visitors to the beach at Leysdown. However there was some conflict between those who wanted to develop Leysdown and those who wanted a local service to Sheerness; the former won.

The company received a Light Railway Order in May 1899 for a branch from Queenborough to Leysdown. The SECR understood that it would cost £52,500 to build, offering to guarantee a return of 2.75% on capital. This sum was less than it offered to other similar ventures in less isolated areas, but there was little risk of an LBSCR takeover! The line was built much more cheaply than the Bexhill branch, even allowing for the easier terrain: it was single, had limited signalling and ungated crossings. In June 1902 the SECR replaced the guarantee terms with an annual rental payment of £1,800 - though it was offered the whole line for £65,000. The SECR declined this offer on the grounds that it had no powers to purchase although these were acquired in its 1905 Act.

By June 1900 William Rigby was at work building the line, with the use of old LCDR permanent way materials and the work was completed for opening on 1 August 1901. SECR directors visited the line in their own saloon, but a celebratory luncheon was delayed until 9 August. New stations were provided at Sheerness East, Minster-on-Sea, Eastchurch and Leysdown. Local delivery sidings were provided at Brambledown, Grove, Holford and Harty

OPENING OF SHEPPEY LIGHT RAILWAY.

This new Railway, which extends from Queenboro' to Leysdown, will be opened for Passenger and Goods Traffic on Thursday, August 1st, 1901, and will be worked by a Local Service from and to Queenboro' as under :—

DOWN.—Week-days.

Distance. M. CHS.		a.m.	a.m.	p.m.	GDS.	p.m.		a.m.	p.m.	p.m.	p.m.	
—	Queenboro' ......dep.	9 5	11 5	2 5	4 20	6 40		11 35	2 10	4 0	6 15	...
1 39	Sheerness East... ,,	9 11	11 11	2 11	4 30	6 46		11 41	2 16	4 6	6 21	...
2 44	E. Minster-on-Sea ,,	...	...	...	...	...		...	...	...	...	...
3 10	Minster............. ,,	9 18	11 18	2 18	4 40	6 53		11 48	2 23	4 13	6 28	...
3 79	*Brambledown Sdg* ,,	...	...	...	CR	...	Call if required.	...	...	...	...	...
4 73	*Grove Siding* ,,	...	...	...	CR	...		...	...	...	...	...
5 47	Eastchurch ......,,	9 28	11 28	2 28	5 0	7 3		11 58	2 33	4 23	6 33	...
6 52	*Holford Siding...* ,,	...	...	...	CR	...		...	...	...	...	...
7 7	*Harty Road Sdg.* ,,	...	...	...	CR	...		...	...	...	...	...
8 52	Leysdown......... arr.	9 40	11 40	2 40	5 15	7 15		12 10	2 45	4 35	6 45	...

UP.—Week-days.

M. CHS.		a.m.	p.m.	GDS.	p.m.	p.m.		p.m.	p.m.	p.m.	p.m.	
—	Leysdown.. ....dep	10 0	12 15	2 50	5 40	7 30		12 30	2 55	5 10	7 45	...
1 45	*Harty Road Sdg* ,,	...	...	CR	...	...		...	...	...	...	...
2 0	*Holford Siding...* ,,	...	...	CR	...	...	Call if required.	...	...	...	...	...
3 5	Eastchurch ......,,	10 12	12 27	3 10	5 52	7 42		12 42	3 7	5 22	7 57	...
3 59	*Grove Siding* ... ,,	...	...	CR	...	...		...	...	...	...	...
4 53	*Brambledown Sdg* ,,	...	...	CR	...	...		...	...	...	...	...
5 42	Minster............. ,,	10 22	12 37	3 30	6 2	7 52		12 52	3 17	5 32	8 7	...
6 8	E. Minster-on-Sea ,,	...	...	...	...	...		...	...	...	...	...
7 12	Sheerness East... ,,	10 29	12 44	3 40	6 9	7 59		12 59	3 24	5 39	8 14	...
8 52	Queenboro' ...... arr.	10 35	12 50	3 50	6 15	8 5		1 5	3 30	5 45	8 20	...

The Trains will run from and to a Bay Road alongside the Up Platform at Queenboro' Station.

The Line is a Single Line, with Run-Round Loops at Queenboro', Eastchurch and Leysdown, and will be worked on the Train Staff and Ticket System as under :—

BETWEEN.	SHAPE AND COLOUR OF TRAIN STAFF.	COLOUR OF TRAIN TICKET.
Queenboro' and Eastchurch	Triangular Brass Bar, Painted Red	Red
Eastchurch and Leysdown	Round Brass Bar, Painted Green	Blue

These Train Staffs are necessary to unlock the Siding Points at the various Stations and Sidings, and any Train having work to do at any of the Sidings must always have the proper Train Staff, and must not be sent out with a Ticket.
The ordinary Rules for Working Single Line by Train Staff and Ticket will apply.

No Engine, Carriage, Wagon or other Vehicle (whether Loaded or Empty) whose weight exceeds **14 Tons** on any pair of wheels must be used on this Light Railway.

At present the short Platform at East Minster-on-Sea, on the Up side of the Line, about midway between Sheerness East and Minster, will only be used on specified occasions, of which due notice will be given to Engineman and Guard.

Inaugural timetable for the Sheppey Light Railway with some advisory notes on the working of the line.

Sheppey branch train at Queenborough with F class 2-4-0T. (R W Kidner collection)

Road; the first and last of these were successful enough to be extended as early as 1903. In July 1904 the SECR decided to buy 0-6-0T *Waddon* for £670 from the LBSCR to use on the line's goods trains, which needed a water supply at Leysdown; this engine became known unofficially as *Little Tich* and served on the island until 1910.

In 1902 a property business known as the Land Company began an attempt to develop an estate at Minster, for which a new station was opened at East Minster although it was to the west of Minster. In 1906 the basic platform there was extended to allow for the running of through trains from London, bringing potential customers to the site. The SECR made its own efforts to develop sparse passenger traffic by introducing the railmotor idea in March 1905, for which new halts were added at Brambledown and Harty Road.

Virtually all passenger services ran to Queenborough where they connected with normal SECR Sheerness line trains. For some people this meant a walk across the tracks, about 425 a day by 1909 so a footbridge had to be provided. This trickle of traffic was eclipsed by the 2nd London Territorials Summer Camp of 1909, for which £2800 was invested in new track and signalling at Queenborough to improve access to the branch. It was even suggested that there should be a direct Sheerness-Leysdown curve. Minster and East Minster stations were heavily used for the delivery of stores.

The railway was a beneficiary of the war, during which its traffic doubled. A new up side booking office was provided at Queenborough so that passengers from the SLR did not have to cross to the down side. In December 1916 a new branch was opened to the aviation school at Eastchurch, the site of which is now a prison.

Another short line in the area was the extension of the SECR into Sheerness Dockyard as authorised in its Act of 1902. This involved clearing away a wooden mortuary which belonged to Rochester Corporation! The line was expected to cost £10,000 with the Admiralty guaranteeing 4%.

Light Railways in Kent and East Sussex

The area of Sussex and Kent borderland south-east of Tonbridge was, in 1890, one of the areas of south-east England least well-served by railways. However it was fairly hilly and the market towns were small, so there was little prospect of rich profits in any scheme. A branch had been opened from Paddock Wood as far as Hawkhurst in 1893 and in 1895 a Tenterden Railway obtained an Act for a line from Headcorn to a point near Appledore, but this was rather too ambitious. The SECR Bill of 1898 included powers to "widen and improve" the Cranbrook and Paddock Wood line, and to extend it to Tenterden and Appledore.

More suited to the extent of likely traffic was the Rother Valley Railway, authorised on 2 July 1896, and planned as a light railway on an easier route from Robertsbridge through to Tenterden although it was only classified under the light railway legislation in 1899; the engineer of this concern was again Holman F Stephens. The line opened to passengers on 2 April 1900, its Tenterden terminus being at the station now known as Rolvenden. This was part of a minor "railway mania" in the region at this time, which included another 1899 scheme for a

Robertsbridge & Pevensey Light Railway with gradients of 1 in 30 and which the SECR firmly opposed - perhaps fearing LBSCR interest - with the Managing Committee showing a firmer interest in the Tenterden Railway. A time extension on this was obtained in 1904.

In 1901 the East Sussex Light Railway received an order for a line from Northiam, on the Rother Valley, to terminate in Rye goods yard, yet it was also opposed by the SECR and made no further progress. The SECR objected to a "junction loop" planned to connect this line into the Rother Valley at Tenterden - again, it perhaps feared an assault by the LBSCR from the west.

Another failed scheme was for a line from Cranbrook to Tenterden, with an original desire to go on to Ashford. This and the Tenterden Railway influenced the route for the extension of the Rother Valley line from Rolvenden to Tenterden Town station in April 1903, which used old SECR permanent way materials.

By early 1901 there was renewed interest in the idea of connecting Headcorn with Tenterden, as proposed by the Tenterden Railway. The SECR discussed the issue with the TR and the RVR, resulting in an agreement that the RVR would build an extension northwards to Headcorn using the TR powers which were acquired by the SER. The SECR agreed to guarantee the RVR a return of 3% after allowing for working profits; the RVR had to pay the SECR £16,000 to cover the promotion of the extension and its expenses. This was a very unwise move, which added substantially to the operating costs of the RVR without a proportionate increase in traffic. Work started on 11 March 1903 and, although it was expected at one time to open in June 1904, this section opened on 15 May 1905, by which time the RVR had become the Kent & East Sussex. Following this, the SER obtained authority to abandon its powers for Headcorn to Tenterden and on to Appledore as authorised in 1899.

Stephens began to become something of a "railway king". He was effectively managing director of a small group of light railways, which he ran from an office in Tonbridge; in June 1901 he reached an agreement with the SECR to put up a telegraph from Robertsbridge to his office. This was at least as much as he deserved, for he could claim to bring extra traffic to the SECR which by late 1901 was enlarging the booking office and extending the sidings at Robertsbridge; yet it is worth considering how much of this traffic was genuinely new to rail, or would have previously joined the SECR at different points. In 1906 the SECR reached agreement with the Kent & East Sussex for their use of Robertsbridge: it was to pay £78 for staff, £15 for water, and rent for facilities on a sliding scale up to £135. In 1921 this agreement was severed by the SECR who threatened to stop the K&ESR using Robertsbridge unless realistic terms were paid - this was agreed by late 1922.

During the 1880s the SER had shown fitful interest in an extension of the Tovil goods branch to Headcorn and even to Lydd. In January 1905 it was approached by another new scheme, the Headcorn & Maidstone Light Railway, asking for financial help in building along a similar route - which was declined. An Order was obtained for this in 1906 and amended in 1907. The intention was to run from a junction with the K&ESR at Headcorn to Tovil goods yard, and then to obtain running powers to Maidstone West - to which the SECR objected successfully in 1908. Unable to raise money, in 1913 the promoters applied to the Light Railway Commissioners for powers to drop the Tovil to Boughton section, but were refused.

In 1901 a Light Railway Order was obtained for a Maidstone & Faversham scheme, an area which had attracted periodic interest before. The SECR considered taking this over in order to build its own line, but would have preferred a route to Sittingbourne. In November 1903 Stephens offered to survey a route, which the SECR agreed to, but it decided not to make an application for a LRO that year although there was renewed interest in 1904.

Another unbuilt line was the Hadlow Light Railway, to the area north-east of Tonbridge, for which the SECR offered some support in 1903.

That there was little wisdom in building any of these lines was shown in the financial performance of the K&ESR's extension; in the first six and a half months, this made a net profit on working of only £50 leaving the SECR to pay out £1814 to meet the guaranteed return of 3%. This fell to just over £22 in the following six months, causing the SECR to "view with anxiety" the K&ESR's interest in a Northiam to Rye extension. In the latter half of 1908 the Headcorn extension made a net loss of £23 so the SECR paid out £1725 for the privilege of receiving the meagre traffic, though the Robertsbridge section did much better - yielding £302 profit.

The situation never improved, so it is surprising the line survived until 1954. The net profit on the Headcorn extension never exceeded £386 for six months (in 1912) and interest demands steadily increased; in the whole of 1919 £106 net profit was made, while the SECR paid £3450 interest at 5%. The Tenterden to Robertsbridge section performed better, recording a net profit £899 for a period of 1913. It is hard to see what the SECR gained from its commitment.

New Lines in North-East Kent?

The SECR used a lot of energy in investigating improved links between Canterbury, Herne Bay and also Whitstable whilst being sensitive to the dangers of an independent local scheme. A Canterbury, Whitstable & Herne Bay Light Railway was proposed and rejected in 1900; it was re-presented in 1901 shorne of the Whitstable extension but still opposed by the SECR.

A report in *The Times* in 1902 mentioned a speech of James Forbes, the former LCDR guiding light, who said that land had been purchased already for a Canterbury to Herne Bay line, but via Whitstable; this suggests the origins of the idea in LCDR/SER rivalry. By April 1902 the SECR was already publicising its scheme for an improved Whitstable station with a loop connecting the two existing lines, thus arguing that a light railway was not needed - yet it received its Order that year.

The Order failed to deliver a railway, so the SECR took other steps to pacify local opinion. An attempt to run a bus service in February 1905 failed due to poor roads. In November 1905 the SECR agreed to subsidise the Herne Bay Motor Co to run a bus between there and Canterbury - at £350 a year; this scheme appears to have been still-born too. In March 1906 the light railway was granted a time extension.

The next step was an offer by a Mr Igglesden to run a bus if the SECR subsidised him at 3d a mile - which was refused in March 1909. On this occasion the SECR was probably wise to commit no further money to a small local problem.

Hythe, Romney and Dymchurch

The SECR presence on the coast west of Folkestone included a short branch to Hythe and Sandgate plus a horse-drawn tramway between the two. Between Hythe and New Romney it had shown only periodic interest in developing a desolate shingle wasteland, although Dungeness shingle had been a useful source of ballast. In 1899 the SECR thought an extension of the tramway would be a good way of connecting Hythe and New Romney if it applied for light railway powers, but in 1900 the SECR obtained powers for a normal line on this route, which it immediately considered might be better as a local tram scheme.

However, by October 1900 a Hythe & New Romney LRO seemed to offer the way forward to the west while a Sandgate, Cheriton & Folkestone Lt Railway offered an unwelcome eastward route with electric trams.

In September 1901 the SECR discussed again whether they should complete the line between New Romney and Hythe and in June 1902 heard of a light railway scheme running from Ashford to Hythe, Dymchurch, New Romney and Appledore. However at this stage the SECR was keen not to divert interest away from its own proposal for a direct route into Folkestone Harbour from the west, without reversal. The SECR was meant to have completed the light railway by 6 August 1903, but instead applied for a two year extension.

May 1904 brought another discussion of the problem. The Managing Committee wanted a diversion on its proposed Hythe to New Romney line and also to extend its tramway along the Dymchurch Road though the Hythe rifle range caused a problem. Perhaps revealing its lack of commitment, the Committee then discussed running a motor bus instead between New Romney and Sandgate station. In November the Committee decided to let the powers for a proper railway between Hythe and New Romney lapse, so that a light railway order could be applied for in future. In the meantime, they would hire two motor buses to "test the traffic" - but by April 1905 another operator had gained the licence for Dover to Littlestone-on-Sea!

The Act which had authorised the Hythe & Sandgate Tramway also allowed its purchase by Sandgate UDC, which was also contemplating handing over the whole operation to two rival concerns anxious to develop electric tramways. A Folkestone, Sandgate & Hythe Tramway Bill was prepared by the British Electrical Traction Company, but the SECR favoured selling out to the National Electrical Construction Company even though it was offering £5000 less as it intended filling the gap to New Romney.

By the end of 1908 the NECC had failed to pay the £18,000 agreed and favour switched to the BET, although in 1909 the former obtained powers to take over the tramway. The scheme, which included an extension into Folkestone, had become enmeshed in technical problems over systems of propulsion allowed within

Earl Radnor's restrictions. In January 1910 the SECR considered a "petrol motor car" instead, but was hardly enthusiastic as the tramway was making a net loss. A new NECC Bill was prepared in 1913, which the SECR agreed not to oppose in exchange for a buy-out of the tramway at £9,000. The NECC seems to have favoured a "rail-less track", or trolleybus, at this stage, but the Bill was dropped in June.

For the 1914 season the SECR decided to run a motor bus from Hythe to Dymchurch as that place was "commencing to develop as a Seaside Resort." War brought an end to such activity and had an almost immediate effect on the tramway - which closed on 7 August. The service restarted in late May 1919, using ex-Army mules, but operating in summer only and without much success; between 1913 and 1921 the tramway accumulated losses of £4,000. On 26 April 1922 the SECR considered running a limited service from 1 June, but found this would cost £600 and yield only £200! Digging out of the tracks began almost immediately, but the tramcars survived to become part of Southern Railway stock.

Thus there never was a direct SECR route from Hythe to New Romney, and it was left to a "main-line in miniature" to fill the gap; but that is another story.

The Kent Coalfield and the East Kent Light Railway

At the turn of the century there was gathering interest in the possibilities of the Kent coalfield. Coal had been discovered at Shakespeare Cliff during work on the Channel Tunnel, and in 1897 the Kent Collieries Corporation was formed to exploit this by sinking Dover Colliery. Difficulties were encountered with soft strata and water, but in September 1903 coal was struck at a depth of 1,190ft. In February 1905 a workable seam was reached.

North of Dover Arthur Burr aimed to get a monopoly of the entire coalfield. He registered as Kent Coal Concessions in 1904 and planned to have all his mines on a grand scale but had financial difficulties. He created the Sondage Syndicate to do the boring and found coal at Guilford and Tilmanstone in 1907, beginning Snowdown Colliery the next year. In August 1907 Burr told the SECR that he hoped to produce 400,000 tons of coal a year in Kent and the SECR expected an increase of £450,000 in its goods traffic. At this stage though, Burr was beaten by his rivals at Shakespeare Cliff, who in October 1907 sent a truckload of coal to Ashford where the Locomotive Superintendent thought it "suitable". Snowdown coal was first produced in November 1912 and was tried by the SECR in April 1913 but further orders were soon cancelled due to the poor quality for locomotive purposes.

Further north, the Ebbsfleet Syndicate, Deal & Walmer Coalfield Ltd and the Anglo-Westphalian Syndicate were active. By 1917 three collieries were active in producing coal - Tilmanstone, Snowdown and Shakespeare Cliff; collieries were being sunk at Guilford, Chislet, Wingham and Stonehall and it was expected that there would be a total of twenty. Yet production was erratic but growing at the start of the war - a total of 1,099 tons in 1912, rising to 59,203 the next year and an estimated 110,000 in 1914.

Tilmanstone was the most effective of the mines at first, starting production in November 1912 and producing 76,000 tons in the first ten months of 1914 although experiencing flood closure; at an average of 2,000 tons a week, it was useful traffic for the SECR. Tilmanstone coal was tried in the SECR cargo boats in 1913 but they lost boiler pressure; "in the case of the *Maidstone* the decrease was apparently dangerous as the pressure fell so low that full speed astern could not be obtained in case of emergency." Guilford was abandoned in 1921 without producing commercial coal. Dover Colliery at Shakespeare Cliff closed 1914 due to water although some ironstone was mined; it produced one train of twelve ten ton wagons in 1912. SECR minutes in June 1912 mention the purchase of 12 wagons of Kent coal, which was of poor quality causing clinker to form and locomotives to lose time. Three months later the same source records the use of Shakespeare coal on the Deal and Hythe lines, but it was poor quality. Stonehall Colliery at Lydden was another failure; work there between 1913 and 1920 produced no coal at all although the concession passed to Stonehall Colliery Ltd in 1922. Hammill Colliery at Woodnesborough and Wingham were both started in 1910 but abandoned by 1914 with little having been achieved. Chislet Colliery, between Canterbury and Minster, was active by 1914 and producing coal by 1916; in 1918 the SECR decided that its coal was the best from Kent.

A further trial with Tilmanstone "best" in late 1913 produced the SECR verdict that its use was "dangerous", although reports in February 1914 claimed that it could at least be used for "gas coal". Two months later the SECR was mixing Tilmanstone and Snowdown coal with best Nottinghamshire to make it fit for locomotives, and in June felt that Snowdown briquettes were satisfactory for locomotives - but not for ships. Only two actual orders were noted by the Managing Committee, both for Tilmanstone coal. However, Kent coal was used to power the Richborough train ferries during the War.

The humble East Kent Light Railway was unlikely to challenge the SECR for passenger traffic - here the first train is hauled by EKLR no.1 with a carriage brought in from the KESR. (R W Kidner collection)

Some of these collieries were situated conveniently for the SECR. Shakespeare was the most easily served and miners travelled to and fro by passenger train, clambering in and out directly onto the track. In April 1913 the mine company requested a halt be built to regularise this arrangement, opened on 2 June 1913, but it was not a public station. A footbridge was provided in 1914 but the SECR had to restate that the halt was not for use by local women and children.

Snowdown and Lydden collieries were served by halts which received a "special service" from 1 January 1914 known respectively as Snowdown & Nonington and Stonehall & Lydden. A halt was also provided for the miners at Chislet and opened in the latter half of 1920, though without the luxury of a footbridge. All of these were open to the public.

Guilford, east of Shepherdswell, was mentioned by the SECR as in need of a siding in February 1907. However, it seems to have been served initially by extending the sidings at Shepherdswell in 1908 whereas Snowdown Colliery already had sidings by March of that year.

Guilford could not be served conveniently in this way and in May 1910 a siding between Shepherdswell and Kearsney (possibly at Lydden) was discussed, with Kent Coal Concessions to pay and this is recorded as having opened in February 1911.

However, in 1910 a new railway system was proposed to serve the coalfield - the East Kent Light Railway, promoted by Kent Coal Concessions who had fallen out with the SECR over preferential rates offered to Kent Collieries. The light railway was to have a "main-line" from Shephersdwell to Sandwich Haven, with a branch to Richborough and a loop back to the ex-LCDR line north of Shepherdswell. It also proposed a line from Canterbury West to Eastry via Wingham and branches to Guilford Colliery, Goodnestone and Northbourne. The SECR thought the Canterbury branch "quite unnecessary."

By November 1911 the first section of line, between Shepherdswell and Tilmanstone, was open but two months later the EKLR suffered the embarrassment of having coal delivered to *it* by the SECR - rather than the reverse. A temporary junction was laid in at Shepherdswell, "Junction no.1" being first postponed and then abandoned. During 1912 the EKLR opened the branch to Guilford, the extension of the "main-line" to Eastry, its Canterbury branch as far as Wingham Colliery and a short branch to Hammill Colliery near Woodnesborough.

In May 1913 the EKLR applied for new orders for lines from Hammill Colliery to Snowdown, Little Mangeham to Deal, Wickhambreux to Canterbury and Coldred (Guilford Colliery) to Alkham. None of these lines was likely to make a profit unless the coalfield succeeded, and the SECR objected to them as senseless competition. The Light Railway Commissioners approved of the Canterbury and Alkham lines only but the SECR also had some pressure from shareholders who thought the EKLR should be taken over.

June 1914 brought the news of another ambitious scheme - to link Wickhambreux to a new quay at Birchington Bay with a connection onto the SECR at Grove Ferry; this was opposed by the SECR as likely to steal traffic away from it. The SECR considered the need for a deep water port to encourage the export of

Kent coal in 1919, favouring Deal as a site.

In 1916 the EKLR started to run passenger services at a time when they were being cut back elsewhere, opening from Shepherdswell to Wingham Colliery on 16 October. The same year it opened an extension from Eastry to Richborough to serve the new port there, although this was opened to passengers only as far as Sandwich Road in 1928. The extension to Richborough opened, to goods only, in 1928.

Amazingly, in 1920 the Ministry of Transport granted more LROs to the EKLR. These were for Hammill to Snowdown, eastwards to Deal, the Canterbury extension, Coldred to Alkham and a few minor connections. Even more amazingly, work actually started on the Canterbury extension though it never got further than the hopefully-named "Canterbury Road".

The EKLR never reached Chislet or Betteshanger collieries. The former had been served by sidings since 1914, though these were much expanded in 1920 when traffic was 5,000 tons a month - and expected to rise to 1,000 tons a day. Betteshanger was the property of Dorman, Long & Co who, in 1922, agreed with the SECR to provide a siding - the SECR paid the costs and the company provided a guarantee on interest depending on traffic levels. S Pearson & Co planned to join Dorman, Long in establishing a steel works on the site.

Other Connecting Lines

The country station of Martin Mill became important during the construction of the Dover naval harbour works by Messrs Pearson. In May 1899 the SECR agreed to lay in a siding for the shingle traffic, essential for the production of huge quantities of concrete. This was to receive shingle from Stonar, which was itself brought onto the SECR at Richborough from a short private line. In 1900 at least shingle was also being received from Rye.

The Martin Mill shingle siding connected into a light railway which ran from Martin Mill to the cliff edge, and then at an angle down part of the cliff-face to reach a point 300ft above the harbour works. Material then used a rope-worked incline to reach the shore level. The railway had its own engine shed at Martin Mill.

The line became redundant when the harbour works were finished and in 1909 it was suggested that it be converted into a narrow-gauge electric tramway with a Light Railway Order being obtained. This plan came to nothing, but the tracks remained until removal in 1937.

The SECR connected with two interesting lines at Sharnal Street, on the Port Victoria branch. One of these was the Chattenden Naval Tramway (authorised by LRO 1901) which ran west to the Admiralty magazine at Lodge Hill, while the Kingsnorth Light Railway ran east to Kingsnorth Air Station and a jetty on the River Medway. The connection at Sharnal Street was opened on 22 August 1904, which would thus seem to be an effective opening date for the Lodge Hill line. The eastern section was not built until 1915.

At its northern edge the SECR was affected occasionally by other proposals. In 1900 the Purfleet & Gravesend Junction Railway proposed a new Thames crossing by tunnel, but failed to interest the SECR, the Midland or the Great Northern so its Bill was withdrawn. The plan was revived in 1904, with a degree of GNR interest. In 1907 a Lower Thames Tunnel Railway proposed a similar scheme.

A few other light railway schemes are worthy of mention, though none of them were parented by the SECR. A LRO was granted in 1902 to the Orpington, Cudham & Tatsfield LR, maintaining a marginal existence until 1906. In 1903 the Aldershot & Farnborough Light Railway was an active scheme and obtained its LRO for a route via North Camp station. A scheme to foster commercial development was the 1907 plan for a light railway from Sandwich station to Sandwich Bay, with a new hotel; the SECR supported this.

Headcorn was photographed in 1950 and a train is seen in the KE&SR platform, waiting to leave for Tenterden. (H C Casserley)

Chapter Eight:

Passenger Services

Although covering only a small area geographically, the SECR operated a wide variety of services - ranging from continental boat expresses to the horse-drawn trams of Sandgate. In terms of passenger numbers it was also one of the largest railways in Britain, though many of the journeys were fairly short; in 1902 it carried 74 million passengers, ranking fourth behind the Great Eastern, London & North-Western and Great Western. However the numbers of passengers were steadily eroded by tram, tube and motor bus competition, especially after the cuts in service of March 1907 which led to a fall in passenger numbers of 2.25million over the second six months of that year. In 1908 passengers totalled 59.5million of which 90% were 3rd class and only 2.8% 1st class, though the latter contributed a higher share of the revenue of £2.48million. These losses were balanced partially by a growth in longer distance commuting, with the Kent coast traffic becoming very worthwhile by 1914.

The SECR certainly extracted its pound of flesh from 1st class travellers. A 1909 comparison of 1st class season rates on different companies showed that a SER season from Pluckley cost £42 whilst a GER ticket from Colchester, a similar distance, was only £31 a year.

At the start of the era, the SECR offered some very remarkable services to the outposts of Kent. For example, in November 1900 Lydd enjoyed ten daily trains to New Romney and four to Dungeness; there were seven to Appledore. The fastest time to Charing Cross was 3hrs 5mins and the 5.15pm from St Paul's had a through carriage that ran all the way to Littlestone-on-Sea. Dorking, which was much better served by the LBSCR, still had 18 daily SECR trains to London although the best on offer was the 7.30am which took 82 minutes to Charing Cross. The 5.08pm from Charing Cross arrived at Dorking at 6.25pm and reached Reading at 8.03pm; one assumes few Reading people used this route to and from work in London! Margate still enjoyed the fruits of SER and LCDR competition with eight London expresses on each route; the 3.15pm from Charing Cross reached Margate Sands at 6pm but the 5.10pm from Holborn Viaduct arrived at Margate West at 6.45pm.

The war years had a drastic effect on SECR services from which some lines and stations never recovered. It also inflated fares to 75% above pre-war levels, although this was reduced to only 50% above on 1 January 1923 - which the SECR estimated would abstract £612,000 from the Southern Railway group's revenues. Nonetheless the era closed with an unexpected compliment from *The Times*, which in March 1922 reported that the SECR had obtained "a reputation for punctuality undreamed of by travellers a few years ago."

Main Line and Express Services

At its formation, the Managing Committee was anxious to create the right impression by speeding up its principal trains and showing the advantages of its new flexibility. Thus in January 1899 a service was introduced from Victoria to Hastings in 1hr 50mins. However savings were made by pruning competitive services, such as the former LCDR through trains between Victoria and Gravesend West Street; these were reduced to one set making two return runs from 1 November 1900.

The flexible use of London termini gradually became a way of tailoring trains to a particular market. Thus in 1910 the 7.05am from the ex-LCDR station at Ramsgate Harbour ran via Chislehurst to Cannon Street for the business traffic, but the 10am ran to Victoria.

The traffic on the longer distance SECR routes was highly seasonal so there were marked differences between summer and winter timetables. The winter 1900-01 timetable combined the former 7.30am Dover and 8.15am Hastings departures from Charing Cross as far as Tonbridge and also cut out seasonal boat trains such as the 2.45pm down and 9.35pm return. The Dover "Car Train" ran at 4.28pm from Charing Cross, but between July and the end of October had a separate portion starting from Cannon Street; for winter it ran in one portion, but via Cannon Street.

A staff group pose by one of the "American Cars" - actually built in Britain - for the Folkestone Car Train and later sold to the Pullman Company. (R W Kidner)

Towns were very quick to criticise any apparent reduction in the quality of service - *The Times* carried letters complaining of the Hastings line winter service in 1900, including one that attacked the down service to Battle - the only pre-2pm departure took 3hr 9mins!

The resort towns were acutely conscious that the quality of their rail service had a major impact on their fortunes. All were helped by new annual 1st class seasons from 1 June 1905. Folkestone's reputation as a genteel resort depended on its quality service, and was encouraged by the "Car Train"; from 1 July 1901 it was served by the 8.55am from Dover, arriving at Victoria at 10.50am with a 5pm return, and a 8.30am to Cannon Street. In October 1905 Herne Bay made a series of demands including the wider availability of 7s returns from London, cheap week-end tickets from the Medway towns, the extension of the Ramsgate to Birchington locals to their town and the running of a "motor car" or railmotor service on the Kent Coast. Sandwich enjoyed a 7.55am Mondays only to London in summer 1909, which ran to catch the weekend golf trade and was non-stop from Folkestone.

After the opening of a new concert pavilion at Margate in 1911 the SECR ran extra fast trains from 2 October to attract visitors during the "off" season. The daily *Cliftonville Express*, reintroduced that year, ran from Victoria at 9.10am to Margate West (slipping two coaches at Faversham) with a return at 5.20pm.

However the SECR could not match the higher speeds of major lines like the Great Western. In its January 1909 edition, the *Railway Magazine* commented on the problems of the ex-LCDR main-line where "heavy loads over a very difficult road, complicated by numerous service slacks" limited speeds; principal trains at the time included the 3.25pm from Victoria which ran non-stop between Herne Hill and Westgate yet averaged only 46.1mph. The 5.10pm from Holborn Viaduct ran non-stop between St Paul's and Margate, achieving only 47.9mph while it was commented that even the descent of Sole Street bank rarely saw speeds exceed 61mph. For 1910 the 5.10pm from Holborn Viaduct, which was limited to nine carriages of which four were slipped, was accelerated to 50.17mph on its non-stop run.

The longest non-stop run on the SECR seems to have been from Deal to Victoria, at 82 miles still too short to yield high average speeds with a lengthy London approach in 1912, when the fastest timing was the 8.27am Paddock Wood to Ashford at 55.4mph.

The Reading line saw little improvement although there were occasional signs of hope. For summer 1910 the 11.45am from Charing Cross conveyed a "fast" portion for the Reading route, which saved 45 minutes from the previous fastest journey to Wellington College - indicating the margin available for im-provement!

The summer 1911 timetables saw some imaginative new services and also some faster ones - St Leonards was brought within 90 minutes of Victoria. An interesting working on the Hastings line was a run from London Bridge to Dover via Hastings. The 9.25am from Folkestone ran via Maidstone on Mondays only as, confusingly, the 8.18am from Sandwich did not call at Maidstone on Mondays. The flexibility of the various SER and LCDR routes was exploited by a succession of trains from Holborn Viaduct to the Kent Coast:
  9.05am via London Bridge and Dartford to Ramsgate Hbr
  10.30am via London Bridge and Hither Gn
  11.25am via St Paul's and Elephant & Castle

Resort towns also required imaginative excursion and pricing policies, which could be used to stimulate trade in slack periods. In 1909 the Metropolitan Railway organised an excursion from Verney Junction in rural Buckinghamshire to Ramsgate. Summer 1910 saw a Sundays-only 9.52am excursion from Victoria for Queenborough and Sheppey. Another feature of the 1910 season was the 7.23am excursion from Reading to Hastings, arriving at 10.28am; the return left Hastings at 8pm and took an even three hours. In 1912 there were Reading to Kent coast trains at 5.50am and 11.05am, with a return from Deal at 1.48pm. During the winter of 1911-12 the SECR ran an extra 9.10am from Victoria to Margate and Ramsgate, which slipped a portion at Faversham for Herne Bay. In the reverse direction it also ran a Thursday "half day excursion" from Ramsgate at 1pm, returning from Charing Cross at midnight. But excursions reached more surprising destinations - there were bank holiday specials to Aldershot for the families and sweethearts of soldiers. Cheap 3rd class tickets were issued any day to Godstone, Merstham, Betchworth, Shoreham etc. for ramblers from 1911.

Another feature of 1912 was an excursion on Mondays and Saturdays from New Cross via the Oxted line to Deal and Margate.

Resorts most needed good Saturday trains, for these made residential holidays possible whereas Sunday travellers were often day excursionists. The summer 1910 timetable included some examples, such as the 9.02am Charing Cross which served virtually every Kent resort between Margate and Sandgate; the 1.05pm from Cannon Street ran on Saturdays-only to bring City gentlemen down to their holidaying families at Bexhill or Hastings for the weekend, Saturday being a half-day at work for many. The 2.03pm from Victoria served Ramsgate in similar fashion, running non-stop to Herne Bay.

Express and excursion traffic was severely curtailed during the war (see chapter 13) and did not return to normal for months afterwards. Some accelerations to coastal towns were made on 1 March 1919 and some new Saturday only trains introduced, such as the 1.15pm Cannon Street to Ramsgate Harbour and the 8.50am Bexhill to Cannon Street.

Substantial improvements were made on 16 June 1919 with many extra fast trains to the coast. These included a 9.10am Victoria to Margate and Ramsgate, which slipped a portion for Herne Bay. The new 10.33am fast to Folkestone and Margate ran via East Croydon while the 1.30pm Charing Cross to Folkestone had a slip portion for Shorncliffe and Hythe. Bexhill was served by fast trains from Charing Cross at 4.40pm and 7.30pm. The weekend traffic at Deal was served by a Mondays only 7.45am up to Cannon Street, arriving at 10.05am; Deal was also served by slip portions on the 2pm from Victoria and 3pm from Charing Cross. The fastest up train from Hastings, the 7.40am, reached Cannon Street in 1hr 35mins while the 8.05am from Folkestone Central took 1hr 30mins to the same terminus. By 1922 it was possible to get from Dover to London in 80 minutes.

Also from 16 June 1919 four spare Pullman cars, not needed for boat trains, were attached to some Folkestone and Kent coast services for a two shilling supplement. These were the 7.55am and 4.50pm up from Folkestone with the return services at 11am and 7pm. The *Thanet Pullman* worked two return trips to Ramsgate, including the 7.45am up which reached Cannon Street at 9.30am. A Sunday working was added from 10 July 1921, the 10.10am from Victoria non-stop to Margate at 11.40am. By August 1922 a Pullman car ran on the 8.05am Margate to Cannon Street and 5.10pm return, the latter taking two hours. The introduction of domestic Pullman services followed many years of experience with the "American Car Trains" running to Hastings and Folkestone.

The 1921 summer timetable further improved the coastal services with trains such as the 10am from Sandwich via Deal and Folkestone to Charing Cross and the 4pm return. A daily Pullman service was run to Deal during the 1922 Golf Championship.

A way of speeding up main line services yet serving wayside stations was the slip carriage; the SECR perpetuated these throughout the period. In 1910 two up Victoria trains slipped portions for Holborn Viaduct at Herne Hill but slips were more common in the down direction such as the 5.10pm Holborn Viaduct to Dover slipping a Ramsgate portion at Faversham. The SECR still operated nine daily at the end of the period - three at Ashford and Faversham respectively, two at Swanley and one at Herne Hill.

Lavish standards were established in the Car Trains, as seen in the ornate furnishings of this vehicle used on the Folkestone service.

Through Services

At the start of the SECR era, the Managing Committee was anxious to improve connections from other parts of the country and in March 1899 was discussing this with the Great Western and the Metropolitan District. Attempts to run a GWR service from Liverpool to Folkestone Harbour were not a success, and in November 1902 Folkestone demanded improved GWR connections, but from 1903 a service from Birkenhead to Deal was established. In January 1904 *The Times* reported that Vincent Hill of the SECR had arranged with the Great Western and the Great Central for through carriages from Manchester and Birmingham to Folkestone and Dover, for which the SECR spent £7000 strengthening bridges on its Reading line. On 29 July it was reported that the Managing Committee found the new train "surpassed their expectations." This encouraged the running of a Bradford to Deal carriage in conjunction with the Midland Railway, starting in 1905 and being withdrawn due to the war in March 1915.

The GWR service to Deal meant that the Kent station required new signalling, including a signalbox, in 1906. The train was smartly timed on the SECR if not elsewhere, with its 1910 run between Tonbridge and Ashford at 55mph being the fastest on the system. The train ran as the 10.38am from Deal and 9.10am from Birkenhead.

A through express from Manchester was photographed on the SECR in about 1922, with a rake of LNWR carriages. (R W Kidner collection)

In March 1911 the SECR agreed with the GWR for through carriages from Wolverhampton and Birmingham to Queenborough Pier, Margate and Folkestone - via Bicester and Victoria, following trial services which commenced on 1 October 1910. This was aimed principally at continental travel. This routing meant that the Deal to Birkenhead was still the only passenger train from the SECR onto the GWR at Reading. From 1911 the LNWR also offered a service via Willesden and Herne Hill to Dover and Deal.

In winter 1913, as trouble loomed in Europe, little Deal enjoyed an enviable service. The 10.38am from Deal offered a through coach to Birkenhead, arriving at 9.15pm after a relaxing 72 minutes in Reading! The 9.05am from Birkenhead reached Deal at 6.30pm. Deal also had through carriages from King's Cross on the 2.41pm, arriving at 5.33pm. The 10.25am from Deal via Herne Hill and Kensington reached Manchester London Road at 6.23pm; the southbound train left Manchester at 10.15am and made possible a Paris arrival at 11.25pm.

Deal lost its through service from Birkenhead in December 1915, the train terminating at Folkestone instead, and it ceased altogether a year later. From 10

July 1922 a daily service was provided from Birkenhead to Ramsgate, Margate Sands and Dover, which also served Deal. A Ramsgate Harbour to Manchester, Liverpool and Kendal train via Willesden also commenced running at that time.

Through services from the Great Northern included regular excursions to Margate from north London, using GNR stock. However from 1 July 1911 to December 1914 there were through carriages from King's Cross to Deal, Folkestone and Dover, with Margate and Ramsgate included from 2 June 1913 until 30 September 1914. In 1911 the train from Deal was scheduled to reach Herne Hill at 1.02pm and King's Cross at 1.25pm, returning from the latter at 2.41pm. The 1913 service ran as the 2.55pm from King's Cross to Ramsgate Harbour and with a 10am up service. From 1 July 1905 to 1 October 1910 a service from King's Cross to Bournemouth had operated via Herne Hill. These services allowed for cross-platform interchange at King's Cross, then reversed at York Road.

A route with long-distance potential that was never really explored was the coastal line via Rye. In February 1909 Lord Brassey led a deputation requesting a through service connecting the coastal resorts, after which the SECR agreed to provide one train a week from Margate to Brighton with cheap fares. From 10 July 1922 a Dover to Bournemouth West was introduced, but this would not have pleased the coastal towns as it was routed via Redhill and Guildford in order to run as a portion of the through GWR train.

Suburban and Local Services

The formation of the SECR was met with some attempts to improve the suburban connections between the systems. This was most effective in outer-suburban areas, with one of the first innovations being the running of some through trains from Charing Cross to New Brompton instead of Chatham Central after 1 January 1899; Chatham Central lingered on until 1 October 1911. Not everyone was satisfied though - there were complaints in January 1899 that the ex-LCDR route from Sevenoaks to Bromley was now much slower due to changes at Otford and Swanley.

One part of the suburban traffic that became controversial under Bonsor's aegis was the "workmen's" services, which offered special reductions for early services into London if large blocks of tickets were bought in advance by employers or trades unions. New united arrangements introduced on 1 April 1899 made these available to London Bridge, Victoria or St Paul's before 8am and reduced the fares from most SER stations. As discussed elsewhere, this traffic was hardly worth the SECR's consideration - yielding an average fare of only 1.34d per journey - and was gradually surrendered to the trams.

In fact inner suburban services were gradually reduced thereafter, notably from 1 March 1907 with sharp reductions of services to Greenwich Park and Crystal Palace although trains to the latter were accelerated by 5 to 10 minutes in 1910; from 1 May the SER Greenwich line also had reductions, the GNR through service to Woolwich having ceased the previous day. The Greenwich line changes saved 150,000 train-miles a year although Charlton station had to be modified to allow for terminating trains. Services from the Midland Railway to Victoria via Ludgate

The humble last chapter in an expensive saga - an 0-6-0T on a motor train working at Greenwich Park in 1912, but not even this economy could save a branch whose whole *raison d'etre* was competition between the SER and LCDR. (R W Kidner collection)

Hill ceased 1 July 1908. However other inter-company London services clung on - the GWR was still running seven daily Southall to Victoria trains in 1913 while the LSWR operated three a day between Richmond and Ludgate Hill with the SECR routing a dozen between Moorgate and Clapham Junction. From 1 July 1907 until 30 November 1915 the Beckenham Junction to Crystal Palace (Low

Most of the SECR suburban services were gradually taken over by Wainwright's "H" class tank engines such as no.550 of 1904. (R W Kidner collection)

Level) service was operated by a railmotor. The SECR also competed by cutting out some stops so that Brixton to the City could be accomplished in 10 minutes compared to 30 by tram and in 1911 provided extra peak period fast trains between Crystal Palace and the City.

Instead, outer suburban services were improved. Beckenham Junction received better services to Victoria and Holborn Viaduct from 1907, accomodated by an up bay extension and an extra up siding. From 2 May 1910 Woolwich Arsenal had an increased non-stop service taking about 15 minutes, while there were extra trains to Addiscombe Road as well.

An interesting service was that introduced late at night for gentlemen of the press from 1 October 1910. This ran at 1.15am from Ludgate Hill to Herne Hill, Penge and Bromley South (arrive 2.38am) and at 2am to Beckenham Junction. From 1911 trains ran at 1.15am, 2am, 3.15am and 5am all to Bromley South at workmen's fares of 5d. There was also a 12.33am Holborn Viaduct to Bromley North.

Inner suburban services suffered particularly during the war years. By April 1915 the Crystal Palace High Level line enjoyed what *The Times* called a "special hourly service" from Victoria in about 70 minutes, although "one exceptional express at midnight performs the journey in 47 minutes. The distance by rail is 9.75 miles." The reduction of this service produced a furore from season ticket holders at the line's stations and at Nunhead, forcing a public meeting to be held at Caxton Hall in December 1916 when it had been learnt that the line was to close altogether from 1 January 1917 - they hoped, joylessly, for the retention of a peak hour service. *The Times* suggested it would be better to cut "women's cheap shopping trips." Services were restored on this line from 1 March 1919, running to Ludgate Hill, but the refreshment room at Crystal Palace stayed closed as it had not been used "to full capacity".

The end of the war was expected to lead to a total revision of SECR suburban practices but this was postponed in May 1919 while the Managing Committee considered the question of electrification. Also some suburban stations, such as Spa Road and Southwark Park, did not reopen and in October 1919 the SECR had to face a deputation led by the Mayor of Bermondsey on behalf of 4500 employees of the Peek Frean's factory. In rural contrast, Cheriton Halt managed a delayed reopening on 14 June 1920 while Grove Ferry escaped a plan to close it in November 1921. Further demands were made late in 1921 but the SECR reasoned that the traffic was "quite insufficient to pay expenses" although the situation might change with electrification.

Also disgruntled about the SECR's failure to return to pre-war services was the Metropolitan Railway, who insisted that the SECR had a legal obligation to resume trains into Moorgate Street and claimed £30,000 losses in October 1922; this case was not finished when the SECR became part of the Southern Railway.

Towns with a good local service found this a benefit in developing a market function, which is why the market towns of Kent which were on main-lines grew much more rapidly during the nineteenth century than those on branches. Maidstone was very conscious of this, so from 1 May 1899 secured special day rates from stations within a limited area. From 1 July 1906 the 11am Folkestone train was diverted to run via Maidstone to improve access to the county town, but this caused an unexpected problem when Robert Horner of Preston Hall claimed the legal right to stop it at Barming under a contract of 9 March 1876. The SECR decided to fight the case and, if it lost, to terminate the train at Maidstone; after a protracted dispute, Horner decided to sell the Hall and dropped the case in 1909.

Estate developers also required a good service and often tried to obtain concession tickets in order to sell houses. In 1903 the SECR refused this to developers of land at Smitham Bottom and Dorking. The developer of the St Germans estate at Hither Green fought to get an extension of his concession arrangement, but the SECR granted only a few extra months of 1912.

A key problem was how to develop little used rural lines or to compete with buses in more urban areas for short distances. An experiment that seemed to offer hope for both problems was the railmotor, with the SECR deciding to order one for trials on the Sheppey Light in March 1904. This followed an unsuccessful experiment with two petrol-electric railcars on the same line late in 1903. After discussion with Kitson & Co, two steam railmotors were ordered, capable of carrying 56 3rd class passengers and hauling a trailer at up to 30mph. These two were tried out on the Sheppey Light and Strood to Chatham Central services with encouraging results, so the SECR eventually ordered six more from Messrs Kitson in October 1905.

Steam railmotor no.2 in its original condition.

The railmotors had long wheelbases so check rails had to be provided on the Sheppey, Port Victoria, Westerham, Hayes and New Romney branches. These made it possible to open new halts on quiet branches, for example Chevening on the Westerham line, and also to develop local services in more populous areas: a Dover to Sandgate service began on 1 July 1907, but required signalling alterations at Sandling Junction. A railmotor on the Sevenoaks to Otford line was an obvious economy while the Gravesend to Port Victoria service made it possible to open six new halts in July 1906 for an outlay of only £338 - at Milton Rd, Beluncle, Denton Crossing, Stoke Crossing, High Halstow and Grain Crossing.

The railmotors were not a great success - some passengers disliked them intensely and they also lacked operating flexibility. The unit on the Hayes branch was soon transferred to the Woodside - Selsdon Road line, then to Beckenham Junction for the Crystal Palace service; the Westerham unit was unpopular and from 1 July 1907 was used on a Hastings to Rye service for which new halts were opened at Three Oaks Bridge, Guestling and Snailham Crossing.

In November 1907 the Locomotive Superintendent, Wainwright, suggested that future railmotors should have a separate tank engine and this design became the "P" class of 1909, being used initially on the Otford to Sevenoaks and Reading to Aldershot services which reversed at Ash.

However the railmotors encouraged the wider practice of building cheap halts to test local traffic potential. In 1908 the SECR decided to widen the experiment to Folkestone-Elham-Canterbury services for which a new halt was opened at Cheriton on 1 May 1908 and one at Warren a month later. December 1908 brought a local request for a similar service on the Maidstone West to Paddock Wood line, resulting in new halts at Teston Crossing and Beltring & Branbridges on 1 September 1909. New halts were rejected at Barming bridge and Luck's Crossing.

Another line to receive this treatment was the Gravesend West Street branch, where Longfield Halt was opened on 1 July 1913 although the improved service ran from 1 June. The Gravesend service was provided by a "railmotor" of one engine between two carriages, shuttling between Gravesend West and Swanley on a pattern previously tried between Otford and Sevenoaks. Other lines receiving this treatment included Ash to Aldershot Town, Beckenham Jct to Norwood Jct, Ramsgate Harbour to Birchington, Margate Sands to Minster, the Greenwich Park branch and the Bexhill branch from 1 December 1915 to March 1916. The history of the railmotors is a chapter of SECR practice that shows an attempt to make a variety of services more attractive to travellers, though those that survived the depradations of the tram fell victim to the motorbus in the 1920s.

Within the suburban area there were very few "special" services that attracted attention, apart from Race traffic on the Chipstead Valley branch. A Pullman service was run on race days from Cannon Street to Tattenham Corner in 1922, proving a success. One of the few destinations that could expect some variety was the Crystal Palace branch, where services sometimes ran for special events; an example of this was for the concerts by the musician Paderewski in December 1898, for which non-stop services from Victoria ran in only 20 minutes. In 1901 the Crystal Palace company tried to set up a Naval & Military Exhibition, for which the SECR contributed £500. However an endemic shortage of modern stock made it difficult to handle special events, especially in the summer, and *The Times* complained of "an utter incapacity to meet the public needs" after the shambles of a Handel Festival at Crystal Palace in June 1909 when no extra trains were provided - 17 passengers were counted in one 1st class compartment.

A potential source of much traffic was the Woolwich Arsenal football team at Plumstead, but the SECR was erratic in the quality of its service.

Another view of a SECR railmotor in service, some time after 1914. (R W Kidner collection)

Carriages

By April 1899 the SECR realised that it had a paucity of main-line carriages and asked for a quotation for 32 bogie carriages from the Metropolitan Carriage & Wagon Company - which priced them at about £2000 each. Within two months the need had escalated to 50 bogie composite carriages and by September a cost of £417,000 was being discussed. These carriages were needed for a variety of types of traffic, including extra summer services to the Kent Coast and for the Victoria to Hastings trains. The SECR also wanted five or six sets for an improved London Bridge to Caterham service, needed stock so it could improve the Chipstead Valley service and even needed extra saloon stock for the boarding school traffic. Another aspect of this review was to spend £80,000 to replace the oil lights in LCDR stock with electricity. By March 1903 34% of SECR stock had electric lights, but there were problems on the suburban trains due to slow speeds and frequent stops. 51% had electric lights by 1910 and all the Mid-Kent stock was converted in 1913-14.

Not all these traffics could be handled efficiently on a railway with seasonal traffic. The solution to the school traffic was reached in 1905 when six saloons were adapted for steam heating for "occasional use" - four of these were "bogie picnic saloons." The carriages could also be used for "Royals" and "VIPs". In 1907 old six-wheel "invalid saloons" had to be replaced by converting two bogie carriages.

In April 1900 the Managing Committee was able to note that four-wheel stock had been eliminated from express services. However it survived elsewhere: in August 1902 *The Times* commented that Sevenoaks to Cannon Street services used old Mid Kent stock "block trains". These four wheelers had three compartments per carriage and were "so soundly and substantially built that they seem to defy decay."

In fact the carriage stock was generally elderly. In March 1903 ex-LCDR carriages numbered 1,251 and ex-SER 3,038 with an average age of 41 years. It was decided to renew 59 per year. Matters were improved after July 1906, when the general manager received authority to use £25,000 from the GPO contract to replace all four-wheelers. At the end of 1908 the SECR had 3102 carriages including railmotors and royal saloons, so clearly a large number of small or old vehicles had been scrapped - made possible by declining inner suburban traffic. However in March 1909 Greenwich stock and LCDR Metropolitan Extension stock was still in use but scheduled for replacement.

The next stage was to reduce the use of six-wheel stock on outer suburban services. In March 1909 74 carriages in block sets with steam heat were planned to be ordered for Victoria to New Brompton, Charing Cross to Maidstone West, Dorking, Tonbridge and Oxted runs so that six-wheelers could be released onto inner suburban runs. The Maidstone and New Brompton stock was ordered first at about £2000 per carriage. From 1 July 1910 new carriages were introduced on Dorking, Oxted and Tonbridge services.

From this date the SECR made regular orders for stock, often dictated by reviews of traffic needs. In July 1913 a new plan was devised for using North Kent stock - there to be 49 block trains and 12 extra six-coach sets. The Mid-Kent line had 13 and a half sets of seven carriages each, which were rearranged into six-coach sets with 44 spare for peak service.

The replacement of carriages was interrupted by the war and did not really begin again until late in 1920 when there was some urgency to get replacements built before the end of Government control of the railways so that the SECR could claim back £1,800,000 for "arrears of maintenance" on stock. By November 1920 work had started on five three-coach sets and six 3rd class carriages, but another fifty 3rd class and twenty passenger luggage vans were needed. To build these at Ashford at this time would have cost £200,000 compared to £80,000 before the war. In the event many were contracted out as Ashford was very busy.

The stock ordered in 1899 was fitted with a communication cord that operated the vacuum brake, following trials on the 10am Folkestone train and return. In May 1900 it was decided that this should be a feature on all SECR stock and by March 1903 48% of carriages were fitted.

Another improvement was the introduction of steam heating. This was included in the boat train stock of 1905 with other carriages having to be adapted to run with them as "bogie picnic saloons". By October 1906 six principal expresses in each direction had steam-heating and it became a general policy from 1907. From March 1909 steam heat was fitted to all main-line stock as it was overhauled, including boat train stock. However steam-heating was not a brilliant success in the winter of 1908-9 and so additional footwarmers were provided for the next winter though demand at Tadworth still exceeded supply. However the adaptation to steam heat continued, and in 1912 30 horse-boxes were included in the scheme.

Toilets became more common too - five new "fixed trains" of lavatory stock were ordered in November 1905 and another 22 3rd class with toilets. By 1906

Westinghouse brakes were being replaced by vacuum brakes.

Window bars were removed from most carriages after the Midland Railway disaster at Hawes Junction and in July 1913 it was decided not to equip new carriages with them.

An issue which caused the SECR some uncertainty was whether or not to abolish 2nd class. This was due to calculations of whether passengers would trade up or down, so in 1911 it believed there would be a loss of £80,000 per year if 2nd class was abolished; gross receipts were about £500,000 a year from the class. However the LBSCR had already decided to abolish 2nd class by this time, having largely eradicated it on the local London services and to Dorking from 1 June 1911.

In January 1902 it was decided to build a new Royal saloon, an order being placed with the Lancaster Railway Carriage & Wagon company at £3070 - though £500 extra had to be spent improving the interior; when delivered in March 1903 the final cost was actually £4170, whereas twelve 1st class carriages ordered three months later cost £1450 each.

Carriages also had to be kept clean, but the breeze of modernity swept in here too. Following trials at Blackheath of a machine bought for £350 in 1903, the SECR decided to buy four vacuum cleaners in 1905.

Passengers' Experiences

A considerable inconvenience to passengers, and a safety hazard, was the practice of "pulling up" due to short platforms. The SECR worked to eradicate this problem, improving Redhill and Sydenham Hill in 1906; the latter was so short that part of a train often stopped in the tunnel. Broadstairs and New Brompton also required attention.

In contrast, the lowest platforms (other than at halts) seem to have been at Wellington College where they were as low as 1ft 10ins - Board of Trade minimum being 3ft. They were raised in 1907.

Another danger was a lack of footbridges. At Bekesbourne, Adisham and Shepherdswell, passengers still crossed the tracks on the level in 1910, using steps cut out of the platform; all were provided with footbridges.

The SECR had to avoid any charge of negligence or it could face hefty compensation claims; in June 1904 a passenger was killed when leaning out of a train near London Bridge, but the jury said the SECR had been negligent as signal posts were too close to the line.

Passengers often claimed damages when injured during a journey in a SECR carriage - though incidents were often not the SECR's fault. In December 1901 Roland McDonald brought an action against a lady whose dog had bitten him while in a 3rd class saloon - but the woman had given a false name and address. More typical was the woman passenger on the Reading line who sued after a goods train derailed, wrenching the door off her own passing carriage and cutting her with glass.

Charles Swinden won £216 after sitting on a wet cushion in 2nd class, as a result of which he got inflammation of the knees. There were also dangers in waiting at stations - a passenger at Dover had a leg amputated after being hit by timber from a passing truck.

There was also the danger of being in a compartment with a dangerous stranger. In March 1911 a Mrs Roberts was attacked by Ernest Smith near Charing Cross, who "feloniously wounded, assaulted and robbed" her, for which he received 18 months in prison. In December 1916 Nellie Purvey, aged 21, was found dead on the line near Windmill Bridge Junction, Croydon, having leapt out of the 4.15pm from Charing Cross. The only other person in her compartment had been Percy Batty, who had had "medical treatment", and it was assumed the woman had tried to escape when he had a fit of some form; "the girl's face bore an expression of terror," it was recorded.

Henry Pearce was charged with behaving improperly to a lady on a train between London Bridge and New Cross on 8 March 1917. Six days later he committed suicide by jumping into the Thames. An even more dramatic case occurred between Crayford and Bexley on 5 June 1917, when Aircraftsman Hurst heard a woman screaming in the next compartment; he climbed out and edged along the footboard to see what was happening, then managed to pull the communication cord. As a result, Bernard Cook was sentenced to five years for an assault on Edith May and Hurst was awarded ten guineas.

The balance of legal battle was redressed in the struggle against ticket fraud. This was made worse when SECR employees conspired in the fraud, an example being Conductor Philpott who allowed his friends to travel on other people's used tickets and corrupted a porter into similar practices during 1902.

In November 1902 the SECR decided to use Shame as a new weapon, by publishing names and addresses of people convicted of ticket fraud. The idea may have been a limited success, as annual convictions fell from 147 in 1901-2 to 85 by 1903-4, although in March 1905 the practice was dropped. The number then increased to 142 in 1906-7.

J Dunckley received a month in prison in 1908 for gumming a new date slip into his old season ticket. Another racket was to collect the unwanted return halves of excursion tickets which people threw away as two excursion fares could be cheaper than a normal return; three Hastings men were arrested in 1908 for picking these up in the street and then selling them for 2s each. However, when a Dover councillor was caught without a ticket in February 1913 the Mayor succeeded in persuading the SECR not to prosecute in exchange for a contribution to the Benevolent Fund. In contrast, a Lt Metaxa was court-martialled for using a false season ticket in 1918.

An unusual offence was committed by Mrs Norton in 1908, by allowing her son to travel knowing that he had scarlet fever; she was fined £5.

Passengers' luggage also caused problems. In October 1903 Elisabeth Grouville was sent to prison for 18 months after taking away another lady's bag at Margate; the court censured the SECR as it had so little luggage space that bags were left piled on the platform. In a contrasting case, Jesse Burroughs was arrested at Tonbridge when he tried to take away his own case which was labelled for Southborough - he won £25 damages. The situation was improved by the setting up of a central lost property system at St Paul's in 1904.

Lost property could sometimes be disturbing. On 24 June 1911 a holiday basket was left at the Victoria luggage office by a woman but opened by police three days later as suspicious; it was found to contain the body of a seven-month old child, covered in chloride of lime. On 11 October 1917 a child of less than three weeks was found with a broken neck in a carriage at Dover.

Passengers were charged for the transport of luggage, but Lady Cecil was rather shocked in October 1908 when her handbag was weighed for a journey from Dover to Hawkhurst!

On 24 April 1914 the Countess of Stafford arrived at Charing Cross by boat train and gave her case to a man she supposed to be a SECR porter. In fact he was an impostor, and made off with jewellery worth £500.

October 1903 brought a shock at Beckenham Junction when two dead people were found in a compartment; they were C Spiller and Miss Alize (sic) Cook, the former having shot the latter and then committed suicide. On 15 June 1907 a Lt Simmons was found at New Cross after shooting himself. A Norwegian sailor shot himself in a 3rd class lavatory in June 1912 and another man on a Charing Cross to Dartford train two months later.

Another death occurred on a Tattenham Corner "up" race special on 24 April 1907, when Robert Choat attempted to get into a full compartment; he got into an argument with Thomas Palmer, a "professional pugilist", who hit him repeatedly in the neck as a result of which he died. Palmer was found guilty of manslaughter. On 28 September 1907 a returning hop-picker was found dead of natural causes in a Staplehurst to Deptford train at Knockholt.

Other hazards of rail travel included drunks and indecent literature. In March 1904 the Navy was concerned that the refreshment bars at Chatham caused annoyance to passengers; about 1,600 sailors travelled up to London for the weekend from Chatham and Sheerness, it being suggested in October 1908 that it would be better if they could be landed at Port Victoria and confined to special trains from there. In October 1905 the SECR reminded W H Smith that it had the right to control types of literature being sold at stations.

Chapter Nine:

Moving the Goods

During the early years of the new century the SECR seems to have made good progress in winning industrial traffic over from the waterways - principally of the Thames and Medway. The period saw the construction of a number of industrial sidings to works already in existence and using water transport. By 1911 the SECR was sufficiently encouraged by a "large increase" in goods traffic that it ordered 300 extra wagons, part of this being to handle heavier flows of coal by rail from the north. However the picture was not entirely rosy: before the Great War broke out, the SECR was already losing some traffic to motor lorries, especially hops and fruit within a thirty mile radius of London. After the end of the war produced a new supply of cheap lorries, this trickle of losses became a flood. The SECR also attempted to improve its regulation of goods traffic by a new system of goods controllers based at Ashford, Tonbridge and Chatham from June 1918.

By far the most important change to SECR goods practices was the opening of the Hither Green yards in January 1899, as a result of a policy pursued by the SER to simplify its goods operation in London. The six miles of sidings allowed goods to be sorted and then forwarded more efficiently to depots such as Bricklayers Arms and Blackfriars. This investment reflected that the main freight task of the SECR was the supply of London's needs, especially of foods from Kent, with some extra continental traffic. Thus among the first significant decisions of the Managing Committee were the extension of the Stewart's Lane goods yard and new sidings at Plumstead (1899), with the construction of a new "inwards" goods building at Bricklayers Arms (1900) complete with hydraulic cranes. However it is notable that the expansion of public goods sidings had almost ceased by 1910 except for a few locations where new building work caused an increase in general traffic; the distance from any point on the SECR to London meant that most of its goods traffic was easy prey for the new motor lorries and traffic losses were already significant by 1921.

Some early changes to Hither Green included installing facing points so that goods trains could run straight in without having to set back. Hither Green also allowed for the integration of SER and LCDR goods working, with the old LCDR sorting sidings at Loughborough Junction being closed and the traffic for Blackfriars being handled at Hither Green instead. By 1906 the SECR was planning the complete closure of the Blackfriars goods depot having transferred much of its traffic in 1900; furniture traffic was transferred away to Stewarts Lane in 1902 and in January 1908 much other traffic to Bricklayers Arms. Blackfriars goods depot was on a site close to the Thames and protected with flood gates, but when it was suddenly inundated on 30 December 1905 the gates were not shut and £1000 worth of champagne was damaged.

The opening of Hither Green brought about a gradual change in goods workings. Not until late 1907 were LNWR goods trains re-routed to reach Hither Green "via Orpington" rather than through London. Traffic at the yard grew steadily and in February 1913 the down yard had to be expanded.

The trans-shipment of goods such as fruit from the SECR heading north was handled at Bricklayers Arms, but by 1910 this depot was often too busy and much work had to be done at Stewarts Lane. Bricklayers Arms was improved with electric lights, and by installing hydraulic power in 1912-3 to replace sixteen horses and one engine. By June 1911 motor lorries were already a common sight at Bricklayers Arms, making deliveries in the central London area. However in 1920 the SECR decided to buy an electric delivery van from the General Vehicle Company, which may safely be claimed as the SECR's first electric motive power; at the same time it took 50 Government surplus lorries for use from Bricklayers Arms and Plumstead. By January 1921 only 26 lorries survived in London and there were seven more in Kent; by using them the SECR saved £1200 a year and so bought another 29 AEC lorries from the Government. A year later it bought a Ford light van for London, to replace two single-horse teams.

There were fewer major investments outside London, one of the few being in a rebuilding of Tonbridge goods yard by 1900. By 1916 further major expansion at Tonbridge was being considered. In April 1903 the SECR decided to build a new goods yard at Merstham, for which they needed to buy land from Lord Hylton. He insisted on a condition that the passenger station should also be improved within a period of three years. It took until 1910 for the SECR to decide to concentrate Margate goods facilities at the Sands station.

As has been mentioned, farm produce was a staple of the SECR goods traf-

The SECR sidings at Folkestone Junction, where all traffic for the town itself was handled. This is a graphic illustration of the sort of conditions men laboured in. (Wakeman Collection, Ashford Library)

fic. Most went by goods train, of course, but some small consignments were taken by passenger if further than 20 miles from Charing Cross as a concession to farmers during the SECR working union Bill; in 1899 the rates allowed for up to 60lbs in boxes. Of all the farm produce, fruit was the most difficult for the SECR as its volatile prices meant that farmers were very sensitive to delay or damage. Farmers banded together to lobby at regular intervals, such as in 1900. The fruit traffic was normally dealt with at Bricklayers Arms, where it transferred to new sidings at the east yard in 1900 - which were equipped with electric light as most deliveries were at night. Fruit was also highly seasonal, so steps like adding an extra siding at Newington to handle seasonal congestion, as in 1913, could hardly have been profitable. Cliffe also gained a fruit siding the same year.

It was unusual for farms to have their own sidings, though a new siding was provided at Clock House Farm on the Chipstead Valley line in 1907 and in 1910 a farmer negotiated for the construction of Langlands Siding, between Swanley and Farningham Road. However there were several sidings which existed to serve a group of farmers in an area without a station, such as Sevington near Ashford; a short siding here is marked on the 1903 Ordnance Survey map although SECR sources refer to the completion of a new siding for fruit and hop traffic at Sevington Intermediate signalbox in January 1906, though this may have been an extension of the existing facility. Traffic of 3000 tons per annum for six years was guaranteed by the producers. Until 1912 Keylands Siding, north of Paddock Wood, was largely used as a "lay-by" but was then extended to serve Swatlands Farm and others in the area. Few purchasers were important enough to have their own siding, but the Army & Navy Co-operative Society gained one at Swanley in 1909. A siding was installed at Beltring in 1909-10 to help win hop traffic away from the waterways, but after barely ten years the traffic deserted to the roads. Hop traffic was very volatile due to its sensitivity to the weather anyway, but there was a sharp decline from £10,000 receipts in 1912 to £7000 in 1913.

A few milk churns could be found on every station, but at Middle Stoke there were more churns than people. The halt there had developed a good milk traffic by 1912 despite lack of good road access or a wooden platform to load the churns from, which was duly added.

Another type of food traffic was in biscuits, largely from the Huntley & Palmer's factory at Reading. Minutes of October 1903 also refer to the construction of a biscuit siding at Sittingbourne. In 1907 the SECR won some sugar traffic to Dover from water carriers. In 1913 Sharp & Co., sweet manufacturers, took over the former Ellis siding at Maidstone Barracks which was improved as "very considerable" traffic was expected. We should also remember beer traffic from Maidstone, Faversham and Canterbury - the Mackeson siding at Canterbury West was taken over by Messrs Simonds in 1921.

Some animal traffic brought problems with prosecutions due to laws about controlling the movement of diseased animals or cruelty. In 1903 the SECR was fined £5 for delivering 42 Scottish sheep to Bickley without the authority of Kent County Council. The SECR was fined £10 in May 1905 after Gravesend porters overloaded sheep trucks so that five sheep died; the senior porter was sacked. Horse traffic for the London area was handled at Rotherhithe Road, where an old wooden platform from Paddock Wood was installed in 1905 to help with cleaning the horse-boxes. In February 1912 the SECR was prosecuted for overcrowding sheep and pigs in a van from Maidstone to Gravesend and fined £106; after this, mixtures of animals were not allowed in a van. In 1921 it was fined £21 for causing suffering to sheep between Tenterden and Gravesend. Sevenoaks UDC set up a cattle market at Tubs Hill in 1918 so the SECR had to expand its facilities there.

Various fox hunting groups were conveyed at discount rates. The huntsman, two "whips", the horses and hounds were taken free if the riders paid full fare; in 1905 this was revised so that those who had travelled free had to pay a single fare.

The SECR undertook delivery of food and other traffic from its depots. This could lead to problems with new health legislation - in June 1907 a Health Officer complained that SECR meat wagons had no covering.

A controversial traffic associated with farming was that in manure, which was taken out of London to the farms of Kent and of which commodity the SECR was the largest carrier in the country. Unfortunately it was almost universally un-popular, and the process of unloading it always attracted opposition. In Swanley manure was still unloaded close to the station in 1903 which caused annoyance as well to the nearby Kent Jam Company. The SECR therefore considered two more remote sites - an extension of May's Siding on the Sevenoaks line, nearly a mile away, or a similar distance towards London on the up side - it being thought that Kevington Intermediate signalbox could be moved to control a new siding for thirty trucks. In March 1904 the SECR decided to buy land at Bournewood Crossing, to the west of Swanley, but to build a new signalbox there (Bournewood Crossing) rather than move the Kevington one. An extension of May's Siding occurred as well. A new manure siding was provided at Eynsford in 1904. By late 1911 the Bournewood Siding was being used for general refuse traffic and a tramway was even considered for it by the contractor working there.

In 1901 the SECR was fined £1 for "allowing manure to remain at Reigate station" on at least six occasions; it was meant to be removed to its destination rapidly, not to be left standing in open trucks in August! The same month there were complaints in *The Times* about "the stench of manure" at Orpington station. However the biggest legal battle was with Beckenham UDC who alleged that the SECR caused a "nuisance" in its handling of manure and refuse there, with it being left standing - causing a smell - or even falling out of wagons. The worst offence was that full, uncovered wagons were left standing at Beckenham Junction on Sundays and eventually a prosecution was brought by the Attorney General. The SECR offered to limit the "standing" period to five hours, then to three, but this was the start of a considerable campaign to force the traffic away from suburban stations. Even when the SECR tried to buy land for a new manure siding at Sole Street in 1903, they found the vendor wisely insisting on a clause banning the unloading of manure.

A large fruit farm could consume sizable quantities of manure. When T Wood asked for his own siding between Otford and Kemsing in 1907 he was receiving 2000 tons of manure a year. Similar traffic could be found at Wood's Siding near

Fawkham which was built in 1904, handling about 2500 tons of traffic a year.

Manure in a different form was transported by sewer. This affected the SECR when a major construction scheme to build a new southern outfall sewer was commenced for the London County Council, requiring two new sidings at Plumstead in 1904. In fact by March 1905 the SECR was anticipating traffic of 100,000 tons, yielding £15,000 in gross revenue; this required further sidings at Angerstein Wharf, Maze Hill and Charlton. It also led to a new siding for the High Brooms Brick Company near Tunbridge Wells, as they had a major contract for the sewer.

In dealing with waste we should also remember the disposal of household refuse, which was transported in large quantities from Southwark to Longfield depot. In 1909 a wagon ran through a wall at Southwark Dust sidings and killed a District Railway inspector. In 1904 Folkestone Corporation decided to build its own refuse destructor, requiring a siding at the Junction. Another offensive traffic was old bones used for glue-making by the Sheppey Glue Co. at Queenborough, where the storage of wagons near the station caused trouble. In June 1915 it was arranged that the Glue Co. would have its own siding to solve this problem.

Another key traffic was building materials, especially cement although the position of many of the Kent cement works on riverside sites meant that the SECR had barge competition in supplying coal and taking away cement. Relations with cement companies were not always cordial; in June 1899 there was a complex legal battle with Martin, Earle & Co who had a cement works south of Strood and wanted to extract chalk from beneath the Maidstone West line. Their argument to do this was based on an assertion that chalk was not a "mineral". At about the same time a siding to the SECR was installed, and this was used in 1900 for stabling wagons used for the Maidstone Show - necessitating the opening of a new signalbox there, Wickham Siding.

Along the Thames, Johnson's cement works between Greenhithe and Dartford gained a 10 truck siding in 1902-3 which seems to have slightly pre-dated the 1907 modernisation of the works; previously much of the traffic went by river. The Stone Court Chalk & Pier Co. was probably connected in 1905 and the nearby New Globe works seems to have received its siding after a request in October 1905. Artillery & Albion works siding opened in about 1908 but closed down soon afterwards. A new works near Stone Crossing Halt was commissioned by the Kent Portland Company and opened in 1921; this had a siding on the down side and a tunnel beneath the North Kent line. Another works which had generally relied on water transport as it was quite remote from main-line railways was that of Francis & Co at Cliffe, which was being improved in 1902-03; the SECR installed a 3 ton crane in Cliffe goods yard and extra sidings for handling cement traffic, but the station was a long way from the cement works.

Bricks and cement were produced by Smeed, Dean & Co between Sittingbourne and Teynham. They requested a siding in 1906 which was opened on the down side in 1907. By 1914 traffic here was expected to reach 25,000 tons a year.

On the Isle of Sheppey, Queenborough Cement Co operated a works to the south-west of the station, which was connected to the SECR by a siding in 1901.

An extra siding was added in 1905 but the area became more important due to the Queenborough Wharf Co which, in 1907, began work on a new deep water wharf at Rushenden Point which required access through the cement sidings. At this time the cement works traffic was about 7000 tons a year. From 1919 the wharf branch was also used to serve a new shipbreaking facility.

Stone and sand also provided useful traffic, especially from areas such as Redhill and various points on the Guildford line. In 1902 Hall & Co were providing 70 tons of sand traffic a day to the LBSCR, so the SECR decided to build its own siding at Redhill to get at this trade. In 1904 a new sand siding was provided at Gomshall and a gravel siding on the down side at Fawkham for Mr Martin of Brockley. Elliott's stone works was opened at Bexhill on a site close to the station yard and provided with its own siding in 1905 as traffic was expected to reach 5000 tons per annum. A site with long-term significance was that owned by Crittenden & Simmons north of Maidstone Barracks, where a stone siding was provided in 1906-07. This was an area that supplied ballast to the SECR from the old Benstead's site just to the south. Kennington gravel siding, between Wye and Ashford, was opened in 1919 for flint and gravel traffic. Ashenden's gained a siding for crushed shingle traffic between Lydd and Dungeness in 1920. The Eggleton & Cochrane ragstone siding, near East Malling, was authorised in late 1922.

A Farnham gravel merchant named Patterson became a significant figure, due partly to his supplying the SECR with ballast. In October 1906 he informed the SECR that he wished to install a "portable railway" for his traffic, that would run into the station yard at Ash. Patterson's gravel pit between Sandhurst and Blackwater was also served by a siding and in June 1914 he wanted a siding at Blackwater itself.

Another building material produced in the south-east was brick. This was an ideal traffic for a railway and the SECR found that firms like the Crayford Land & Brick Co (Messrs Martin) could drive a hard bargain; in May 1899 the SECR agreed to pay £1162 to provide a siding, probably their Fawkham one which handled bricks and refuse, and the firm would pay 5% interest on this if revenue did not reach £1000 per annum. In 1902 Lawrence & Son called for a down side siding between Wellington College and Wokingham for their brick and stone traffic, this being opened in 1903 although the SECR asked for changes in the contract when it was discovered that they still used the LSWR for most traffic. Their traffic increased to about 15,000 tons a year from 1911 to 1915, but then fell again.

In January 1907 the brickworks of A Lawers at Grovehurst, on the Sheerness branch near Sittingbourne, requested a siding. This was built by February 1908, at which point the brickworks went into liquidation. Cremer's Siding at Hartlip served another brickworks in this area.

A tile and hearthstone works east of Reigate belonging to Mr Taylor was provided with a siding in 1907, for which a new signalbox was built. The siding serving Nutfield brickworks was out of use during the war years as the firm had closed, but it was taken over and the siding put back in service in late 1918.

An unsuccessful siding had been provided for the East Sussex Brick Company in 1889 near Doleham. When local people requested a public siding in their area in 1908, it was decided to rent the private siding for £15 a year. However receipts for all of 1914 were only £21! A similarly remote public siding was Churn Lane, on the Hawkhurst branch, although it was referred to as "Taylor's Siding" when poor use was discussed in 1917; its main use was forwarding fruit.

During the period roads were being much improved. Although this increased competition, it also provided extra traffic as Chart Siding was extended in 1911 due to a local contractor supplying 30,000 tons of "tarred macadam" to Kent County Council.

Of course the SECR also delivered building materials to where they were needed, and there was a great boom in this traffic after the War. In October 1920 Woolwich Borough Council informed the SECR that it wished to use two sidings at Well Hall and connect them with a light railway to deliver building materials while the same month Robert MacAlpine informed them that he needed sidings at Bellingham for LCC housing.

Paper making was a key industry in Kent and was largely the reason for the existence of the Tovil goods branch in Maidstone. Traffic there was still expanding in 1901, with Reed & Co requiring further facilities. In later years, though, the Medway Valley below Maidstone was to become the dominant centre of the paper industry in that area with Dartford and St Mary Cray also important. In 1903 Townsend, Hook & Co had a siding for their paper traffic at Snodland built, then promptly rebuilt their factory and demanded alterations.

Dartford mills provided newsprint for *The Daily Telegraph* and other journals; this traffic was worth £4000 per year in 1900, so over £5000 was spent improving handling facilities. The Imperial paper mills at Gravesend West Street gained sidings in 1910. By 1913 these mills were contributing part of the SECR's annual paper traffic of 90,000 tons, worth over £24,000, so that extensions were needed to the paper loading shed at Dartford and the warehouse at Bricklayers Arms; a new paper warehouse was opened there in 1918.

Northfleet paper mills made use of the wharf there, to which the SER had opened a siding under an 1874 agreement; this had to be revised to account for the new traffic there. East of Greenhithe, the Empire Paper mills at Ingress Park were opened in about 1919 and connected into a long siding provided earlier for the War Office on the down side. Paper traffic at Chartham was also growing in 1913.

At the end of 1919 the SECR learnt of proposals by the Reed paper business to build a huge new mill at New Hythe where there had once been a small cement siding. This eventually opened in 1928, but the SECR expected traffic to be at least 50,000 tons a year in outward business alone.

Coal was an important traffic, though less than it might have been had the Kent coalfield lived up to expectations. Much of the coal was delivered to gas works, most of which gradually acquired their own sidings especially in larger towns like Reading. For example, the Yorktown & Blackwater Gas Co. gained a siding in 1907 as its traffic was worth more than £1000 a year. The Sevenoaks Gas Co. at Bat & Ball was connected in 1902. The Wadhurst Gas Co. applied for a siding between Ticehurst Rd and Etchingham in 1905. A siding for Herne Bay Gas Co. was completed 25 March 1914. Dover Gas Works near Buckland Junction was

The unsuccessful Guilford Colliery near Eythorne in about 1912; it was abandoned in 1921 without ever producing any commercial coal. EKLR no.1 can be seen. (R W Kidner collection)

connected in 1917 whilst a down siding at Maidstone Barracks served the gasworks there from 1918, although this still received most of its coal by water; the South Suburban Gas Co. at Belvedere was connected the same year and the Broadstairs Gas Co. in 1920.

Small amounts of coal were delivered to other concerns. A siding was put in at New Romney in 1904-5 for the Littlestone Water Co.'s pumping engine. Tramways also consumed coal to generate electricity and often had sidings such as that near Broadstairs for Thanet Tramways installed in 1900; Hastings Tramways gained a siding at Ore in 1905. Of course electricity generation gradually became a major business consuming much coal; the South London Electricity Company had a large works on the down side between Cambria Rd signalbox and Denmark Hill, which was connected in 1907.

A siding was provided for the LCC tramways depot near Angerstein Wharf in 1912. Beckenham UDC opened its own electricity works near Clock House in 1920, which also had a siding for coal.

Virtually every station had its own coal siding, where local merchants usually operated. Some larger merchants had their own facilities such as Plimsoll at Elephant & Castle, though this yard was leased to the Great Northern in 1907. One of the most important points for coal traffic was Beadle's Wharf at Erith, used by Cory & Co. to unload coal from the north-east - much of which was used by the SECR, and having sidings extended in 1907. A new coal depot was opened at Charlton in 1909-10 and Cory had two sidings installed for their Rochester wharf where traffic was expected to reach £50,000 a year. The latter was correctly named as it was in Rochester, but adjacent to the wrongly-titled Chatham Goods depot.

Some of the coal delivered by the SECR originated on the LNWR and GWR but the SECR had occasional problems collecting what it was owed from these concerns; writs had to be served on them in 1907, after which the LNWR paid over £40,000 but continued to dispute the balance. In November 1908 the GWR finally paid up the debts it had accrued between January 1900 and June 1908 - £78,337, but at the same time attempted to negotiate a new deal with the SECR that all through goods should be exchanged at Longhedge. The SECR rejected this as it would have lost money, but by October 1908 the GWR was trying to buy land nearby for its own goods depot at Battersea Low Level on the site of an old reservoir and filter beds, close to which the Midland already had a coal depot. Connections from this to the SECR were opened in 1909, the first traffic being in milk, although it was not fully opened until 1911. This resulted in increased exchange of traffic at Stewarts Lane, where a number of new sidings were needed in 1912.

The LNWR brought an action against the SECR in November 1910, alleging that it showed "undue preference" to the Great Northern in forwarding goods. The 1864 agreement between the GNR and LCDR obliged the latter to "do all in their power" to use the Farringdon route except if it would damage the GWR. The LNWR lost the case on 1 November 1910. The GWR was increasingly exploiting its strong position, with its own coal depots at Addiscombe Road, Hither Green and Lewisham whilst the agreement was to be expanded by the SECR to include the Great Eastern and Great Central. The Great Northern opened a coal siding of its own at Addiscombe Road in 1911, and the sidings there for Harris & Bailey were extended in 1920.

Sir Frederick Harrison was then employed to sort out the complex financial entanglement of SECR-LNWR affairs; he found that the SECR should pay back £83,000 to the LNWR. However this bitter pill was sugared by a rapid expansion of the coal traffic in 1911-12 so that 500 extra coal wagons were ordered from Hurst, Nelson & Co. in 1913.

A developing traffic was in oil and oil products, especially as cars became more numerous. The Anglo-American Oil Company was particularly active in expanding its facilities and installed a siding at Bromley North in 1901-2, when the chance was also taken to add a new coal siding. They opened a siding at Ramsgate Town in 1902. By late 1902 the Caucasian Petrol Export Company had established a depot at Angerstein Wharf. In 1913 BP opened a bulk petrol store at Addiscombe Road and the Bowring Petrol Co. at Hither Green; BP added a bulk spirit store at Addiscombe Rd in 1919.

Occasional special events produced heavy traffic. The 1899 Maidstone Agricultural Show required two extra sidings and an unloading road at Maidstone East as well as auxiliary signalboxes at both Maidstone stations. The 7-10 June 1904 Agricultural Show at Guildford caused the SECR to install two new sidings at Shalford.

Military supplies and equipment were significant at many sites, especially around Aldershot, Dover and Chatham. In 1902 extra sidings and a loading road were added at Farnborough in anticipation of a new barracks. In 1909 the SECR was anxious to win more of the traffic from Farnborough and Aldershot as this was dominated by the LSWR, so it built a loading dock at the former site. The exten-

The working timetables give much additional information about goods traffic; several interesting workings are listed here.

CHATHAM DOCKYARD LINE.—GOODS TRAIN SERVICE.

A Goods Train (worked by Day Pilot) will run between New Brompton and the Dockyard on Week-days, as under:—

DOWN.	arr.A.M.dep.	arr.P.M.dep.	UP.	arr.A.M.dep.	arr.P.M.dep.
NEW BROMPTON	... 7 30	... 3 30	CHATHAM DOCKYARD	... 8 10	... 4 0
CHATHAM DOCKYARD	7 40 ...	3 40 ...	NEW BROMPTON	8 20 ...	4 10 ...

SPECIAL INSTRUCTIONS.

The Line is worked by Train Staff, which must be kept in the Signal Box at New Brompton when not in use, and no Train or Engine must enter on the Single Line without this Train Staff.

The Train Staff is round in shape, on an Iron Bar; it is coloured green, and marked "Chatham Dockyard Branch."

No Train or Engine must travel at a greater speed than 4 miles an hour over that part of the Line between the first over-bridge leading to the bathing place (where a Notice Board as to speed is fixed) and the Terminus in the Dockyard, or at a greater speed than ten miles an hour over any other part of the Branch Line.

Engine Drivers must keep a good look out for Hand Signals from the policeman in charge at the office near the Main Level Crossing to the Dockyard.

FAVERSHAM CREEK BRANCH.

Goods Trains will run, if required, on Week-days, as under:—

	a.m.	p.m.		
Faversham, dep. for Creek	10 0	3 30	...	...
Faversham, arr. from Creek	10 45	4 15	...	...

SEVENOAKS LOCAL GOODS TRAIN SERVICE. (On Week-days only).

		p.m.			p.m.
Sevenoaks (Bat & Ball)	dep.	2 45	Sevenoaks (Tub's Hill)	arr.	3 5
Sevenoaks (Tub's Hill)	arr.	2 50	Sevenoaks (Bat & Ball)	dep.	3 10

NOTICES AND SPECIAL INSTRUCTIONS.

CONDITIONAL GOODS AND G.V. SERVICES.

Special Wool Train (when required). Stewart's Lane and Blackfriars to Dover.

DOWN.		Not Sats. arr.P.M.dep.	Or Not Sats. arr.P.M.dep.	Or via Oat- ford Loop. arr.P.M.dep.	UP.		arr.A.M.dep.		
STEWART'S LANE	...	... 12 5	... 1 30	... 2 15	DOVER PRIORY	... ...	... 7 0		...
Factory Junction	...	... 12 7	... 1 34	... 2 17	Canterbury	... ...	7 50 8 5		...
Brixton	... ...	... 12 11	... 1 41	... 2 23	Faversham	... ...	8 35 9 20		...
Herne Hill	...	12 13 12 14	1 43 1 44	2 25 2 26	Sittingbourne	... ...	9 40 10 5		...
Loughboro' Sidings		12 17 12 43	1 47 2 13	2 30 2 55	New Brompton	... ...	10 30 11 15		...
BLACKFRIARS	...	12 53 2 0	2 23 2 58	3 10 3 43	Chatham	...	... 11 21		...
Loughboro' Junction	...	... 2 12	... 3 8	... 3 53	Meopham	... ...	C ...		...
Herne Hill	...	... 2 15	... 3 11	... ...	*Longfield Siding*	... ...	C ...		...
Beckenham	... ...	... 2 31	... 3 25	... ...	Swanley	... ...	... 12 20		...
Cambria Junction	...	... ...	... ...	... 3 59	Beckenham	... ...	... 1 5		...
Nunhead	... ...	... ...	... ...	... 4 10	Herne Hill	... ...	... 1 20		...
Shortlands	...	... ...	... ...	... 4 26	*Sorting Sidings*	...	1 25 2 0		...
Bickley	... ...	... ...	... ...	... 4 49	Herne Hill	...	2 5 2 10		...
Swanley	...	... 2 50	3 50 4 5	... 5 3	STEWART'S LANE	...	2 20 ...		...
Chatham	...	3 37 3 40	4 45 4 48	5 50 5 55					
Sittingbourne	...	... 4 8	... 5 12	... 6 22					
Faversham	...	4 25 4 40	... 5 32	... 6 40					
Canterbury	...	... 5 13	6 0 6 20	7 10 7 30					
DOVER HARBOUR	...	6 0 ...	7 10 ...	8 15 ...					

Inspector PHILLIPS to provide Guards.
It is important this Train should run punctually.

C Call at Meopham and Longfield Siding when necessary; will run to Blackfriars when required to take in Empties.

This Train must keep clear of all Passenger Trains. On Saturdays it must wait at Sorting Sidings until the afternoon traffic is over.

GRANDE VITESSE TRAIN.—DOVER TO HOLBORN.

A G.V. Train will run, if required, at times as under:— (P 9,797).

UP.		arr.A.M.dep.			DOWN.		arr.P.M.dep.		
DOVER HARBOUR	... ...	... 6 10	...	BLACKFRIARS	... ...	... 1 0		...
Dover Priory	...	... 6 12	...	Loughboro' Junction	... ...	... 1 10		...
Canterbury	...	... 6 35	...	*Sorting Sidings*	... ...	1 13 ...		...
Faversham	...	... 6 51	...	This Train will run from Holborn to Blackfriars immediately. It is unloaded, and the Engine must turn and will there attach traffic, and will run from the Sorting Sidings as soon as possible after arrival, and will take down Empty G.V. Vans and other traffic. On Mondays the Train will convey Cattle from Sorting Sidings to Stations as required.				
Sittingbourne	...	... 7 4	...					
Chatham	...	... 7 20 7 23	...					
Swanley	...	... 7 49	...					
Bickley Ballast Pit	...	... 7 56	...					
Beckenham	...	... 8 2	...					
Herne Hill	...	... 8 11	...	*It must not be allowed to interfere with business Passenger Trains.* Dover to provide for the working.				
Loughboro' Junction	...	... 8 13	...					
HOLBORN	...	8 20 ...	...					

sion of Sandhurst College in 1909 allowed the SECR to supply building materials via a new siding and temporary tramway. Unusually, a siding installed at Beluncle Halt for the Admiralty during the War was taken over by the SECR for public use on 1 January 1920.

Like all railways in the country, the SECR carried domestic mails for the Post Office which was governed by a flat rate contract which was £25,000 initially. When this was due for renewal in 1901 the GPO offered £30,000 per year though in July 1904 the SECR was asking for £65,000. No agreement had been reached by 1908, though the SECR was prepared to accept £50,000. £65,000 was eventually agreed, earning the SECR a useful sum in back payments, and then increased to £85,000 from January 1913. Parcels were often taken on passenger trains - in 1919 the SECR decided to provide electric lights in the guards' compartments so that they could sort parcels *en route*.

Another common traffic was newspapers, which from 1912 were priced according to annual contract rather than being weighed by staff. A leading paper like the *Evening News* could be worth £1750 a year, but others like *The People* were worth only £525. The former was worth over £3000 in 1913, but the SECR had lost much of the suburban London newspaper traffic by this time. However in 1914 it calculated that the *Daily Chronicle* was actually overpaying by about 14% - but said nothing!

The SECR had virtually no "freight-only" lines, although the Dungeness branch must have seemed like this in the winter. It did, however, operate the Faversham Creek branch which belonged to Lord Sondes and yielded healthy interchange traffic with coastal vessels; in 1901-2 it carried 38,248 tons of goods in 12 months. Its own equivalent was the Angerstein Wharf branch, where even the wharf itself was part of the SECR. The Tovil branch was hardly longer than a siding, but carried heavy traffic in paper.

Where goods were lost or delayed the SECR had a responsibility. In August 1901 it had to pay £7-6s for "non-delivery of a fortune telling machine," which could perhaps have been put to use in predicting a more reliable means of transport. It was sued in 1909 for having taken ten days to deliver a roundabout from Margate to Chatham; it is tempting to comment on the sort of route that could have been used. A van load of drapery caught fire near Faversham in 1912, as sparks got into it through the ventilators; the SECR had to pay damages of £460 as drapery should not have been in a ventilated van at all.

An interesting legal problem was posed by the 1921 railway strike - were railways still liable for perishable goods that had to be disposed of due to delays? Ellen Reader of Brenchley delivered two large consignments of apples to Churn Lane Siding, on the Hawkhurst branch, in June 1921 for delivery to Bolton. The first load got as far as Willesden but the second was caught up by the strike while at Hither Green and the SECR sold them. The Company insisted that it had been prevented from delivering them and the apples had become subject to the official Food Controller under the 1915 Defence of the Realm Act. The SECR brought the proceeds of the sale into court and observed that there had been a backlog of 2000 wagons at Willesden, with only two men working. They also asked what they were meant to do when instructed by the Food Controller - "Were we meant to have a stand-up fight?" Counsel asked.

There were also attempts to defraud the SECR by giving incorrect weights or falsely describing the nature of goods. The Crayford Land & Brick Co "systematically understated" the weights of goods despatched from Fawkham in 1908-09, owing the SECR £1542. Complex charging systems also created opportunities for fraud - a Blackheath firm which sent breeding fowls by rail saved money by declaring them as for consumption.

Of course goods were also prone to theft. In April 1917 PC Scott was patrolling near Kenley station with his dog at 1am when the dog began to bark, and it led him to discover two men stealing bacon from a truck in the goods yard; at their homes, similarly pilfered brandy and whisky were discovered. In 1919 a man suspected of stealing whisky from Gomshall station committed suicide.

Although the SECR's main competitor for goods traffic was to become the motor lorry, it was threatened by a 1911 attempt to improve the Medway to Tonbridge - which it opposed.

The fickle and seasonal nature of SECR goods traffic seem to have caused it difficulty in retaining the necessary numbers of wagons to cater for underlying traffic growth. Early in the era, the SECR tended to hire in or buy secondhand when under stock pressure - it hired 200 goods wagons in July 1899 and bought 45 secondhand ones in June 1901. By March 1904 it had a stock of 11,440 - 81% of these originated with the SECR. However some wagons were very old - one involved in an accident at Bromley South in January 1912 had been built in 1864. In the years of strong traffic growth just before the War, the SECR made several large purchases - 100 cattle wagons in January 1912, 500 goods trucks from Hurst, Nelson in August and bought 200 secondhand trucks the following month. A further 500 were ordered from Hurst, Nelson in 1916.

Chapter 10:

Incidents and Accidents

Traffic Accidents

There was a popular belief, not entirely justified, that the SER and LCDR had been accident-prone due to their financial problems. Thus, when a guard was injured at Dover SER in 1898 and the cramped conditions were blamed, it was commented in the press that the new relationship between the SER and LCDR would make such incidents a thing of the past. In fact the SECR was fairly successful and an article in the *Railway Magazine* in January 1913 calculated the two railways as being the safest in Britain, on the basis that only five passengers had been killed on them since 1890 - out of 59.3 million carried.

There were occasional accidents when shunting of goods trains caused a passenger train to come into collision, but passengers were rarely injured in an actual shunting accident. An exception was at Appledore on 26th December 1899 when a horsebox was being added to a train; the shunt was too violent, resulting in three serious injuries and sixteen minor ones.

The more typical pattern of shunting accidents is exemplified by that near Sevenoaks Tunnel on 11th July 1900 which occurred in the same place as the 1884

A destructive derailment of a troop train occurred at Gomshall in February 1904; remarkably, no-one was killed. (Wakeman Collection, Ashford Library)

accident. A goods train was shunted onto the main line by mistake, in front of an up Margate train. The line was closed for twelve hours and injury claims for £2988 were submitted, though these were eventually settled for £1445.

On 18th June 1918 at Penge, a goods train was shunting when some trucks became derailed across the main-line. The down 10am from Holborn Viaduct ran into the derailed trucks, causing the engine to derail and the leading carriages to telescope. There were ten injuries, including one severe, with the line being blocked until late the next day. Alfred Johnson had both legs broken in the accident and claimed damages against the SECR, who very meanly objected on the grounds that he had given £15 to Charing Cross Hospital - which depended on charitable donations. Johnson won his case spectacularly, taking away £1000.

One of the most persistent patterns of accidents in SECR history is of incidents caused by signalling error or fog in the heavily congested London district. On 9th October 1899 both factors were combined at Blackfriars, leading to the death of a guard five days later. Lt Col Yorke, the Inspecting Officer, found that the signalman had returned the signals to danger without having actually ensured that the train had passed - causing it to stop and be hit in the rear by another. He recommended that the Sykes "lock and block" system at Blackfriars Junction should have treadles and track circuits added.

Fog was always a severe strain on the SECR in London. *The Times* of 18th November 1901 set the scene for its description of the previous day's accident at Brixton by recording that "a dense mass of fog rolled over the railway embankment enveloping everything in darkness and completely obscuring a signal post." In these conditions the 6.02pm from Victoria stopped at a signal and was hit in the rear by a Victoria to Greenwich Park train. The rear carriage of the 6.02pm was destroyed, but it happened to be empty; nonetheless, there were sixteen injuries according to *The Times* and 57 claims for compensation. Another rear end collison occurred at Snow Hill on 9th November 1904, a SECR Victoria to Moorgate being hit by a Midland Railway train to Kentish Town. In 1919 the SECR decided to try fog detonator placers in the wake of another fog-bound accident at Parks Bridge Junction on 13th January.

One of the worst fog-related accidents happened at Waterloo Junction on the morning of 25th October 1913. The morning business trains were running very late because of the weather, and the 7.35am Blackheath to Charing Cross stopped at Waterloo Junction station at about 8.50am. It was then hit in the rear by the 7.32am up from Elmers End, killing three passengers and seriously injuring another three; there were 55 claims for damages. One damages claim, by a widow and her child, was settled for £2250.

The causes of the accident were studied by Major Pringle and received publicity within two days of the accident; he found "irregularities" in the work of the signalling staff at Waterloo and it was revealed that a boy "booker" often helped with the signalling instruments. An inquest on the dead found that the accident was due to the negligence of signalman Moore, although this was not to the extent of being "felonious". Moore had used the key to unlock the Sykes system without correct precautionary measures, although the inquest also felt that all signalboxes in the London area should have train describers. It was also concerned about the track arrangement west of Waterloo Junction station, which switched the paths of Mid-Kent trains.

When Moore gave his evidence to Pringle in early November, the Inspecting Officer finished by saying, "I hope you will not make any more mistakes." The report, published on 3rd January 1914, certainly blamed Moore for using the releasing key incorrectly, but Pringle also felt that the weight of the levers in the busy Belvedere Road box contributed to excessive strain on the signalmen. He also felt that the whole area needed to be track-circuited, although the SECR was only planning to do this work between Waterloo and Waterloo Junction boxes and to remove the latter, and cautioned drivers to proceed more slowly in fog.

The accident at New Cross on 15th December 1915 was never satisfactorily explained, it being clear that something had gone wrong with the signalling system although Lt Col von Donop failed to establish the precise reason. The 5.20pm Cannon Street to Dartford was hit in the rear by the 5.17pm Charing Cross to Maidstone West. The second and third coaches of the former were telescoped, so that there were three serious injuries and nine other people needed medical attention. The signalman insisted that he had set the signals against the 5.17pm, but it was discovered that an intermittent fault had occurred on the blocking instrument a few weeks earlier, causing a train to "disappear". Von Donop was unable to prove whether the cause of the accident was this intermittent fault or the signalman's error.

The complexities of working in the Borough Market Junction area led to an accident on 11th October 1910, where trains were allowed to be exempt from absolute block working if they were slow. On this occasion "not slow enough" was the verdict, though there were no injuries. There was another collison there on 5th September 1914 caused by a train failing to stop at signals, though with only minor injuries. Two rear end collisions occurred on 5 September and 10 November 1914.

Another fatal accident due to a driver misreading a signal occurred at Cannon Street bridge on 27th June 1914. The 9.18am to Hastings passed a danger signal and, travelling at 7mph, collided with the middle of a local train from Plumstead. One carriage overturned and the guard's carriage was titled against the signalbox, killing one passenger and resulting in 49 claims for injury. The Hastings driver, Harrison, admitted that he mistook the signal - it was his first accident in 42 years service. However a letter to *The Times* signed "Blackheath" blamed the accident on the scissors crossing at Cannon Street which was "just a death trap".

Signalling error was a common factor in many accidents outside of London as well. On 20th January 1899 a London to Maidstone special was hit in the rear by a light engine while standing at Strood, throwing one young man called Vane out of the window and onto the platform. The special was carrying E G Falcon's theatre company to Maidstone for a season of *Dick Whittington*. Damages were settled at £350.

A bizarre signalling accident occurred at Chatham Goods on 4th June 1914. A goods train was ready to leave from the layby siding on the embankment beside the main-line, but instead the signalman set the points so that it ran down the steep incline to the goods depot. It crashed through the buffers and across the public road, fortunately without injury - though the signalman suffered most with a 2s a week pay cut.

Driver error was also a common cause of disaster. On 23rd November 1900 a Sevenoaks Bat & Ball to Victoria train passed a danger signal near Swanley and was derailed on the catch points. Although there were problems with the brakes on the leading engine, the Inspecting Officer also felt there had been a "lack of caution". On 15th November a Midland Railway goods train hit the buffers near Southwark Street bridge on the Blackfriars loop - it was the driver's fault but the guard was injured.

On 12th August 1902 one man was killed when a SECR train entered Bo Peep Tunnel against the signals, colliding with a LBSCR goods train already inside. The inquest recorded a verdict of manslaughter but the magistrates discharged the driver.

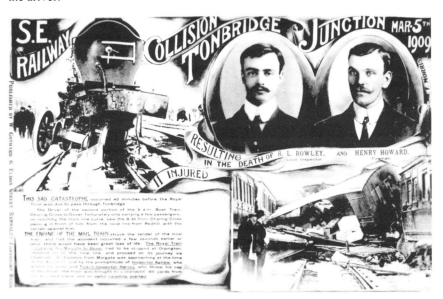

Commercially produced postcard showing the destructive accident at Tonbridge in 1909. (Wakeman Collection, Ashford Library)

There was a significant accident at Tonbridge on 5th March 1909. A down Cannon Street to Dover and Margate train was approaching Tonbridge at the same time as the 8.30am Dover, which ran via Redhill. The latter passed a signal at danger which led into the immediate danger of a collison with an up express which was signalled to cross its path. Two men on the footplate, Robert Rowley and Henry Howard, jumped off hoping to save themselves - but fell into the path of the fast train from Cannon Street which was running more or less in parallel, and were killed.

The line was blocked by the two trains, and an Inspector and a signalman acted swiftly to prevent a fast up Margate train running into the wreckage. The

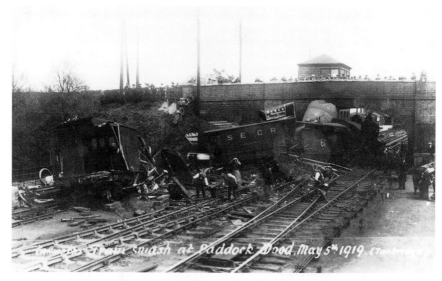

Another commercial exploitation of disaster - this time, the 1919 goods train accident near Paddock Wood in which two railwaymen were killed. (R W Kidner collection)

accident also affected the King, who had left London on the way to Dover, but had to be rerouted from Orpington back to Bickley and onwards via Chatham. Rowley was an Inspector, the actual driver of the train being named Moore; he survived, but was sacked in May 1909 when Pringle placed the blame upon him.

An SECR driver and fireman were killed in a collision between two goods trains at Keylands Siding near Paddock Wood on 5th May 1919, which set off an extensive fire. Driver Smith, in charge of the Folkestone goods, was blamed for ignoring signals - though it was noted that he had only driven over the route twice before.

Hitting the buffers was a fairly regular event. On 22nd January 1903 the 6.50am Charing Cross to Tonbridge hit the buffers at its destination, injuring five. On 22nd May 1912 four passengers were injured when the 5.38am from Orpington ran into the buffers at St Paul's. There were thirty injuries when a Bromley North train arrived too rapidly at Cannon Street on 18th June 1915.

The most famous accident in SER history, the Headcorn disaster in which Charles Dickens could have died, was due to the error of the permanent way staff. This was a rare problem in SECR days although the Holborn Viaduct to Queenborough Pier train was derailed at Elephant & Castle on 17th August 1902. Major Pringle blamed Ganger Miles, who had not followed the rule book in removing an "obstacle" from the line.

Like all railways, the SECR suffered occasional derailments. On 15th December 1902 the 3.40am up Dover Mail derailed at Chislehurst, carrying Post Office employees but no passengers. There were seven claims for injury. In February 1904 three soldiers were injured when a troop train from Gravesend to Southampton derailed at Gomshall.

A very unusual disaster could have occurred to the 11am Victoria to Dover boat train on 15th October 1901, which was seen passing Canterbury East with the underframe of its rear carriage on fire. The signalman managed to get the train stopped at Kearsney, where it was discovered that a hot axle box had ignited the underframe beneath a carriage full of passengers!

No major incident was caused by deliberate attempts to derail trains, but the practice was a persistent worry. On 11th March 1899 an attempt was made to derail the 9.50pm up Folkestone boat express near Sandling, with iron chairs placed on the line. On 8th October 1920 the 7.18pm Hastings up train hit some railway sleepers and an iron bar on the track at Southborough, though without serious effect. A man found "loitering" nearby was arrested.

The most significant "natural disaster" to effect the SECR, the collapse of the line between Folkestone and Dover on 19th December 1915, fortunately involved no injury to any person; however it did leave "D" class no.742 and a short train marooned for nine days and the line itself out of use until 1919. Disasters of this sort were rare, one of the few significant ones being due to heavy flooding between Ticehurst Road and Etchingham on 27th October 1909. The turbulent River Rother undermined the foundations of the bridge north of Ticehurst Road, causing it to collapse under the weight of an up goods train - the engine of which ploughed twenty yards into a field. There were many flooded cottages nearby. The line was blocked by this and also by a heavy slip between Wadhurst and Ticehurst Road four days later, traffic operating via the LBSCR and also via Ashford.

On 17th July 1918 a violent storm struck the south-east suburbs and flooded the lines at Woolwich, where an up Gravesend train was derailed by debris washed onto the track. Heavy rain also caused a slip between Canterbury East and Bekesbourne on 6th March 1919. The 5am Dover Priory to Faversham ran into the slip and was derailed, then being hit by the 2.23am GNR demobilisation train from Clapham Junction to Dover despite the frantic efforts of the first train crew to warn it by lighting a newspaper; there were no casualties.

A broad definition of "natural" causes of accidents could include the effects of heat, which derailed an up Bexhill express near Crowhurst viaduct on 7th August 1910 due to buckled track. There were no injuries. Perhaps a similar explanation lay behind the "rail creep" which derailed the up Granville Express near Graveney on 19th June 1912.

In the early days of railways exploding locomotives were fairly commonplace, but this was a rarity in SECR days. Nonetheless, no.206 suffered an explosion whilst working an empty stock train from Tonbridge to Tunbridge Wells on 24th September 1912. The firebox crown and stays overheated, causing severe scalding to both of the footplate men who were blasted onto the ballast although their lives were saved by a goods guard who poured oil on the burns. The driver lost his memory and the fireman spent four months in hospital.

Death at Milton Range Halt

A very serious accident occurred at the lonely Milton Range Halt on 21st August 1922, killing five men and injuring at least 59 others. The Halt was being used by workmen rebuilding the London to Strood road, which was a post-war job creation project. Each morning one train from Charing Cross and another from New Cross brought men out of London and distributed them at various points along the line, from where they could walk to the road.

On the fatal morning there was dense fog, so that the Charing Cross train approached at Milton Range Halt at 6.35am but failed to stop in time and overran the platform by forty yards. This was a common problem, as the site was notorious among drivers for its lack of landmarks and consequent problem of stopping correctly in fog.

The worst traffic accident on the SECR was at Milton Range Halt in 1922, with some of the wrecked carriages pushed through the wooden platforms into the Thames & Medway Canal. (Lens of Sutton)

The driver was going to "set back" to the platform, but the men had other ideas. As there was no footbridge at this basic station, the men normally got out of the train to cross the line in front of their own engine - which they did on this occasion, even though the train had missed its proper stopping place. Their normal practice was to rush out, causing problems for the ticket collector, and this stopped the driver from setting back to the platform.

As the crowd of men was crossing the line, a light engine from Strood suddenly emerged from the foggy swirl, killing one man on the spot and carrying two others fifty yards along the track - they died later in hospital. It was so foggy that the driver of this engine was unaware of any accident. The light engine had whistled as it approached, but this was merely a custom that had begun when the Halt was busy with soldiers during the War.

Meanwhile the Gravesend signalman had given the second workmen's train an instruction to "advance on" to his advance starting signal, but its driver had never stopped there in twenty years experience and assumed that he was alright to continue forwards. The men who were still in the first train suddenly realised that the noise behind them was the New Cross train approaching; there was a frantic scramble to escape, some men leaping straight from the train into the parallel canal. The second tragedy then occurred, as the New Cross train crashed into the Charing Cross one, telescoping its carriages and pushing wreckage across the track and men into the canal. Later some of the carriages were pushed into the canal to help clear the line. Two of the passengers were killed.

A woman living at Bridge House on the canal side tore up her sheets to use as bandages, and some of the wounded were put onto a train to be taken to hospital in Rochester. Henry Boot & Sons, the road contractors, awarded gold watches to two men for trying to stop the second train and organising the rescue.

At the inquest, the jury complained that Denton signalbox should have been open at such a busy time and criticised the use of such a dangerous spot to detrain large numbers of men - noting that workmen from Strood came by road.

Charing Cross Roof

An extensive rebuilding of Charing Cross station roof was under way when, at 3.45pm on 5th December 1905, two spans and the screen at the river end began to collapse. When the whole section came down a few minutes later, some of the brick wall on the western side of the station collapsed outwards taking the iron of the roof with it. Two men working for the SECR on the roof were killed and an advertisement cleaner employed by W H Smith. However the brick wall fell onto the Avenue Theatre, which was also under repair, killing three workmen there.

This picture shows the extent of the damage to Charing Cross roof and also illlustrates how serious loss of life might have been.

A sketch of emergency repairs taking place at night shortly after the roof collapsed.

The timing of the accident saved the SECR from a more serious disaster, for although a Hastings train was preparing for departure the platforms were not crowded and the accident happened at the down end - people had less need to walk out that far at a quiet time of the afternoon. In addition, there had been a significant time lapse between the first signs of imminent disaster and the actual fall.

A faulty tie-rod was diagnosed as the cause of the disaster, but the disruption was considerable and the costs enormous. The owner of the Avenue Theatre brought a case against the SECR, which was settled in June 1906 for £20,000. This fee compares interestingly with the compensation paid for the three dead and 27 injured among the men working on the Avenue Theatre - £1,750. By January 1908 it was calculated that the disaster had cost the SECR £106,000. The station had no passenger trains until March 1906.

Another serious accident to affect workmen on the system occurred in 1913 during the rebuilding of Margate West station which was in the charge of the contractor Rigby. A new wall was being built and some men were excavating at its foot, without having taken care to reinforce it. The wall collapsed and killed four of Rigby's workmen.

Other Incidents

The most frequent cause of death on the SECR were people who got onto the line through various reasons, of which we can include suicide attempts. It was often difficult to decide whether a fatal accident had been a suicide or not, and because of the social distaste for suicide coroner's often avoided the verdict. Relatively commonplace incidents such as the solicitor run over and killed at Rochester Bridge on 2nd August 1902 therefore have no certain explanation.

On 9th October 1904 W Bosanquet was run over and killed near Sundridge Park. This may have been suicide, but the verdict was that "deceased suffered from the effects of alcoholism and drug-taking and apparently wandered onto the line unconscious of his whereabouts." Similarly no-one knows the real story of Miss Mary Money, aged 21, who was found in a mutilated condition in Merstham Tunnel in September 1905, though it seems likely she jumped out rather than fell.

This incident is very similar to the death of Marion Aitken, aged 30, who was found dead in Penge Tunnel on 16th March 1909. The train had arrived at Penge station with a door open, and it was assumed that her death was an accident. Penge Tunnel was the scene of regular suicides. A boy was killed when he fell out of the train in Tyler Hill Tunnel in January 1918. There were more tunnel deaths in April 1922 when two Chatham naval ratings fell out of a down train in Higham tunnel - probably due to drunken frolics.

Suicides on the SECR were about 24 a year in the period leading up to the War - most being people who simply jumped in front of a train. More chilling still, perhaps because of the evident determination involved, was the case of Miss Leiter, a 21 year old German governess who committed suicide at Penge in 1913. She got down onto the track as a train pulled out of the station and placed her head on the rail.

There was a spate of suicides in 1914, at places as diverse as Farningham Road, Penge Tunnel and Ramsgate. One man shot himself in a carriage at Bromley South. In August 1915 a wounded soldier committed suicide at Westenhanger and in April 1918 a soldier killed himself in Gillingham Tunnel having been depressed by his war experiences and wounds. More unusually, a fireman who killed himself on the line at Sheerness in 1919 was found to have committed "suicide when temporarily insane following influenza." Another military victim was Lt Col Lyonbichitch of Serbia, who jumped out of a train near Orpington on 18th October 1919.

Occasionally passengers had genuine accidents while waiting for a train. In January 1904 a man fell off the platform at Spa Road just as a train was arriving. The train was stopped and a search made, but the man was not found. After the train had gone he was discovered, but rather than get a doctor the station officials sent him on the next train to Guy's Hospital where he died. The Coroner censured the SECR for this action. On 15th September 1904 two lady passengers waiting at Elephant & Castle were hit by shards of broken coal scattered from the bunker of a down boat train; with serious facial injuries, they were able to claim £1400 damages.

On 5th September 1917 a passenger was killed at Maidstone West when trying to jump off a moving train. A few weeks later a "stowaway" was killed when he fell off a goods train near Whitstable. In October 1920 a man was pushed off the platform by a crowd of hop-pickers and run over with fatal consequences.

On occasions the passengers endangered themselves by getting onto the track. In January 1902 the 7am GNR train from Barnet to Victoria stalled on the incline at

THE LEVEL CROSSING

" Are there no more trains this evening on the up line, porter ? "

" No, mum."

" And no more trains on the down line ? "

" No, mum."

" Is there no *special* train ? "

" No, mum."

" Nor an *excursion* train ? "

" No, mum. The gates are to for the rest of the evening."

" You're quite sure ? "

" Yes, mum."

" Then come, Amelia. We can cross the line ! "

The contrasting attitudes of the public to level crossing safety are shown in these two cartoons.

PRIVILEGES OF HIGH RANK

Railway Gatesman. " It's agin the rules, my lady, openin' o' the gate like this ; but it ain't for the likes o' me to keep yer *ladyship* a waitin'."

Noble Countess. " Why is it against the rules, my good man ? "

Railway Gatesman. " Well, my lady, the 5.17 down express has been doo these ten minutes ! "

Snow Hill. A pilot engine was summoned from Ludgate got derailed, causing the line to be blocked for an hour. Several passengers on trains to Crystal Palace and Victoria got out and walked along the line to Ludgate Hill.

Level crossings were especially notorious locations of accidents, though it was rare for the railway passengers to suffer. Pedestrians often attempted to dash across the line in front of a train with fatal results, as at Broadstairs in October 1899; in this case the Board decided to provide a footbridge. In January 1901 three horses were killed at Tonford Crossing near Chartham.

A crossing with a history of problems was Willesborough Crossing, near Ashford. There was a fatal accident there in March 1907, at a crossing used by over 800 people a day, so a footbridge was moved down from Erith.

In July 1910 a grain van was hit by a train on an occupational crossing near Kenley, with both the horse and its driver being killed. The grain merchant had to pay compensation of £203 to his employee's widow, which he claimed back from the SECR along with £50 for the horse and van. The SECR defence was that occupational crossings were covered by different laws than public ones, but the merchant was able to prove the SECR knew the crossing was used regularly by the public and won most of the damages.

Because of these dangers the SECR sometimes tried to close crossings or replace them with bridges. In 1909 the SECR got into a legal battle for control of a crossing at Barden Park, near Tonbridge. A crossing had been opened there in 1866 and used for carrying loads of hops across the line, but at some stage after 1890 the landowner, Mr Abrey, gave the keys of the gates to the SECR. In 1908 he let some of the land out for market gardens and the rest as allotments to Tonbridge UDC, deciding that he needed the keys back. The SECR argued that the crossing was dangerous - at the foot of a steep bank and on a sharp curve. However in February the Judge ruled that Abrey and his tenants should be able to use it and that the SECR had to ensure their safety.

On 29th January 1910 two people were killed at Crabtree Crossing, Erith, one of a number of crossings that had regular fatalities. At one crossing in Lower Sydenham six people were killed between 1906 and 1911, and at another crossing in the same area there had been three deaths, including a young girl who was run over by three trains. This led to a discussion at the Home Office about forcing the SECR to erect a bridge. In January 1912 a man and a child were killed at College Crossing, Shalford.

In July 1912 there were fatalities on successive days at the crossings in Selling and Staplehurst though it was always difficult for the SECR to replace crossings with bridges due to legal restrictions. In April 1913 it managed to push through a scheme to close two pedestrian crossings at Hastings and replace them with a subway at a cost of about £1,750. Matters got worse as motor cars became commonplace - in August 1913 one crashed into an SECR crossing and overturned - killing one man, though others were saved by the signalman. On 22nd June 1917 a tractor broke down on a level crossing near Pattenden Siding, Goudhurst, and was destroyed by a train.

In October 1918 retired Commander Strickland was killed on a public crossing at Sheerness due to a combination of factors - "somewhat deaf" already, a raging gale made it impossible for him to hear an approaching train.

The SECR was legally responsible for any accident where negligence could be shown. In January 1920 a man was knocked down at the crossing at Slades Green after having gone through the pedestrian wicket gate. He sued for damages, claiming that the gate should have been fastened if it was not safe to cross, and won £550 plus costs.

Another legal battle occurred after a man was killed at Hanging Banks crossing near Canterbury West in 1921. His employer sued for compensation, the SECR contesting the right to use the crossing but lost the case.

However, though crossings were more dangerous than bridges, not even bridges were proof against disaster. In June 1899 a traction engine with three trucks was approaching the bridge west of Sandling Juntion when it got out of control and plunged onto the tracks, killing its driver. An approaching boat train was stopped by signals.

There were also incidents when people got onto the line. In April 1913 a ten year old boy, the son of a policeman, was found decapitated on the line at Kenley and in October 1919 the 16 month old child of the bridgekeeper was killed at Swale - he got onto the line through a hole in the fence made by the Army. Nobody ever knew how General Sir George Wolseley came to be on the line near Wateringbury in May 1921, but he became one of the most illustrious victims of the SECR trains.

The First World War resulted in many soldiers being stationed to guard the railway, occasionally with tragic results as discussed in chapter 16. On 6th October a Territorial Army soldier was knocked down at St John's, dying soon afterwards. There was much criticism of the ambulance service, for the poor man was wheeled by hand through the streets and it took 25 minutes to get him to hospital.

Of course it was not only people that got onto the line. In October 1917 the SECR got into a legal battle with the owner of a bull, which got onto the line near Marden and was killed. The owner claimed £45 damages as the SECR should have maintained fences or hedges to prevent his bull getting onto the line, while the SECR counter-claimed for £11 as the bull was supposedly "enraged" and had damaged the SECR's hedge. The railway company lost. There were also numerous occasions when cows and sheep got onto the line, such as the events of 14th October 1921 when the "up" Flushing boat train from Dover ran into a herd of cattle near Sevington Crossing, killing two.

A Fictitious Accident

The most famous accident of South Eastern Railway days was the Staplehurst disaster, which involved Charles Dickens in a non-fatal capacity. The SECR also had its connections with novels and novelists, and the directors of the system cannot have been pleased when their railway appeared in a fatal accident in Arnold Bennett's 1907 novel, *The Ghost.* In it the "hero" takes the Dover boat train on the ex-LCDR route, but changes carriages at Sittingbourne due to a rather frightening man in his original compartment. As the train is approaching Dover Priory, there is an accident:

"Then, in the fraction of a second, as it seemed, there was a grating, a horrible grind of iron, a bump. a check, and my head was buried in the cushions of the opposite side of the carriage, and I felt stunned - not much, but a little.

'What-what?' I heard myself exclaim. 'They must have plumped the brakes on pretty sudden.'

Then, quite suddenly, after an interval, it occurred to me that this was a railway accident - one of those things that one reads of in the papers with so much calmness. I wondered if I was hurt, and why I could hear no sound; the silence was absolute - terrifying.

In a vague, aimless way, I sought for my matchbox and struck a light. I had just time to observe that both windows were smashed, and the floor of the compartment tilted, when the match went out in the wind. I had heard no noise of breaking glass."

The hero, a doctor, clambers out of his carriage and finds a railway official who tells him what has happened:

"'There was a goods wagon got derailed on the siding just beyond the home signal, and it blocked the down line, and the driver of the express ran right into it, although the signal was against him - ran right into it, 'e did.'

Other people were crawling out of the carriages now, and suddenly there seemed to be scores of spectators, and much shouting and running about. The engine lay on its side, partly overhanging a wrecked wagon. Immense clouds of steam now issued from it, hissing above the roar of the wind. The tender was twisted like a patent hairpin in the middle. The first coach, a luggage van, stood upright, and seemed scarcely damaged. The second coach, the small, old-fashioned vehicle which happily I had abandoned at Sittingbourne, was smashed out of resemblance to a coach. The third one, from which I had just emerged, looked fairly healthy, and the remaining three had not even left the rails."

Bennett's tale seems to have been influenced partly by the Grantham disaster of 1906, where a train inexplicably ran through signals and led to all sorts of rumours about why the driver failed to slow down. In Bennett's disaster, the "stoker" complains about driver Bill:

"'Bill, 'e was all dazed like - 'e was all dazed like. I told him the signal wasn't off. I shouted to him. But 'e was all dazed like.'"

Chapter Eleven:

The Battle against Trams and Buses

When the South Eastern and Chatham railways came together in 1898, it was generally supposed that railways were - and would remain - the pre-eminent form of transport in Britain. This was especially the case in passenger transport where the very shape of British cities, and London in particular, had been the creation of the railways in the Victorian period. Yet by the outbreak of war in 1914, the SECR had lost virtually all of its inner suburban traffic so that many services withdrawn during the War never revived after it. The cheap and convenient tram exposed a company which had little idea of how to compete and which, perhaps, had no real desire to fight to retain a troublesome traffic that yielded few profits but blocked up the stations which might be better used for longer-distance customers.

This proved to be but the prelude to a battle between rail and various forms of road transport (in which we might include street trams) that has lasted for the rest of the century. As will be shown, the SECR's supposition that it could abandon the inner suburbs since the outer reaches of the Metropolis would yield rich pickings proved a risky strategy in the light of the motor bus boom in the immediate post-war years. In the same period the end of World War One released a flood of motor lorries which began to challenge rail's control of the goods market. Throughout this period the SECR failed to make any significant innovations, delaying electrification and slow to adjust its fares structure.

The SECR was slow to react to the rising challenge from road, even when the main competition was the humble horse tramway. Losses in the 1890s were meant to be stemmed by simple measures such as adjusting the fares on workmen's tickets, which was done on 1st April 1899. They were valid on any arrival at Victoria, London Bridge or St Paul's before 8am and had to be bought in blocks of fifty by employers or trades unions. Under the marital rearrangements of the SE and LCDR, workmen's fares from most SER stations were reduced by a penny and by the same amount to the stations on the LCDR's Greenwich branch. Because of these changes the SECR sold an extra 805,000 tickets at 1.34d each on average - a yield of only £4,500; perhaps there was a message here about the traffic being worth the fight.

Apart from the vastly expensive widenings of lines in the London area, the SECR did little else to encourage inner suburban traffic so that the condition of stations like Ludgate Hill, Deptford and Woolwich Arsenal became the cause of much bad feeling. Fog was also a notorious problem, causing much delay through minor collisions and rendering operations like shunting in and out of Cannon Street a nightmare. Crowds of up to a thousand passengers waiting to leave Spa Road at eight in the morning were not unknown.

The 1890s had seen a slow increase in competition from horse trams and

Woolwich Arsenal station was rebuilt by the SECR but the district was also well-served by trams. (E. Course collection)

horse buses, but the new century brought a more potent threat in the form of the electric tram. In February 1900 the SECR decided to petition against the South East Metropolitan Tramways scheme and five months later was concerned about electric tramway schemes in Sheerness, emphasising the need to be concerned about short distance traffic in all the larger towns as well as London itself. However there was also the possibility of profit as the tramway power stations would need supplying with coal - in the same month the SECR discussed a proposed siding at Camberwell New Road for a tramway generating station. Back in March the SECR had also decided to install a siding between Margate and Broadstairs for the Isle of Thanet Electric Tramways & Lighting Company, a scheme which affected the SECR in another way as a new bridge had to be installed for it at Broadstairs in 1901. Two years later Hill complained that "tramways were a great peril which had caused a considerable fall in traffic on the railway between Margate, Broadstairs and Ramsgate."

The first electric tramways did not open in the south-east suburbs until 1903, but by the end of 1900 the horse-drawn variety had already had a serious impact on SECR traffic. At General Meetings Bonsor made a regular complaint about the problem; in January 1901 he reported to shareholders that some stations within six miles of London were experiencing a net decrease in passengers while in August he reported "a large diminution of short journeys through other means of locomotion." The main concern was London, but there was also worry over competition between Margate and Ramsgate.

An extra edge was given to the question by the role of London County Council in promoting the electric tramways. In February 1902 the SECR considered acting together with the London General Omnibus Company in a bid to frustrate the LCC scheme for a tramway linking Blackheath, Lewisham and Camberwell.

In May 1902 the SECR held a conference with the LBSCR to discuss the threat. The proposed London Electric Company was planning a network of suburban trams which would feed into tube routes under the congested central areas, and Bonsor hoped that the SECR and LBSCR could unite to promote aggressive schemes in defence of what they already held - an extension of the East London line being considered. He even suggested that the SECR would promote its own underground lines. William Forbes of the LBSCR felt that competition was only significant within the six mile radius and that Croydon was quite safe. "Mr Bonsor agreed, adding that in his view a railway could not compete with tramways in London and the immediate suburbs." There was some concern that any attempt to compete would plunge both railways into a "low fares policy", the wisdom of which had been called into question by the workmen's tickets experiment.

In July 1902 Bonsor felt vindicated as he reported that outer suburban gains were outpacing inner suburban losses to the trams, but the following year the electric tramway idea was proposed in Chatham, Erith and Maidstone - the latter proposal running out to Barming. However Bonsor remained optimistic, noting a slight increase in 3rd class ticket sales and commenting that "The tramways had more or less had their day..."

This, of course, was a major error as the electric trams were just about to enjoy rapid growth. In fact by January 1904 Elephant & Castle had become a major focus of tramways and from 24 January it was possible to journey from there to Greenwich by electric traction.

A route that suffered badly from the competition of the Metropolitan District Railway's electric trains, was the system of links between Charing Cross, Cannon Street and London Bridge. On 1 June 1904 1st class season tickets were reduced from £7 to £5 for a year, or £4 for the shuttle between Charing Cross and Cannon Street. 3rd class ordinary fares were also reduced. This effort led to an increase in passengers but a decrease in revenue.

These changes were perilously close to the "low fares policy", but passenger traffic in the first half of 1904 was down in total by £4,500 and one station alone lost 600,000 passengers in that period. The second half of the year saw 3rd class passengers down by 1,871,000 although the actual revenue loss was only £2,496 - very short distance traffic indeed! These trends continued into 1905 and by the end of 1906 the SECR calculated its total losses to trams since 1900 as 3.3m passengers and £42,000.

In December 1904 the LBSCR announced its intention to fight the trams by electrifying the South London Railway from Victoria to London Bridge, but the SECR planned economies instead. From 1 March 1905 Borough Road station opened only from 7am to 10.30am and from 12.30pm to 7pm Monday to Saturday. It was also decided to close Cannon Street after 9.16pm and between 11am and 4.30pm on Sundays to save about £9 a week.

In June 1905 further consideration was given to station closures but Kidbrooke and Beckenham Hill proved to be legally protected by agreements with landowners. Receipts at Kidbrooke per annum were only £83 against expenses of £273; figures at Beckenham Hill were £187 to £201. Loughborough Junction experienced a sharp fall in City traffic so the tracks there were realigned and on 13 March 1907 the SECR decided to close Borough Road station entirely after 30 March due to "tramway competition" - although the platforms remained for some time afterwards. This station closure marks a turning point in the struggle.

On 27 March 1907 the Board discussed a number of measures - all retreats. From 1 March they had cut the service on the Metropolitan Extension to Moorgate Street as well as the Crystal Palace and Greenwich Park services. Proposed cuts from 1 May were to include many inner London stops and the Charing Cross-Cannon Street section of the Gravesend services. It was also suggested that services to the Great Northern should be stopped and the Beckenham to Crystal Palace line be worked by a motor train.

Thus the last regular Great Northern trains ran through to Woolwich on 30 April, the Victoria service ceasing from 30 September. When the Midland Railway service ceased on 1 July 1908, the line between Ludgate Hill and Farringdon Street lost its passenger service altogether. However rail connections were possible between London Bridge and Kings Cross by tube railway from 12 May 1907. On 31st July 1907 Bonsor told the shareholders that electric trams at Brixton, Camberwell and Clapham had "emptied their trains"; yet, only four years before, he had prophesied the decline of the tram. The service from the Mid Kent line to Victoria finished on 1 July 1908, partly a tram victim as many of the passengers came from the Brixton area.

Bonsor's confusion was still evident in January 1908 when he told shareholders, "There is still a general improvement in the outer suburban traffic, but the receipts for short-distance traffic continue to be affected by the increased tram and motor omnibus competition; there are indications that some passengers that left the railway for the tram are now returning."

Provincial tram competition was almost as worrying. In June 1908 the SECR considered the threat posed by Sheerness tramways with a scheme to extend as a light railway to Minster-on-Sea. This was opposed by the SECR as it would have paralleled the Sheppey Light, and the Light Railway Order was refused in August. In October it was decided to try and fight the Dartford and Gravesend competition from 2nd November by issuing cheap tickets from that date and opening new halts at Stone Crossing and Swanscombe. Fortunately the fact that services based on these towns were operated by rival companies Balfour Beatty and British Electric Traction prevented a through service being introduced across the intervening one and a half mile gap; BET put on a through bus service in 1913.

Only three months after this decision to compete, Bonsor told the General Meeting that "it was impossible to compete with" trams. The effect of them may be judged from figures he presented:

Table 4: SECR Passenger Receipts

Year	No. of passengers	Passenger receipts	Receipts per passenger	Season ticket receipts
1899	71,116,000	£2,375,000	7d	£309,000
1908	59,515,000	£2,465,000	9.5d	£396,000

In July 1909 Bonsor was still bemoaning "the loss of traffic by Tramway competition has become a very serious matter," and announced that 3rd class season tickets would now be available to some parts of the ex-LCDR system as they were on the ex-SER lines. Stations like Catford, Sydenham and Dulwich thus received the benefits of the "cheap fares policy" though Bonsor cautioned that "the decline has been rapid and, if the innovations were successful, the recovery would henceforth be slow."

This decision was a response to fierce criticism of the SECR management by shareholders such as Mr Drucker and Lord Weardale, who wanted two "expert" directors added to act as managing directors. The apparent lethargy of the Board in facing the tram competition was one of the reasons for this, but Bonsor tried to argue that the trams created social factors that benefited the SECR. His defence was that trams reduced the value of property and drove the middle classes further out, where the SECR could benefit. This was partially true and matched ideas now enshrined in urban geography, but the SECR had also been at fault in assuming that the better-off would pay more to be segregated from their economic inferiors when travelling to work.

By July 1910 the Board was claiming that the only line showing poor results was from Victoria to Snow Hill or Nunhead; this was affected partly by the LBSCR's South London electrification which opened on 1 December 1909 and which attracted former SECR passengers to some of its services.

Optimism was ill-founded of course. The danger in the outer suburbs was revealed by a Bill for "Rail-less electric traction" to run from Purley to Merstham or Caterham in 1910 and the "Croydon & Southern District Rail-less Electric Traction Bill" of 1911. Trams were also being extended to Catford, Herne Hill and in Dartford. The trams claimed a second victim when Grosvenor Road station closed from 1 October 1911, though some measure of revenge could have been claimed in February 1912 when a bolt fell off the SECR's bridge at Southwark Bridge Road and derailed a tramcar.

In January 1912 it appeared that Bonsor had decided to oppose the cheap fares policy, declaring that "the general fact remained that short journeys in the Metropolitan area meant a considerable number of passengers, but very few sovereigns." Another worrying trend appeared at this time - 5000 hop-pickers had been "lost" to road transport the past season.

At East Malling many people were voting with their feet against high SECR fares by walking to Barming from where they could catch the Maidstone trams rather than the trains; cheap workmen's fares were available before 8am. The SECR decided in October 1912 to open a halt in the hope this would help convenience to triumph over price; this opened in 1913.

By 1913 the motor bus was becoming as significant a problem as the tram, and probably more so in the outer districts which Bonsor had believed sacrosanct. In January 1913 he bemoaned tram and bus competition in the same breath, but maintained the "no fighting" stance - "It would not be wise...to incur large capital outlay in order to endeavour to regain the passengers they had lost - " by which he meant electrification. Yet the SECR was involved in electrification, for the LCDR was paying 12.5% of the costs of electrifying the East London Railway.

Shareholders became increasingly restive about the motor bus competition, with letters being sent to the Board in October 1913. An enlightened shareholder, E Walford, saw an opportunity for development though; at the General Meeting in February 1916 he pointed out that "omnibuses might very well be feeders to the Railway. They might run along the cross roads and bring traffic to the stations."

During the War itself, SECR services were restricted but there were significant fare increases - up by 75% between 1914 and 1921. This put the SECR in an exposed position when the end of the War released a flood of motor vehicles, though it was helped by the increasing tendency in post-war Britain for shops and offices to standardise their hours of work. This caused a crush as the "rush hour" became concentrated, having been spread between 7am and 10am during the Victorian period. The buses and trams reacted to this with some fare increases, which delayed temporarily rail's decline.

Services that were cut and stations that were closed during the War included a high proportion of those that were losing the fight against the trams. Some of these did not reopen, such as Spa Road and Southwark Park - both well within the six mile zone - which closed to the public from 15 March 1915 though some staff stops were still made. Walworth Road closed from 3 April 1916 as did Camberwell, Loughborough Junction (west platforms), Clapham (SEC only), Brixton (SECR) and Wandsworth Road - at the latter two LBSCR electric services were preferable anyway. The Greenwich Park branch succumbed from 1 January 1917, but this was a duplicate line in any case although affected significantly by trams.

A continental express, including several Pullman vehicles, passing the site of Wandsworth Road's SECR platforms in about 1923 - this was one of the stations that could not cope with tram competition, although the situation was worsened by the LBSCR's South London electrification. (R W Kidner collection)

In the immediate aftermath of the War, buses were the key danger. By 1919 London County Council was applying for powers to run its own buses and in June 1920 there was an hourly bus service running between Charing Cross and Lower Kingswood - the heart of the prosperous outer suburbs. Buses proved adept at winning leisure traffic in such areas, especially the middle class ladies who liked to go up to London for shopping. From 1st December 1921 the SECR therefore introduced cheap return "shopping tickets" for journeys of up to 15 miles into London; these were on the same restrictions as the LBSCR's - 10.30am to 4.30pm and after 6pm only. In October 1922 the SECR discussed acute bus competition in the suburbs on Sundays - again reflecting the sensitivity of the leisure market rather than business travellers.

The LBSCR also suffered. It wrote to the SECR in July 1922 about the electrification to Coulsdon, which had been delayed by the War. The letter complained of "the loss of business now being suffered in consequence of the competition of road transport."

SECR policy is shown as largely inadequate in competing against tram and bus services. Though Bonsor was correct in abandoning the "six mile" zone as one where railways could not compete - and where it was hardly worth their while - the SECR proved to be reluctant to invest in its outer suburban services and left these dangerously exposed to buses after the War. The fiasco of electrification is discussed in another chapter.

The New Fashion of Travelling in Motors

In October 1902 *The Times* was using its Letters columns to vent anger on the inadequacies of the SECR when E H Cooper wrote a prophetic letter; "the problem presented by this scandalous line," he opined, "will be solved by motor cars."

The threat of the car remained very restricted until 1914 as they were unreliable, expensive and dependent on roads of varying quality. However even a few cars could be annoying to the magisterial Bonsor, who complained in January 1907 of a decline in traffic to the seaside due to "the new fashion of travelling in motors instead of by the much more comfortable means of railway carriages...He did not think, however, that this fashion would last for ever." Wisdom is easy for those who come later, so we must forgive Bonsor this notable error.

World War One proved a turning point for cars. Whereas rail services were severely curtailed, especially after December 1916, rich people with cars were virtually unrestricted and got into the habit of avoiding slow and overcrowded trains. The position was worsened by huge rail fare increases, but even in 1922 the car was still far from being a means of mass transit.

Chapter 12:

The Motive Power

At the start of the era the SECR was purely a steam railway, and it still was at the close despite several years of agonised discussion of the benefits of suburban electrification. In this respect it lagged behind its neighbours, the LBSCR and LSWR, a situation which served to complicate relations at the formation of the Southern Railway.

The locomotives were placed in the charge of Harry Wainwright, formerly in charge of the SER's Carriage & Wagon department and insufficiently experienced in locomotive work. In fact much of the subsequent designing of SECR locomotives was the product of Robert Surtees, the ex-LCDR chief draughtsman, while Wainwright gradually lost control of the running department to Hugh McColl. A particularly colourful description of Wainwright deserves repetition:

"He was a man of supreme Edwardian elegance and was partnered by a most attractive and fashionable wife. A meticulous man of high principle but also a very human one whose moustache would bristle with displeasure at the sight of poor working conditions and who is reputed to have devised many ingenious methods for reducing the discomfort of his workmen."

Wainwright's sense of style, perhaps developed whilst designing plush passenger carriages, could be seen in the Brunswick green livery and elaborate lining of the SECR locomotives.

The start of 1899 found the SECR with too few modern locomotives among its stock of 674. There was a particular problem on the LCDR route, but this was partly due to inadequate bridges restricting the size of locomotives that could be employed; this problem was addressed, but it was to be many years before substantially heavier engines could be fully utilised on this route.

The immediate needs were identified as goods engines and modern bogie tank locomotives, the latter primarily for suburban passenger services were an off-the-shelf LCDR design built by Sharp, Stewart & Co. By May 1899 it had also been realised that at least 40 goods engines were needed, the eventual "C" class, in order to improve the goods service offered to the whole region. These 0-6-0 engines were built at a variety of places including the works of Sharp, Stewart & Co and included the last engines to be built at Longhedge works in Battersea.

Attention then turned to passenger engines capable of express work, so twenty of the new "D" class were ordered in September 1899 although the class eventually numbered 51. The first did not arrive until February 1901 and the lack of power gradually became an acute embarrassment - twice in a fortnight the new "luxury" Folkestone train got stuck in Sevenoaks tunnel. This was made worse by the performance of Robert Stephenson & Co who were due to deliver their five locomotives in August 1902, although they actually reached the SECR on 18 February 1903. Under the contract Stephensons were liable to a fee of £20 per week

"C" class 0-6-0 no.255, built in June 1900.

The first Wainwright passenger class for the SECR was the "D", here with no.741 of 1903. It is shown at Battersea in simplified wartime livery, but still with a copper-capped chimney. (Lens of Sutton)

but this was waived "as an act of grace" according to Minutes of May 1903, and then in June changed to an insistence on a penalty of £2260. Vulcan Foundry were also late with their delivery, though Dubs were on time with theirs.

In 1903 work began on designing a type of steam railmotor for lightly trafficked lines like the Sheppey Light, the first two of these being introduced in 1905. Bonsor told a General Meeting in July 1905 that the first two railmotors were ordered as an "economy" and were "satisfactory" enough to justify six more, which were ordered in November. Although these units did save money compared to a traditional train, they lacked operating flexibility and were all out of service by February 1920.

By June 1903 the locomotive stock had risen to 734 and 34 "duplicates". They were a substantial investment, costing £183,000 to repair in 1902 alone. The SECR added to this stock with one or two unusual purchases, notably a Terrier tank engine from the LBSCR in August 1904 which saw some subsequent use shunting at Sheerness and on occasional Sheppey Light goods services. Another unusual addition to the roster was the purchase for £400 in 1904 of *Middleton*, a shunting engine belonging to the contractor William Rigby, which was employed at Folkestone Harbour.

The next stage was to renew the fleet of tank engines for shorter distance passenger work, so that the "H" class 0-4-4Ts were built between 1904 and 1915.

The mixed results of the railcar experiment led to Wainwright's plan for a free-standing Terrier-type small tank engine, which became the "P" class. The first

"H" class 0-4-4T no.269, built in November 1905.

two of these were built at Ashford in 1909 and used on the services to Ash and on the Sevenoaks Bat & Ball line. In June 1909 the SECR ordered six more for the Bexhill branch, Paddock Wood to Maidstone West, Strood to New Brompton, Birchington to Ramsgate Harbour, and Norwood Junction to Beckenham. Here we see another attempt to alter the economics of marginal railway services, though one doubts the discussion about economising by abolishing brass domes on engines - in July 1910 - would have made any more significant difference.

Between 1905 and 1909 Ashford works built the "E" class for the heavier, steam-heated trains such as Continental and Pullman services. They also commonly worked Royal trains, such as the unusual working on 16 August 1913 from

Liverpool Street to Dover for the King of Denmark. On 26 December 1918 one of the class worked a special to Victoria conveying President Wilson, which actually had an air escort.

Introduced in 1913 was a class of 0-6-4Ts, the "J" class, and these were heavily employed on semi-fast workings to Tonbridge, Dorking and Hastings.

The "L" class, introduced in 1914, were built specifically for service on the SE section due to the increasing expense of further improvements to the LCDR main-line and following concerns about the lack of appropriate power for summer services. These were the last engines designed under Wainwright's charge, though

The diminutive "P" class were intended for railmotor use although no.754 was completed in full Wainwright passenger livery in 1909. (E Pouteau)

"E" class no.507 was built in 1908 but soon modified with extended smokebox, as shown here in a 1911 view. (R W Kidner collection)

his position by this time was most insecure and he "retired" on 30 November 1913 only a month after the SECR had decided to order twelve from Beyer, Peacock & Co. In fact Wainwright had taken three months off due to illness at the end of 1912 and was granted an allowance of £1200 a year on retirement.

His replacement was R E L Maunsell who had been working in Ireland, and who took up office on 1 January 1914 but a guiding force in locomotive work continued to be R Surtees. Maunsell was appointed on a salary of £2500 plus the use of Alfred House at Ashford, but unlike his predecessor he had no charge of the running department. It was Maunsell who suggested getting some "L" class engines built outside of Ashford as there was an urgent need for more locomotives, and contracts were signed with Beyer, Peacock and with Borsig & Co of Berlin for delivery by June 1914. The latter contract provoked some press interest as the only previous imports of German locomotives had been a few small engines for contractors' use; the SECR defended its action on the grounds that UK builders were too busy to guarantee delivery whilst the Germans had offered "a favourable price" - they cost about 10% less than the Beyer, Peacock engines.

The Borsig engines reached England in May and June 1914 and on 12 August the SECR decided to defer payment as war had broken out. The SECR's debt remained unpaid for several years, eventually coming within the Clearing House (Enemy Debts) arrangements, under which £49,202 had to be repaid in late 1920.

Maunsell's own plans were delayed through the need to assemble his own team at Ashford and then the dislocation caused by the War, but by January 1915 he was planning new designs of passenger tank and express goods engines. The first examples of "K" class, a 2-6-4T, and "N" class, a 2-6-0, both appeared in 1917 but further builds were delayed until the end of the War. The "K" class became known as the "Rivers", infamously so after an accident in 1927 that led to a wholesale rebuild. From 1919 "D" and "E" classes were rebuilt for use on the LCDR section, Maunsell achieving a considerable increase in the locomotives' power without adding significantly to their weight.

The lack of new building was highlighted when the SECR featured in the trial of a man for stealing a tarpaulin from it in 1917; the man argued that the SECR

Maunsell 2-6-4T "K" class no.790 in its 1917 official works photograph. This locomotive was later named *River Avon* but, like the rest of its class, was converted to a 2-6-0 tender engine after a series of accidents. (R W Kidner collection)

"lost" engines and that its German ones "go away for repairs and don't come back."

SECR locomotives had a tendency to fall foul of the law in the London area as they emitted too much smoke. In June 1901 the SECR was fined £5 for "permitting engines to smoke" at Dulwich. In 1902 it was prosecuted 73 times and lost 58 cases, with fines totalling £226. In August 1910 it was fined due to "dense black smoke" emitted by engines labouring up the 1 in 100 from Herne Hill to Sydenham Hill. As late as July 1922 the LCC was still prosecuting the SECR for smoke nuisance at Woolwich, though the magistrates advised that it was not possible to have a locomotive that produced none!

The Railway Fires Act of 1905 also forced the companies to fit new spark arresters to their engines when the law became effective in 1908. In June 1909 a building at Marley Lane, Battle, was burnt down due to sparks from an engine as a result of which the SECR decided to expand an experiment with Tiddeman Spark Arresters. Nonetheless the dry spring and summer of 1911 brought fires almost every day, an especial problem being sparks igniting the beds of straw used to cultivate strawberries and rhubarb. 127 claims cost the Managing Committee £1634 and 900 other reports did not result in claims, though there was £1000 damage to railway fences.

Electrification

Since 1903 the SECR had had powers to use electrical working and in February 1905 Bonsor suggested at a General Meeting that the SECR might try electric trains on its "Metropolitan" line in a similar way to the Metropolitan District Railway. At another meeting in January 1911 a SECR shareholder commented that the jointly owned East London Railway was in a "slough of despond" and should be electrified.

Six months later Bonsor was openly agreeing on the East London electrification idea, but he was much more lukewarm about electrifying the SECR itself to Dartford. He doubted such a scheme "would pay", but felt it might be necessary if steam working at Cannon Street and Charing Cross became too complicated - noting that it took 7 to 10 minutes to "form" a train at Cannon Street thus reducing station capacity.

However Minutes of a meeting in January 1912 suggest that Francis Dent was concerned to get the issue moving forwards, "either entirely or for the suburban area only." Dent, who favoured overhead electrification, felt that congestion at Cannon Street was the main consideration and any economies were a secondary factor. Bonsor seems to have been largely opposed to electrification, at least in as far as it was deemed to be a way of competing against the trams. It was decided to get Mr C Mercz to investigate, for which he charged £1500. The report was submitted in June 1913 and was extensive in its coverage, including observations on the working of the Channel Tunnel and advocating a 1500V dc system, but further consideration was halted by the onset of hostilities. In the meantime, the LBSCR began to run electric trains on its South London line using the 6000V overhead system - and the possibility of conflict was created.

Later in the War the SECR felt confident enough to return to the theme and chose Alfred Raworth to be its electrical engineer, "an officer who could give an unbiased opinion on suggestions for electrification," who already had extensive experience with the British Electric Traction Company, Brush and the LSWR. Raworth decided in October 1918 to study electric railways in the USA and left Liverpool on the 1st December at about the time when the Ministry of Munitions & War announced that electrification would be considered in post-war reconstruction applications.

Raworth returned on 8 March 1919 and the Managing Committee attempted to establish government attitudes to electrification before redesigning its summer timetable for that year. The government eventually decided to pay 5% on capital works or new stock after 1 May 1919, if approved by them. This seemed to encourage electrification and Raworth submitted his Report in October 1919.

In November the Ministry of Transport requested a report on the SECR's electrification proposals. The Minister, Sir Eric Geddes, set up an electrification committee the following year.

The Government wished to stimulate employment in the post-war era, while the SECR wished to proceed with suburban electrification but lacked the capital; its scheme to electrify all lines within 15 miles of Charing Cross would cost £5m, but 70% of this would be wages and the scheme could employ as many as 6,500 men for three years. The SECR's desire for electrification was still based upon the lack of capacity on the London lines, especially between 8am and 10am. Under the Trade Facilities Act the Government offered to guarantee loans on approved schemes, so in November 1921 the SECR decided to apply. After a meeting with the Advisory Committee, the SECR agreed to set up a separate company to organise the electrification with its own capital of £5.5m although the method of electrification had to await Ministry approval.

However, by this stage the amalgamation of the SECR, the LSWR and the LBSCR to form the Southern Railway was in an advanced state of preparation - but the three companies disagreed on the method of electrification to be used. Sir Philip Nash was appointed by the Minister to untangle this complex web and met representatives of the three companies in January 1922. The LSWR especially was strongly opposed to the SECR's chosen electrification system of two rails carrying 1500V dc, which it denounced as non-standard "either in this country or elsewhere" and a danger to staff or public - though the SECR attempted to patent its own "Live Rail Protector". The SECR system was reckoned to be both cheap and safe by Raworth.

By June 1922 the SECR's plans were advancing. Land was to be bought at Angerstein's Wharf for a 60,000KW generating station and 220 track miles were to be electrified at a cost of £6.5m. The first Board meeting of the South Eastern & Chatham Construction & Power Company was on 2 June. Later that month the scheme came before the Electricity Commissioners, who regulated the electricity supply industry, with the West Kent Electricity Company suggesting that the supply could come from its own works at Belvedere. The Electricity Commissioners decided that £1m could be saved on the SECR's scheme if it used existing electricity suppliers.

No doubt this set back was a relief to the other partners in the Southern Railway, who hoped to stall the SECR's plans but as late as November 1922 the SECR was still discussing moving ahead with its own system and on 20 December looked at the effects of electrification on the Greenwich Observatory. Significantly, the Government's own Electrification Committee advised in favour of a third-rail system and the adoption of this for the SECR lines was to be one of the earliest significant decisions of the Southern Railway. Ironically, Raworth went on to plan and introduce electrification across wide swathes of the new Southern system.

Chapter 13:

The Strains of War

Because of its unique geographical position, the SECR carried vast quantities of men and munitions throughout the course of World War One. This was done at a time when wages were spiralling and normal maintenance was severely reduced by the lack of available employees and materials. In fact the system came close to collapse for a number of reasons - "At one time...it looked as if we would have to suspend the passenger traffic." By the end of the War the SECR was thus in a weakened physical position - but also financially strained as well so that it could not afford to embark on an electrification scheme using only its own resources. This weakness left it ill-prepared for the new era of road transport that was launched virtually as soon as the War ended, and which had a sharp effect on the carriage of light goods and short-distance passengers. The world of the railways was never to be the same again.

The regulation of the railways in wartime was governed by the Regulation of the Forces Act, 1871, which provided for the setting up of a Railway Executive Committee combining the ten general managers of the leading British railways; this was formed in 1912 and included Dent of the SECR. The railways were covered financially by a Government guarantee of pre-war revenues; when war eventually broke out, these were fixed on 1913 levels - which was a good year compared to its predecessors. "Railway shareholders have been treated most generously by the Government."

The first war to affect the SECR was actually the Boer War which, though fought in South Africa, required much extra traffic. In December 1899 the Government requisitioned 5000 trucks to help serve the bases at Woolwich, Chatham and Aldershot; during one particular week of that month, the SECR ran 51 special trains.

The 1871 Act gave the Government the ability to take control of certain assets as well as the management of the lines. Thus, in 1905, they informed the SECR that the ships *Mabel Grace* and *Empress* would be asked for "in national need", whilst 100 of the SECR's horses could also be requisitioned. Three years later the War department inquired into plans to protect bridges and tunnels between Higham and Chatham - this being a key route of supply between Woolwich Arsenal and Chatham Dockyard.

When War with Germany finally broke out in August 1914, the SECR was immediately "taken over" by the Government. The initial phase of the war then involved the shipping out of the British Expeditionary Force by the SECR and LSWR ("without loss of man or beast" according to J Thomas, MP) and the receipt of Belgian refugees in large numbers from 20 August.

There was a phase of concern about German activity in England. On 9 August a SECR troop train was fired on at Edenbridge and windows broken; Kent

Police described the suspect as "tall and dark, with a sallow complexion and a moustache...he has a slouching walk." Under the headline "German Spies in England" *The Times* reported that a train had been shot at near Graveney on 15 August 1914. On 24 September an attempt to wreck a Boat Train at Grove Park was foiled by a policeman who found an iron chair fastened securely to the track - this was supposed to be German work. However anti-German panic did not penetrate all corners of the SECR - as late as August 1916 German language signs were still displayed at Charing Cross!

Defence of the line was in the hands of the War Office, who paid for extra footbridges at Lydden Spout, Shakespeare Cliff and Dover to improve access. The signalbox on Admiralty Pier became an Admiralty guard house, which was appropriate.

One of the SECR's main problems was how to handle increased traffic with fewer men - the solution being to take on large numbers of women, especially for goods handling in the London area.

War produced an apparent increase in "earnings" for the SECR, with the profit division between the SER and LCDR for 1915 being £20,000 more than in 1914.

War had a significant effect on staffing of the SECR, with an acute shortage affecting the SE London area and made worse by a regulation of March 1915 that the railways were not to take on men of military age. By the end of 1916 4000 employees had "joined up" and been replaced by 1300 women, mostly as clerks and porters. There were problems - as late as January 1916 the 440 female porters at Bricklayers Arms had no toilets of their own. The final total of SECR staff who enlisted was 5,222 of whom 461 were killed. Some of the replacements were found amongst Belgian refugees, who were taken on as platelayers based at Longhedge and Blackheath in 1915 with houses leased for them. One of the men fell into the Thames while working at Angerstein Wharf in 1916. Extra staff had to be found for unusual jobs - Mr Taylor was paid £100 a year to be "Censor of telegrams." By February 1916 the SECR had spent over £6000 on their hotel costs.

However staff shortages were a constant problem for managers like Tempest, and influenced his recommendations for the closures of January 1917. Thus the closing of the Crystal Palace HL branch released 33 men, 11 were released from the Bat & Ball line and a further 20 from the Bexhill branch. By this stage there was an acute shortage of goods shunters, and signalmen commonly worked 12 hour shifts - a situation made worse in October 1918 when 'flu struck London signalmen.

It did not help when employees were "lost" for other reasons. A porter at Sidley was sacked after being found guilty under the Defence of the Realm Act - he turned on a light while sweeping the station at night!

The war also caused inflation of wages with the first "war bonuses" being agreed in February 1915; prices more than doubled by 1920. When SECR headquarters staff joined the Army, the railway "made up" their salaries to the normal level.

The SECR also contributed to the war effort in other ways. Ashford works built many goods wagons for the War Department and made damping gear for 18lb guns. By 1915 the SECR was producing much material for the government including artillery wagons and munitions; the munitions work reached as high as £80,000 a month in 1916 and £104,000 in 1917.

The First World War was also the first time when the railways of Britain were attacked from the air. London Bridge station was altered with a new wooden staircase leading beneath the railway viaduct as a shelter for over 300 people from nearby offices. Admiralty Pier was hit by three bombs on 9-10 August 1915. On 19 March 1916 air raids killed ten people in Ramsgate and Dover, causing some minor damage to the SECR. On 25 February 1917 the Kent coast was bombarded, a shell falling 100yds west of Margate West, damaging the down line and track circuit wires. It left a crater over four feet wide. Slightly further west there was another crater in the up line, but traffic had been restored by 5.40am.

On 25 May 1917 there was a raid on Folkestone which threatened the safety of the 4.30pm down express as it neared Smeeth; six bombs were dropped as the

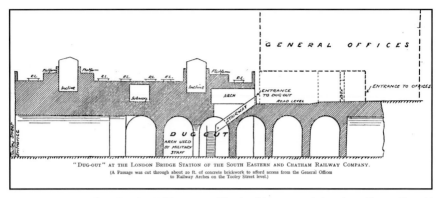

"Dug-out" at the London Bridge Station of the South Eastern and Chatham Railway Company.
(A Passage was cut through about 20 ft. of concrete brickwork to afford access from the General Offices to Railway Arches on the Tooley Street level.)

An attempt was made at London Bridge to provide air-raid accommodation that office staff could reach quickly.

Germans gave chase until the driver stopped in Sandling Tunnel - a grateful passenger sent £25 to the crew, while the driver of the Hythe bus was given 10s after bringing his frightened horses back under control. Half of the bombs dropped by 17 Gotha bombers fell within 400 yards of Central station, killing 77 people in the town and 18 at Shorncliffe.

On 7 July 1917 an air attack smashed the glass roof of Cannon Street station whilst a "large" bomb fell on the track near No.2 Signalbox. It sank five feet into the ground but did not explode, whilst there was damage to signals at Spa Road and Bricklayers Arms.

Ramsgate suffered an attack on 22 September, when a bomb landed at the London end of the Town station's arrival platform, passing through the roof. Much

Map of Folkestone showing the bombing raid of 25 May 1917; the Central station seems to have been a key target, but the harbour area escaped.

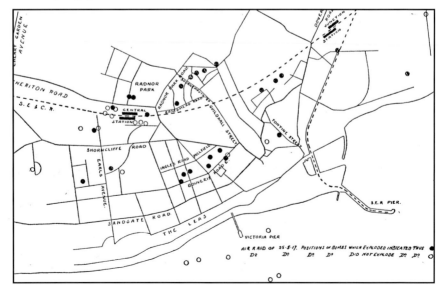

of the station roofing was badly damaged and two men were hit by debris. On 24 September a bomb fell on the up line near Buckland Junction.

On 29 September 1917 a spent shell fell on the down loop platform roof at Hither Green while an unexploded shell buried itself in a ballast siding at Tonbridge. A bomb landed 300yds on the down side of Sheerness East and blew the rails into a field. The following night there were more raids: the lines were damaged between Margate East and West and near Woolwich Dockyard, while there was slight damage to the Port Victoria station building by an unexploded shell. Glass was broken at Charing Cross, Waterloo, Cannon Street and London Bridge. After these events it was decided to buy a small car for Percy Tempest so that he could get about visiting all the damaged places.

Grosvenor Road bridge was damaged by the flames from a broken gas main after the raid of 1 October 1917. On 19 October bombs hit houses on the up side of the line near Hither Green, blocking the railway for three hours. The same raid demolished the home of SECR labourer Welch in Camberwell - he was given £10 by the Committee. F Merlo, a SECR porter at Calais, lost his house to a bomb while on active service and was given 500 francs. That night a Zeppelin dropped bombs on either side of the 7.45pm Ashford to Dover train between Grove Ferry and Minster.

The night of 31 October brought widespread raids though it seemed that shells fired at the Germans did as much damage as the bombers themselves. Bombs damaged bridge 638 near Erith, Eddington bridge near Herne Bay and an embankment near Folkestone whilst an incendiary device landed in Fawkham goods yard without igniting. Shells damaged the track between Herne Bay and Birchington, the decking of Rochester bridge, a bridge near Allington and the roof of Charing Cross.

The raids of 6 December caused minor damage and delays at many London stations including Victoria, and also at Sheerness Dockyard, where the engine shed was hit, and Whitstable. 18 December brought damage to Cannon Street, Angerstein Wharf, Southwark Park, Margate East to Broadstairs and Bekesbourne. Empty carriages at Cannon Street were hit by a shell on 28 January 1918 while the next day there was damage at Margate West, near Chilham, and between Nunhead and Greenwich Park.

London Bridge and Angerstein Junction were damaged by shells on 16 and 18 January 1918. On the former date Female Porter Gregory received a citation for "praiseworthy conduct" as she had lowered the Shortlands station lights during a raid.

On 22 April 1918 a plane crashed on the line between Upper Warlingham and Sanderstead, the two airmen being burnt to death; the line was closed for half an hour only.

The night of 19 and 20 June saw a series of raids. At Hither Green a bomb landed on the down line while a shell hit the track between Shooter's Hill and Welling. At Dover Priory a bomb fell in the locomotive yard, a bomb broke wires between Whitstable and Herne Bay, and a shell damaged the station roof at Faversham. Two nights later Port Victoria, London Bridge, Waterloo, Cannon Street and Charing Cross all had shrapnel damage.

On 17 July 1918 four incendiaries fell on Hawkesbury Street crossing and a bomb in the Dover Priory goods yard.

The end of the war arrived with huge backlogs in routine maintenance so that in November 1918 the Railway Executive Committee was trying to order supplies of steel rails.

In March 1919 the SECR discussed a suitable memorial with an Institute at Ashford being a popular suggestion. Baring, who had achieved General status during the war, wanted a memorial at Dover and cast iron lists of men killed at stations. Mr W King was employed to sculpt a memorial for Dover Marine station. On 10 November 1920 the "Unknown Warrior" was brought from Boulogne to Dover by *HMS Warrior*, then carried by SECR to London. The SECR war memorial at Dover Marine was unveiled by Cosmo Bonsor on 28 October 1922, listing 556 names.

Bad feeling about the Germans did not end with the hostilities though, as an added extra detail shows from the SECR's record of a tragic accident in June 1920; the Knockholt stationmaster was out shooting with his son when the boy was hit in the back, the inquest verdict being "accidental death due to a defectively made German sporting gun."

During the war, the SECR received compensation for shortfalls in revenue, which guaranteed levels of income but not dividends. This money was usually paid monthly, but about six weeks in arrears. At the same time wartime regulations meant that the SECR no longer published full accounts, and when its traffic profits for the first half of 1915 proved to be up by £43,000 it kept this information to itself - perhaps betraying a suspicion that levels of compensation were generous. As an example, actual net receipts in May 1913 were £152,706 whereas in May 1916 they were £38,721 - to which the government added £250,485; however this picture was also distorted by the rapid wartime inflation. For the whole of 1916 the SECR believed that it had actually gained half a million pounds which it regarded as a "temporary advance" against arrears of maintenance.

Government regulation continued after the war, when the SECR became notably less confident. Government control of passenger fares and also of staff salaries squeezed normal working profits for many months after the end of hostilities; in November 1920 the SECR was complaining that compensation arrived late, whilst weekly cash income was only just above actual expenditure.

By February 1921 the railway companies were feeling the acute financial pressures resulting from wartime stress and were seeking compensation for a decline of earning power - specifically blamed on rising wages during the war. This was exacerbated by the eight-hour day regulations enforced from 1 February 1919. Further pressure was caused by an end to government control of coal prices in February 1921 whilst government control of the railways themselves ended in August 1921.

The Sea and Overseas

Continental travel was widely disrupted by the war. All civilian services via

Dover ceased on 4th August 1914 and there were no sailings to Ostend once it had fallen to the Germans on 14 October. LBSCR Newhaven to Dieppe services were diverted to Folkestone from 12 August 1914. From 22 February 1915 the 8.30am Victoria to Boulogne and 12.30pm to Calais resumed running, but neither was suitable for journeys to Paris; Calais was only open to the military, Red Cross and people visiting the wounded. By November it was only possible for civilians to use the LBSCR service from Folkestone to Dieppe.

One of the immediate tasks of the SECR was the handling of Belgian refugee traffic, with as many as 6,000 landed in one day at Folkestone. Belgian railway officials were accommodated at the Charing Cross and Cannon Street hotels; the Zeebrugge harbourmaster was accommodated at Folkestone. The crown jewels and other Belgian treasures were also brought to Dover in total secrecy. *Invicta*, *Victoria* and *Queen* left Ostend laden with refugees on the day the Germans arrived.

The whole of the Dover harbour area became a military zone and so Dover Town station closed on 14 October 1914 and from 11 October 1915 civilians needed special permission to visit the town. Huge efforts were made to get Dover Marine ready for traffic and it was used for wounded and refugee services, though there were no civilian services and it was soon found to be too incomplete; instead it began handling ambulance trains from 2 January 1915 after additional work. From July 1917 it was used for soldiers going to and from France and from 17 November 1918 for returning prisoners of war. Demobilised soldiers continued to stream through until 20 March 1920.

With leisure travel to the Continent depleted, the SECR handed over many of its vessels - and their crews - to military control. *Engadine* and *Riviera* were taken over by the Admiralty Air Department as seaplane carriers and "so completely altered that it was doubtful whether they could ever be re-adapted to the cross-Channel service." Both ships took part in the Cuxhaven raid in December 1914. *Engadine* played a key role in the Battle of Jutland, being the first to sight German ships on 31 May 1916 and sent up a seaplane to warn of this, then was "mentioned in despatches" by Sir John Jellicoe for assisting the survivors of the *Warrior* by trying to tow the stricken vessel back to port rescuing 675 men from its boats, whilst Captain Hancock was awarded an OBE.

Empress was refitted at Chatham dockyard, seeing initial service between Sheerness and Ostend. Then it became part of the Harwich patrol and took part in the raid on Cuxhaven on 24 December 1914, during which it was attacked by airship L6. Then *Empress* too was refitted as a seaplane carrier, at Calshot, and went on to save 300 lives from the SS *Hesperian*. All three seaplane carriers were then sent to the Mediterranean.

Hythe became a troopship taking over some of the first British troops to Le Havre, then working regularly between Dover and Dunkirk. In March 1915 it and *Folkestone* were sent to Malta to take part in the landing of troops in the Dardanelles.

Amiral Ganteaume, a French ship, was torpedoed off Boulogne in October 1914 with 2,500 men and women on board but many of the lives were saved through

Repatriated British troops pose for the camera as an up train stands under the multitude of shunt signals at Dover Marine.

the action of Captain Carey and *The Queen*; Carey was given a gold watch and the OBE, and his crew received six days extra pay. In June 1916 he was awarded the Cross of the Chevalier by the French President and a few months later the *Queen's* ticket clerk received a silver medal. *Queen*, the first turbine steamer to cross the Channel, was sunk by a U-boat on 26 October 1916 but was fortunately in ballast at the time and also insured for £81,750. Also in October 1914, the *Invicta* rescued survivors of the torpedoed *MMS Hermes*.

In late February 1915 a Boulogne to Folkestone passenger ferry carrying 92 passengers was attacked near Boulogne by a U-boat, with a torpedo passing 30yds ahead. By this time Boulogne itself was effectively an English military town and the SECR had been doing extensive War Department work there with extra sorting sidings or the ammunition yard and Royal Engineers' Park. The SECR was asked if it would operate the port traffic, which involved shipping five engines over to France.

Hythe was involved in a collision with another ship and sunk in the Dardanelles in late 1915, the Admiralty paying £12,500 compensation; 10 crew were lost and many troops drowned. *Calais*, which the SECR had sold in 1911, was sunk by a U-boat on 26 February 1916. *Achille Adam* was lost with five men and a boy when it was captured and sunk by a U-boat off Newhaven on 23 March 1917; the victims included two men killed in the fighting, whilst the others perished after being set adrift in a boat for 28 hours. Three widows received £300 under the Workmen's Compensation Act, with a small pension. *Deal* was slightly damaged by an enemy shell while moored at Calais in April 1917.

On 19 December 1917 *Walmer* was damaged by a bomb while at Boulogne. *SS Galacum*, loaned to the SECR, was attacked by a U-boat between Folkestone and Boulogne on 6 April 1918; two torpedoes were fired but the ship was able to negotiate a way round them! Another hired vessel was hit by a bomb while at Calais on 22 July.

TSS Onward caught fire while berthed at Folkestone on 24 September 1918 and had to be sunk where it was. The fire was never explained, but the ship was recovered after the war and enjoyed further service to the Isle of Man!

Biarritz was launched in December 1914 and taken over by the Admiralty as a minelayer. In late 1916 the Admiralty decided to reduce its hire charge for this vessel by 30%, sparking a furious row which the SECR seems to have won. This vessel was unusual in being "chartered" by the Admiralty rather than requisitioned. It was stationed in the western Mediterranean and laid the mines that blew up the German raider *Breslau* and damaged the *Goeben.*

The *Maidstone* was returned by the Admiralty in April 1916. However the SECR was still short of vessels and in December 1916 the Admiralty chartered the *Shotton* to operate the Army Mails service between Folkestone and Boulogne - crewed by the SECR.

Maid of Orleans was launched in March 1918 and became a troopship straight away, though as normal it was crewed by the SECR when involved in a minor collision in October. Its maiden voyage was on 16 August and it was based at Southampton. It was sunk by a mine in 1944.

In 1919 the shipping of troops across the Channel reverted from the Ministry of Shipping to the SECR and on 1 November 1919 Folkestone was returned to SECR control. Dover Marine station opened to the public for the first time on 18 January 1919 and the public service to Ostend resumed. Paris services via Boulogne began on 3 February and the Flushing service about the same time.

The Richborough Ferry

Richborough Siding opened early in 1916 to serve the rebuilding of an old wharf for continental traffic known as Pearson's Wharf, which opened in May 1916; trains for it were sorted at Paddock Wood and used an 1898 connection, the wharf having originally been built to handle materials being used in the Dover harbour construction project. This wharf proved inadequate and in June 1916 work began on another new wharf (opened 16 September 1916), for which the Inland Water Section of the Royal Engineers diverted the course of the River Stour to create a new channel. At first barges were loaded at Richborough which then crossed the Channel and used the Belgian or French canal network. A fleet of 50 tugs and 232 barges was based at Richborough and many barges were also built there. 20,000 cross-Channel barge trips were made carrying 1.8m tons of materials. The effect was virtually the creation of a new town, with a workforce of 19,000 at its peak and 14,000 soldiers living on the site, many of whom were there for training purposes.

The huge increase in rail traffic necessitated replacement of the original connection with a new one closer to Minster in September 1916 and with sorting sidings at Weatherlees Sidings opened on 14 May 1917.

However in January 1918 the Cabinet approved a top secret project, already under construction, to operate a train ferry from Richborough, which necessitated

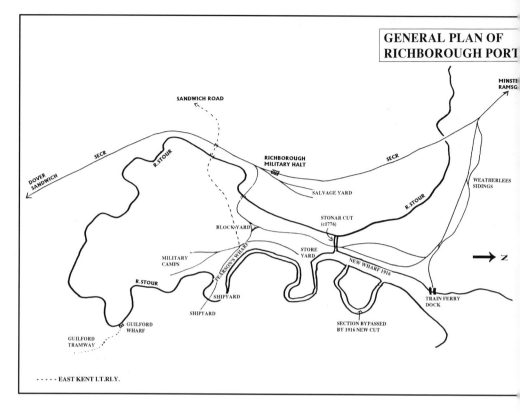

widening a section of the Stour to 500ft wide. By June 1918 there were at least eight major trains a day under the "Imperial" codes and the system was much improved when the train ferry came into operation on 6 February 1918, running to Dunkirk. The train ferry made 269 round trips to November, although outward traffic was three times greater than inward. Three vessels were built of which two operated from Richborough to Dunkirk and one from Southampton to Dieppe, each 363ft long and capable of 12 knots; they had four lines of track and could carry 54 10-ton wagons. During February 1918 alone the train ferries carried 150 locomotives, 6208 new wagons for the WD, 328 brake vans, 685 tanks and four 14inch railway guns. Returning traffic included much salvage material and the RAF had a salvage depot on the site.

The existence of the train ferry was revealed as soon as the war was over:

"Two heavy goods trains were shunted in position with only two shuntings, the wagons were chain-locked to the deck and the vessel at sea again within 25 minutes, during which time the vessel had been supplied with oil fuel and water. One contrasted this achievement with the busy dock-sides of the less fortunate ports where trucks have to be off-loaded and the contents either man-handled or slung by crane into a ship's hold."

The site was divided into several distinct yards such as Weatherlees Yard which could handle 1500 wagons a day, Train Ferry Yard, Saltpans Yard and

Richborough Yard as well as the Salvage Transit Depot for returning materials. There were 80 miles of railway sidings which eventually handled 540,000 wagons - cared for by a maximum of 20,000 men.

By January 1919 the military authorities were anxious to offload the responsibility of working Richborough onto the SECR and the site was also inspected by the Port of London Authority on 19 February 1919. From 10 February civilian workers were employed there, brought in by train from Dover and Margate; these gradually expanded and for a time included separate men's and women's trains! They ran onto the site to a point near the wharf. The operation of Richborough was transferred to the SECR on 28 February 1919 but then to the Ministry of Munitions on 12 December.

The opening of Richborough put extra pressure on Sandwich station, where minor changes were made in November 1918. The War Office paid £32 for a Halt to be opened at Richborough 29 June 1918; this was so cheap as it only had a down platform, which must have given rise to some morbid jokes among troops bound for France, although its main use was to bring in workers from the Thanet towns. There was also temporary housing provided at Richborough.

As has been noted, the SECR was very cool about train ferries before the war and showed no interest in taking over Richborough after it. By January 1919 there were already rumours that the ferries were to be used for Southampton to Le Havre, or even for Irish cattle traffic. Attempts to develop the port were a failure and the workmen's passenger service ceased in 1921; the lifting gantry from Richborough was sold to the GER for use at Harwich, but the link span remained in situ for many years. Even this survival was by chance, for the barges taking the Southampton equipment to Harwich sank, and it proved impossible to salvage the lifting gantry. In 1925 some of the facilities were bought by Pearson, Dorman Long Ltd as part of the development of the Kent coalfield.

A more successful port developed during the war was Ridham Dock, though this originated before the hostilities. There was a large trade in munitions at Ridham, bringing bigger vessels through the Kingsferry bridge and resulting in a correspondence with the Admiralty in 1917. The Admiralty refused to pay for extra piling to protect the bridge, and the SECR was obliged to do the work itself. From November 1917 passenger trains for munitions workers ran from Sittingbourne into Ridham Dock.

Wartime Goods Traffic

One of the most obvious results of the war was the increased traffic carried by the SECR, which by early 1916 amounted to an average of a hundred extra trains a day of which the vast majority were goods. Much of the extra traffic was material for the Army and Navy, though there was also extra traffic due to wartime dislocation - inshore coastal shipping in the Thames and along the Kent coast virtually ceased. This meant that coal via Blackfriars Junction increased to a million tons a year, much of it taken to Angerstein Wharf or Rochester for transhipment to barges though up to 400,000 tons was delivered per year to the Channel ports. Cannon Street was closed partially to allow the exchange of goods crews and locomotives there instead of Herne Hill, Hither Green or Blackheath. The extra traffic affected some places acutely - traffic from the Bexley and Woolwich area, the heartland of the munitions industry, was five times greater in 1917 than 1913; goods clerks at Woolwich increased from 11 to 48 and a new office had to be built at Plumstead for a further 52. Clerks at Chatham Dockyard were less fortunate - they got a new iron hut in 1917. However other traffic was lost - the regular Ashford Cattle Show was abandoned, for example. Not all the extra traffic was weapons of war, however, for there were many supplies such as bread from the government's bakery at Ashford.

Some of the additional traffic was handled by extra scheduled trains, some by regular specials that came to have a schedule of their own, and much by individual special workings. Woolwich was the focus of much military traffic and also received inwards consignments of extra coal from Nottinghamshire. Traffic from there included up to five daily workings to Redhill and even a through vans train to Woolwich from Liverpool Street.

From January 1917 the longer distance traffic was reorganised to give it greater priority and speed. Much of this traffic ran via the Redhill route whilst there were regular trains to Southampton and Portsmouth.

Messrs Vickers had a munitions factory at Crayford for which large extensions were planned by November 1914, when they asked for a new siding on the down side towards Dartford to handle the increased goods traffic and also large numbers of workmen who were causing capacity problems at Crayford station. It was in use by next January and was extended in 1916. Vickers also had a factory on the up side at Erith, which they added to by building on the down side. In 1916 the two parts were linked together with a double-decked footbridge, accomodating people on one level and the handling of goods on the other.

To accommodate all the new munitions workers, a government housing scheme for 957 houses at Well Hall was pressed forwards from February 1915 and new sidings laid in by March 1915 to handle the construction traffic; the contractor also laid in a tramroad. A maximum of 190 wagons were handled in a day and over 25 million bricks from Fletton unloaded.

In April 1915 it was decided to build new sidings at Aldershot North Camp and Ash. Two months later it was agreed to extend the Ordnance depot sidings near Dover Pier but this was not completed until July 1916.

A key point was Plumstead, which already handled most of the Woolwich Arsenal traffic, and which was expanded in stages - nine extra roads opening on 1 December 1914 and others the following June. Fourteen new sidings were laid out to the east of the existing yard and opened in early 1916 and a new siding added nearby at Abbey Wood in January. However by February 1916 the SECR could not handle the volume of traffic for Woolwich Arsenal and needed extra "holding depots"; these were provided in the shape of extra sidings at Kidbrooke and Blackheath. A new eastern connection into the Arsenal was known as the "Marsh Siding". Chislehurst, Grove Park and Eltham were also used as auxiliary depots.

The Thames Ammunition Works was situated on the marshes north of Slades Green and was served by a new light railway connection known as the "Trench

Warfare Light Railway" opened in June 1916. This was worked by the SECR, who were paid monthly, and after the war was used for a short time for refuse traffic. Another such line extended the Chattenden Naval Tramway south-east from Sharnal Street to a pier on the Medway; this was opened in 1915 and maintained by the SECR, and also served an Air Station; it was reopened in 1927 as the Kingsnorth Light Railway.

Not all munitions installations gained a branch. A remote one - justifiably given its appalling safety record - was the explosives works of Curtis & Harvey on Cliffe Marshes. In October 1915 they asked for a light railway connection to Cliffe station - three miles away, and with a difficult ascent of a chalk cliff to consider. Percy Tempest was to act as engineer and the work to be done on a cost plus 10% basis, with traffic of 2000 tons a week expected. The line was dropped by the Ministry of Munitions.

The supply of coal to Woolwich Arsenal and other installations in the area was improved by the opening of Crabtree Sidings near Belvedere in about December 1915, with extensions in mid-1916. This network connected both the Cory coal depot and a munitions works east of Crabtree Manor Way.

An extension was provided at Longfield Siding in 1916 and let to the EC Powder Co. for supplying gun cotton. In 1916 the goods shed at Bat & Ball was taken over by the Army as a chaff-cutting depot while the Hythe tramway depot was also let to the military. By February 1918 the SECR stores depot at Longhedge had to be moved to Bricklayers Arms so the War Department could take over.

A siding on the down side west of Abbey Wood was opened in January 1917 for the King's Norton Metal Works and the National Filling Factory; the factories closed in 1920. At Bellingham a siding was laid in to the serve the Canadian Army timber depot.

Towards the end of the war the bottleneck at Redhill became an increasing problem and two extra down side sidings were laid in at Reigate and opened in October 1918 to allow the "stacking" of goods trains unable to pass through the former. Redhill itself saw extensions to the track circuiting to help handle the traffic safely.

Very little military traffic was ever sent to France via Dover, which was essentially a Naval port with a role in Channel protection. Due to this, the disastrous Folkestone Warren landslip in December 1915 had no military significance; the track was not restored as there was "difficulty in obtaining labour and getting anyone at present to undertake a contract" which would hardly have applied in the case of a national emergency. However, by December 1917 new loops were being constructed "for the government" at Canterbury, "for the emergency movement of troops and materials." Another loop proposed to improve goods flows was suggested west of Dartford on the orders of the War Office in 1918, but not built; this was paid for by the Ministry of Munitions in April 1920.

In fact the Shakespeare Cliff tunnel became an ordnance store for the rest of the war, a function which was also considered for the nearby colliery.

This was the first war in which aviation played any significant role, and the SECR played a small part in this. From March 1918 it ran a daily train of three vans from Charing Cross conveying officers' small arms, which then crossed the Channel by plane - presumably from Lympne. In January 1915 it was discussing a proposed branch to the Naval Aviation Establishment at Grain, with land having already been leased for the purpose, but construction amounted to little more than a siding. In December 1916 a siding was laid in from Eastchurch, on the Sheppey Light, to the new Royal Naval Aviation School; a dock extension was opened from this in 1918. Large numbers of women were employed here but the SECR did not consider providing a ladies' toilet until March 1920 - then decided it was too late!

In October 1917 the SECR was involved in planning a branch from Westenhanger to Lympne aerodrome which was completed by August 1918 and paid for by the Air Ministry.

The SECR installed a siding and junction at Upper End Farm near Birchington as a link to the Manston Camp Light Railway, signalled by a new box Birchington "A". This line opened in July 1918, but passengers from Birchington had to change trains at Upper End Farm. Sidings for the Air Ministry were also installed at Kidbrooke in 1918, close to the extensive range of sidings opened in 1917. Petrol and spare parts for the aeroplanes in France were sent out via Dover.

The heavy wartime traffic in dangerous goods was not handled entirely without incident. On 23 May 1915 a military goods train from Bricklayers Arms was passing Coulsdon when a spark from the engine set fire to a truck loaded with petrol, wood and steel. The driver stopped the train and its crew managed to isolate the wagon before a disaster could occur - they were rewarded with £1 each.

The end of the war brought heavy return salvage traffic, much of which came via Richborough. In late 1918 a salvage depot was suggested for Hither Green, but this was dropped. However the return of peace did not bring an end to improvements - sidings at Folkestone Pier were extended by November, the Admiralty paid for improved connections to the dockyard from the Prince of Wales Pier branch in December 1918, the junction at Sharnal Street were improved in January 1919, a connection to the Admiralty test site at Yantlet Creek paid for and the Admiralty there supplied with secondhand track for the branch. The Air Ministry was paying for sidings at Kidbrooke and Manston as late as April 1920.

Military mail to France usually went via Victoria and Folkestone in a train of 30 box trucks, which sometimes ran in two portions. This was loaded in Victoria from 11am to 11.30pm each day, but inward mail was also handled at Charing Cross and Cannon Street. Over 4 million letters were handled in 1917.

Army greatcoats were handed in at SECR stations after demobilisation whilst unwanted food supplies were brought back to Deptford. From the outbreak of war until the end of 1914 the SECR carried over 20 million tons of government materials.

Wartime Passenger and Troop Traffic

For civilians, passenger conditions progressively worsened during the war. This was due to a combination of reduced services, total closure of some lines, and a government policy of raising fares to discourage travel. Special services were occasionally put on, in contrast, for senior officers such as Sir Roger Keyes in

April 1918 during the cross-channel raids. The most famous trains were the "Imperial As" from Charing Cross or Victoria, which ran with only two carriages on an as-required basis for top officers; the service was used by Sir John French on 14 August 1918, reaching Folkestone in 80 minutes, and altogether there were 283 runs.

The first station closures were Dover Town (14 October 1914) and Sheerness-on-Sea (8 November 1914). Various measures were intended to discourage leisure travel and the through trains from the north ceased in December, although the GWR Deal service was first cut back to Folkestone in April 1916 and then taken off altogether in December. From 22 February 1915 excursion and cheap day tickets were withdrawn.

On 15 March 1915 the SECR closed Spa Road, Southwark Park and Deptford stations due to the coal shortage, though the first two retained a staff-only service until 20 September 1925 when closure became total; Deptford was reopened to the public from 19 July 1926. Bingham Road and Spencer Road halts closed the same day in 1915, though the former was restored to public use from 30 September 1935.

On 1 December 1915 the SECR further reduced local services due to a shortage of men and locomotives, although "business trains" were retained. Cheriton Halt closed altogether and Sunday trains ended on the Victoria to City line and the Gravesend West Street and Greenwich Park branches; *The Times* reported that the Crystal Palace Low Level to Beckenham Junction service had ceased altogether from 1 December.

The next set of closures were Battersea Park Road, Camberwell and Walworth Road which all closed after the final services on 1 April 1916 as the SECR withdrew its Victoria to Moorgate service which had, in any case, been in ill-health for some time due to tramway competition. As this was a Sunday, the first official day of closure was 3 April. This meant that the spur into Moorgate lost all its SECR services as did Clapham and Wandsworth Road stations. Holborn Viaduct Low Level closed from 1 June 1916 and Ludgate Hill lost all but peak hour services at the same time. St Lawrence station, near Ramsgate, also closed from 3 April.

From 1 January 1917 there were reductions in the services to Bromley, Orpington etc. which received some comment in the press as the owners of motor cars did not suffer similar inconvenience. The SECR also closed completely the Crystal Palace High Level line, the Greenwich Park branch, the Bat & Ball line and the Bexhill West branch - although the latter retained a slim coal train service. The Beckenham to Norwood passenger service was withdrawn and SECR services over the Oxted line were also cut. Other stations deprived of their passenger services that day included Selsdon Road and Coombe Lane(W&SC), Smitham, Reedham Halt, Box Hill, Rochester Bridge, and St Leonards Warrior Square. Sunday services were withdrawn from many lines and a few stations on "open" lines were also closed on Sundays. On the same date fares were increased by 50% though the effect of this must be balanced against raging inflation. Starting the war with 436 daily departures from London, the SECR had only 280 by 1917.

By May 1917 the SECR had realised that closed stations had a lower rateable

View of the then-closed Holborn Viaduct Low Level station in the mid-1920s, with a B1 class backing empty stock into Snow Hill carriage sidings. (R W Kidner)

value, which could be reduced still further if they were demolished. It therefore drew up lists of which closed stations were to be demolished or not; those identi-fied to enter oblivion included Loughborough Junction, Walworth Road, Battersea Park, Clapham Road, Wandsworth Road, Camberwell Road, Spa Road, Southwark Park, Deptford and Box Hill. In October 1917 the SECR got a rebate of £7-7s from the Coulsdon poor rates on account of Reedham and Smitham being closed! Curi-ously the stations of the Bexhill branch were not mentioned in this list, especially as the Managing Committee discussed the possibility - in June 1917 - that the rails and fittings of the entire line might be sent abroad! However the line reopened with a limited service later that year, though Sidley stayed closed.

From December 1914 there was a daily service for refugees from Folkestone Harbour to Holborn Viaduct via Orpington and Herne Hill.

The provision of extra passenger services for troops had less of a physical effect on the SECR than the expansion of goods traffic. In April 1915 the War Office requested a new halt to serve a rifle range between Gomshall and Dorking. This was opened as Westcott Halt in May 1916 and was paid for by the W.O.; it survived the post-war cuts due to use by local TA riflemen. In July 1916 it was decided to widen platforms at Canterbury West to help load troops there.

One of the largest camps was at Westenhanger, which also generated regular leave trains from August 1915. These were woven in with the regular leave trains between Victoria and Folkestone Harbour.

Many of the extra munitions workers travelled by train. At the start of the war about 5000 workers went to Woolwich Arsenal by SECR, rising to 32,000 by 1916 with shifts staggered to start at 6, 7 or 8am. The SECR also provided some passenger carriages for workmen's trains at Woolwich Arsenal in 1916. Church

A crowd of munitions workers gather on the platform at Kidbrooke on their ways home in about 1918. (Alan A Jackson collection)

Manor Way Halt, near Plumstead, was opened on 1 January 1917 for wartime workers and was used by about 9000 workers each day; the halt had its own signalbox and some services started or terminated there with the Ministry of Munitions paying for a footbridge in 1918. It closed on the last day of 1919. A further 6000 travelled to stations between Abbey Wood and Crayford.

An initial attempt to use Admiralty Pier for hospital trains was soon abandoned. Dover Marine was used regularly for ambulance trains from 2 January 1915, and the old Town station was used to berth them. Altogether nine ambulance trains were based there, including two SECR sets. The SECR handled many ambulance trains but it was worried at the decision in late 1916 to convert the former Canadian camp at Westenhanger into a hospital for soldiers with venereal disease! In April 1917 it was converting carriages into kitchen cars for ambulance trains.

Hospital trains had several destinations on the SECR including Shorncliffe, Gillingham, Well Hall and Ingress Park Siding near Greenhithe. Later Preston Hall near Aylesford became a hospital and some trains were also handled at Farningham Road or Fawkham. SECR men also unloaded ambulance trains at West Croydon, though not on their own system. Hospital trains continued to run long after hostilities had ceased, Sidcup being a destination until at least 1920. 78,883 wounded were unloaded on the SECR.

Dover Marine also handled some of the soldiers on leave from 21 July 1917 but most commonly they were routed via Folkestone, and then went to Victoria. From November 1914 there were three or four leave trains a day between Victoria and Folkestone, rising to 12 later in the war. Weekend leave trains also operated from many bases on the network and nearly 14 million men used SECR local services. Dead officers' kit was sent to Holborn Viaduct or Cannon Street.

A unique feature of the SECR's work was the Money Exchange set up at Victoria. This received francs from homecoming troops and despatched them back to the Base Cashier at Boulogne, the total sum sent out amounting to £14m by its closure on 31 October 1919. By February 1916 up to 14 separate offices could be functioning to handle the leave trains.

Special facilities for soldiers were also provided at Victoria. In November 1915 it was decided to install a rest room for 62 soldiers over the Customs House, which the YMCA contributed to. In July 1918 the Victoria rest room was converted to the Army Pay Office. The soldiers' buffet operated in the Metropolitan booking office at Victoria from 15 February 1915 until 30 June 1919 and was visited by the King and Queen on 27 March 1915; it had 12 million customers.

Charing Cross Hotel became a "great convenience for officers going to or returning from the Front, and for some it seemed almost a military establishment," *The Times* reported in January 1917. For much of the war there was a daily officers' train from there to Folkestone. The Hotel has also attracted attention as the place that Admiral Lord Fisher chose to hide after his sudden resignation in 1915. Perhaps this explains why the Admiralty had tried to take over the Hotel for officers, but it had been rebuffed on account of the chronic lack of officer-class accommodation in central London.

The total number of soldiers carried by the SECR in the war was 26 million. These were carried in 101,872 special trains, though some also used scheduled services to get to places like Milton Range Halt; there were also 7,515 ambulance trains run.

Box Hill, Reedham Halt and Smitham reopened on 1 January 1919, whilst the Bat & Ball and Crystal Palace High Level lines reopened on 1 March as did Warrior Square. Selsdon Road reopened on 16 June with the new summer services. Sheerness-on-Sea station reopened on 2 January 1922, with Dockyard closing instead.

After the war the Pullman Car Co. was able to reclaim its premises at Longhedge although there were complaints in 1922 that the whole site had been left in a "deplorable" condition.

Chapter 14:

The Managing Committee

The dominant figure in the SECR was always Cosmo Bonsor, who combined chairing the Managing Committee with the same role on the SER Board. At first the SER and LCDR continued to have separate general meetings, but once these were combined Bonsor's public dominance was complete. Bonsor was born at Great Bookham, near Leatherhead, on 2 September 1848, with a wealthy father who was able to send him to Eton and bequeath £300,000. Bonsor's first career, and the source of his wealth, was actually brewing for he was a partner in Combe & Co when barely 21 and Chairman at thirty. He was elected to the Board of the SER in 1894, became deputy-Chairman in 1895 and Chairman in 1898. There he was credited as "having originated and carried through the amalgamation..." of the SER and LCDR. He was "a man of commanding physique and charming personality" and "even his big frame seemed too small to contain the large heart he was known to possess...", a fawning obituarist concluded.

It was at Combe & Co. that Bonsor made his name, through an aggressive expansion founded on the control of tied houses during the 1880s and 1890s. He then oversaw the creation of the Watney Combe Reid combine in 1898, of which he was Chairman until 1928. However this business failed to expand as rapidly as its predecessor, so that by 1928 Bonsor was widely considered to have allowed it to stagnate. A criticism was that he had failed to rationalise its operations, and it is tempting to compare this with his work on the SECR. As a Chairman Bonsor was less bombastic than Forbes or Watkin had been with the LCDR and SER, whilst he also avoided the excessive complications of a parallel career in politics - although he sat as a Conservative MP from 1885 to 1900 but then renounced political ambitions. Although a Director of the Bank of England, he turned down the chance to be Governor. Bonsor, though, latterly seems to have become remarkably timid in his control of the SECR; typically, he prevaricated on fundamental decisions such as electrification and train ferries, wasting energy on minor diversions such as Pullman trains.

Bonsor does seem to have been aware of the need to improve the SECR's public image, and this can perhaps be traced in the notable improvement in SECR building standards. A number of major stations like Victoria and Tunbridge Wells were reconstructed, whilst the Bexhill and Tattenham Corner branches had a some fine stations. These were mostly the work of Alfred W Blomfield, the SECR chief architect from 1905 to 1918 at the end of which he joined Bonsor's other major interest - Watney Combe, Reid & Co..

Bonsor was not the only Chairman that the Managing Committee ever had; the first Chairman was Sir George Russell, who died in March 1898 and was succeeded by Bonsor. The first General Manager was also of the old school - Alfred Willis, who retired at the end of 1900. In another break with the past, Sir Edward

Watkin's retirement from the SER Board was announced shortly before his death in April 1901. However his erstwhile arch-enemy, Forbes, was guaranteed to be paid as an advisor for ten years.

Bonsor's record as the Chairman of a railway business was probably helped by the fact that professional railway managers were becoming more influential without becoming dictatorial. Both Watkin and Forbes had been railway "professionals" who had evolved, too grandly, into magnates, but Vincent Hill, Percy Tempest and Francis Dent avoided these dangers. Hill had started with the LCDR in 1862, becoming manager of the Hull & Barnsley Railway in 1884; in 1901 he came back to the SECR as general manager. Francis Dent was the son of Admiral Dent, who took up a post as Marine Superintendent on the LNWR after leaving the Navy. The younger Dent joined the same company in 1884 and rose to become goods manager of the SECR in 1907. He became general manager in 1911 until 1920. Tempest, the son of a solicitor and then a Leeds University graduate, was chief engineer of the SECR from 1899 and became general manager in 1920.

The management of the SECR soon came in for some criticism, though of course this was traditional. It was noted by the press that working expenses for the first period of 1899 were up £71,000 and that for the SER expenses per train mile had risen to nearly 61% of receipts - they had been 51.8% in 1889. This was due to a considerable increase in services, largely put on for political reasons. However, one of the strongest arguments for joint working had been that it would create efficiency and this should have been reflected in a consistent reduction in the proportion of receipts consumed by working expenses; progress in this area was fitful as the following table demonstrates.

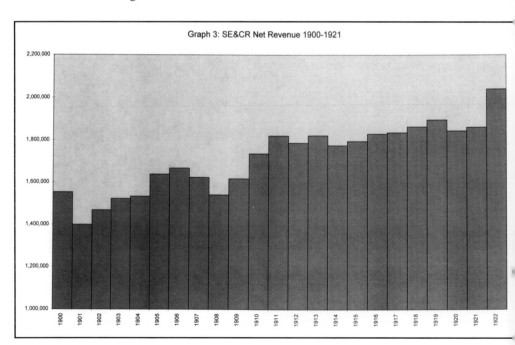

There was also a shortage of capital. In November 1899 a Bill was presented to raise £3million whilst two months later the LCDR was unable to meet payments on a land purchase and had to borrow from the SER at 3%. In August 1900 the SER meeting was told that improvements planned for Charing Cross, Tonbridge and Ashford could not be afforded. This was the uncomfortable position into which Vincent Hill stepped as General Manager in January 1901.

Initial news was not good for Hill. The first half of 1901 produced net revenue down 21% on the same period of 1900, due largely to huge expenses increases such as coal and £41,000 extra on wages.

Lord Harris resigned in July 1901 as he was acting as assistant adjutant-general at Johannesburg, being replaced by Sir William Hart-Dyke (a former Conservative politician) of Lullingstone Castle. In 1902 the size of the Managing Committee increased from nine to fourteen with the SER gaining three representatives - Lord Hothfield, Colonel Charles Surtees and Sir Alfred Watkin. Deputy Chairman was Aretas Akers-Douglas of Chilston Park, Maidstone who had been Conservative Chief Whip and entered the Cabinet in 1905; he was Home Secretary from 1902-1905. George Wyndham, another former Conservative Cabinet minister, sat on the Committee until his death in 1913.

The financial decline steadied, but did not cease, in the latter half of 1901 when the SECR was paying £163,000 in rates and duties - nearly 8% of gross income. The position was helped by a fall in the price of coal, so that Hill was able to receive a 25% salary increase to £4000.

In February 1905 A Gathorne-Hardy resigned from the Managing Committee and was replaced by Colonel John Mellor, who was related to the Watkin family by marriage and chairman of a Lancashire spinning company. He can be seen as a representative of the "Manchester interest" until his death in 1916.

1907 was a bad year for the Committee with net revenue sharply down, and this led to unrest among shareholders. A major scandal hit the SECR management in August 1908 when the *Investors' Review* published an article that some of the directors considered libellous. It dealt with allegations raised by a SECR shareholder named Drucker, who claimed that the Committee was paying too much for its coal - the *Review* commenting that "we suspect the solution would lie in what the Americans call 'graft'." George Gilligan acted as a shareholders' representative in talks with the Board, arguing for two new "expert" directors in a "managing director" style - which can be seen as a criticism of Bonsor who was lacking in professional railway experience. However *The Times* in January 1909 felt that the net revenue was the real problem and that "explanations from the Chair have been so chronic that there is little need to wait for another instalment." The last half of 1908 produced a £16,000 fall in goods revenue and another 1 million passengers lost to the trams with which, Bonsor said, "it was impossible to compete."

An attempt by Drucker to force through a no confidence vote in the Managing Committee was lost despite Lord Weardale's support, and then in February a vacancy was created by the death of Lord Burton. He was replaced by Colonel Baring, a financier with no railway management experience. In June Sir David Salomons, a financier with considerable electrical interests, retired (temporarily) and the opportunity was grasped to invite Sir Frederick Harrison to join the Committee. Harrison was the recently retired Managing Director of the London & North-Western so brought a wealth of experience; it was also noted in the press that Francis Dent, another former LNWR man, had become assistant general manager and there were rumours that the LNWR might be planning to take over the SECR. This did not occur, though in June 1911 there were rumours at the Stock Exchange about a link with the GWR. Sir Arthur Yorke, former Chief Inspector of Railways with the Board of Trade, was a director of both the GWR and SECR - and from 1916 also of the Grand Trunk of Canada.

By July 1909 the committee of shareholders was being led by Sir Robert Perks; it included three MPs, Brassey, and the former chairman of an Argentine railway, but Drucker was still active. His complaints included a claim that the SECR had taken on 2000 extra staff since 1898, though this was partly due to legal changes in working practices, lack of co-ordinated train services, and the failure to compete properly with the trams - though on this point Bonsor could marshal a strong defence on economic grounds. Perks complained that Harrison was too old (he died in 1915) and that the SECR was used by "popular comedians" as an example of inefficiency - though this was hardly an innovation!

Francis Dent was one of the new generation of professional railway managers, but he seems to have left the SECR before his ideas had been fully developed.

Pressure on the Committee was eased by much improved figures for 1910, which Bonsor saw as evidence that "the Committee's policy was right in doing what they could to encourage the railway traffic outside the London area and in reducing unremunerative trains within that area." Here was a strong antidote to the Drucker view.

Photo]   [Stereoscopic Company.
MR. FRANCIS HENRY DENT.
General Manager, South Eastern and Chatham Railway.

At the end of 1910 Vincent Hill retired from management and was soon elected to the Committee (in the place of Sir Alfred Watkin), though he died in 1913. His managerial role passed to Dent and the Superintendent of the Line post passed from William Thomson to Edwin Cox on 1 June 1911. Another piece in this new management team was laid in 1912 when A Jones of the Lancashire & Yorkshire Railway became Outdoor Locomotive Superintendent, charged with improving discipline in the men and reliability in the engines. Dent was a strong individual, "inclined to rule by fear rather than persuasion."

The improvement of the business was seriously damaged by the coal strikes in the first half of 1912. The SECR carried 3.5m fewer passengers and cost it

£75,000 in lost traffic and higher coal prices. Bonsor felt that "an anxious half year" had seen the "return to prosperity...seriously retarded by labour unrest and the strikes." The SER dividend payment was only 1.25% for the half year, but this recovered to 4% for the whole of 1913 before dipping again at the start of 1914 due to increased wages and a fall in traffic.

The outbreak of war completely changed the SECR's financial arrangements though annual net revenue stayed remarkably stable - it was £1.7m for 1914 and £1.86m for 1918. Of course these figures included the sums granted by the REC - actual cash receipts from traffic being as little as 20% of 1913 levels by 1916. Dent received a knighthood in the New Year Honours List that year and was engaged in much Government work at the time. Bonsor also found official employment - in 1920 he was in charge of the International Commission for the division of Austro-Hungarian rolling-stock.

Even before the end of the war, the politicians were already considering the future of railways and a Commission had been set up. In November 1917 the SECR complained that there had been no consultation via the Railway Companies Association. However the SECR was a struggling company by this time, suffering especially from a lack of capital that meant that - by 1919 - projects like the Charing Cross bridge were in danger. At this critical point the SECR lost the services of Dent, who retired on a £2000 pension on 31 March 1920 "because of a disagreement with his Chairman." Dent had been, according to the *Railway Magazine*, "an exceptionally capable chief executive officer." Percy Tempest replaced him, though it was clear that the post would be only temporary.

The SECR had little ability to increase its profitability with fares set by the Railway Passenger Fares Order of 1916, wages also controlled by the government, and all major investments requiring government approval. In February 1921 SECR fares were up 75% compared to 1914 and goods rates up 112%. There followed a period of sharp decline, with actual passenger numbers falling from 98m in 1920 to 83.5m in 1921.

Although the SECR made some protests about Government-led reorganisation of the railways, one gains the impression that the management was almost too tired to make a serious fight of it. By November 1921 Tempest was meeting with Forbes of the LBSCR and Walker of the LSWR to discuss arrangements; Bonsor's plan was for the SER and LCDR to amalgamate first on the basis of the 1920 accounts to form a proper SECR, though the LSWR had at first assumed that it would swallow up the others on the basis of net income. Discussions in May 1922 assumed a new SECR would be comprised 58% of SER stock and 42% LCDR but this step never took place. However, the SER did have to absorb the nominally independent London & Greenwich Railway, Victoria Station & Pimlico Railway and Mid Kent (Bromley & St Mary Cray) Railway. The companies agreed to proceed with all proper maintenance on their systems, but not to embark on major new projects.

Although there was discontent over the electrification issue, plans proceeded smoothly until the arcane subject of LSWR access to Ludgate Hill arose. This was governed by an agreement of 1865: the LSWR had made a contribution and in exchange was allowed to keep LCDR portions of fares from Richmond or Wimbledon until they reached £11,060. The LSWR felt it was owed the balance by the LCDR and the matter had been further complicated by government compensation.

Shortly after this, Bonsor displayed public doubt about the railway reorganisation. Part of this was on principle as he believed a government had no right to interfere in private property, and he doubted the benefit to the public. "The more I see of the Railways Act 1921, I am bound to confess, the more I dislike it," he observed in August 1922, before discussing the complex problem of LCDR stock valued at £11m that paid no dividends.

The formation of the SR included an agreed valuation of the SER and LCDR that allows us an insight of what an actual SECR might have been divided up as - 56.9% to the former, 43.1% to the latter.

Reflecting on the history of the SECR, the *Railway Gazette* saw some credit as being due to Bonsor - "Through all the trying times Mr C Bonsor pursued the policy of improvement with a determined optimism which entirely justified itself, and he had the satisfaction of handing over to the new Southern Railway Company a first-rate property." This Company came into existence on 1 January 1923.

Several figures from the SECR lived on to influence the Southern Railway. Its new Board contained familiar names including Brigadier-General Baring, who became its Chairman in 1924. E W Mellor, William Newburn, Sir David Salomons, Charles Sheath and Dent were all to be found at the table. Percy Tempest, though, retired from railway management after one year with the Southern though he was consoled with a knighthood in 1924. The SECR also bequeathed one name destined to be of significance in the longer term for Britain's railways - Eustace Missenden, who joined it in 1899 and in 1949 became Chairman of the nationalised Railway Executive.

An analysis of the SECR's net revenue performance over the years 1900 to 1922 shows very little real growth. In fact, if wartime inflation is allowed for then the net revenues of 1919-22 were substantially less than those of the pre-war era. In addition, for many years expenses formed over 65% of income, a ratio that was much higher than on many other UK railways.

Chapter 15:

The Way, Works & Signalling

Engineering Workshops

The Managing Committee took over a system with two full sets of engineering workshops at Longhedge in Battersea and at Ashford. One of the greatest attractions of the SECR was that it could make substantial savings by closing one of these operations down or by rationalising where work was done. The time scale, though, did not work favourably so that in October 1899 the SECR was forced to plan a major rebuilding of the boiler shops at Longhedge when an earlier decision on joint working would have made complete removal to Ashford much cheaper.

By January 1899 the SECR was buying 60 acres of land at Ashford and in 1900 agreed on an £80,000 scheme to centralise the Carriage & Wagon shops there. These were opened in 1902. The whole operation could be presided over by Wainwright from his official residence at Alfred House, Ashford.

In February 1910 the SECR considered moving the locomotive shops at Longhedge to Ashford, which would save about £5000 a year though the cost was likely to be £60,000. It was felt that this would be partially offset by selling some of the London land. An extra factor was that locomotives built at Longhedge tended to be about 20% more expensive than Ashford ones. In July 1910 it was felt that some of Longhedge could be rented out, but the eventual scheme was to concentrate all new locomotive building at Ashford and use Longhedge for repairs. This

Part of the extensive SECR works at Ashford. (Wakeman Collection, Ashford Library)

S 13746   Junction and Railway Works, Ash...

R S Surtees is seen with the Ashford drawing office staff. He was a veteran of Longhedge Works and prospered at Ashford. (Wakeman Collection, Ashford Library)

was announced in February 1911, Wainwright telling the press that about 2,500 extra staff would be needed at Ashford. Ashford required a new erecting shop as well as an extension of the old one, a new tender shop, new electrical power station and many additional houses.

Former LCDR M1 class 4-4-0 no. 636, after being reboilered in 1903; it was withdrawn in 1912.

The SECR also then considered reorganising the Locomotive, Carriage & Wagon department into separate sections for running and "manufacturing". No doubt Wainwright felt this as a snub at a time when relations between him and the Committee were not good.

Some staff left Longhedge for Ashford in June 1913, by which time 62 new houses had been let and the SECR decided to build 45 more. By that stage a new girls' school had also been provided.

Parts of Longhedge were let to the Pullman Company, Nestle's, the Anglo-Swiss Condensed Milk Company and a company called Silverthorne. In 1916 parts were taken over by the Canadian Forestry Corps and then the Motor Transport Corps, which reduced the ability of the SECR to repair wagons there. The position of Pullman at Longhedge was strengthened after the war when they gained extra space and erected their own buildings on the site.

Late in 1919 work was begun on re-equipping Ashford boiler shops so that new boilers could be built there. At about the same time work began on a new locomotive shed, delayed since 1914, and at Battersea locomotive depot a coaling plant and lifting shed were provided. A further concentration of work at Ashford was encouraged by the burning down of the Tonbridge wagon shop in June 1919, an old carriage shed at Ashford being adapted for the purpose.

The SECR maintained its Ashford level of activity right up until the end of the era - reroofing the SECR laundry at Ashford West in 1921, extending the carriage shops in 1922 and even buying the old military bakery in New Town Road. However one sphere of operations passed away when the Ashford schools were sold to Kent County Council in 1922.

The major development of a locomotive depot in the period was at Slades Green, begun by the SER as part of a concentration on outer rather than inner suburban traffic. The depot there opened on 27 October 1902 although the station serving the area had opened its doors on 1 July 1900. Deptford locomotive shed closed in October 1904, displacing nine engines. From late 1905 the coaling of engines at Woolwich Arsenal was transferred to Plumstead and this made it possible for the coaling stage at the charmingly named Nog Siding, Cannon Street, to also be closed.

In July 1922 the Strood locomotive depot was closed and its facilities transferred to Gillingham.

Ballast

The SER's traditional source of ballast had been the shingle banks of Dungeness, but by the 1890s this was unacceptable in general use and in 1901 Tempest made clear his preference for broken stone. The SECR took early steps to improve its mineral supplies, buying a ballast pit at Shorne - which was in reality Hoo Junction - in 1899; this provided only gravel although it could also be used for dumping used ballast, so in 1901 the SECR bought some land on the north side of the line near Sevenoaks Tunnel for ragstone, then in 1902 purchased 39 acres at Allington Quarry for £18,000 from Lord Romney and this became its principal source. Allington became of immediate significance as it was intended to provide the ballast for the Orpington to St John's widening, which was to be taken out in a tramway and loaded at Bensted's Siding. This siding was effectively taken over by the SECR, so a new facility had to be provided for Bensted's themselves.

Dick, Kerr & Co also installed a narrow-gauge line at the Sevenoaks ballast quarry, and much of the ballast for the widenings must have come from here as Allington did not open until 1903.

In SECR care, the Allington quarry was rapidly developed. A stone crushing machine was installed in 1903. What was then needed was a better way of getting the ballast to the track than painful shovelling so in 1911 a hopper ballast train was ordered. This began work in 1912 and was so much quicker than the old methods that it outpaced Allington's production! A second train was ordered in October 1913

Sand for locomotives had come from a cutting at Reigate, but from 1900 this came from Gomshall.

Signalling

Four types of signalling work dominated SECR activity. These were the extension of signalling when lines had been built or quadrupled, the improvement of current installations to allow for changes in technology or safety standards (notably the use of electricity), the installation of additional signalling to allow for extra traffic, and attempts to economise on the staff costs in signalling.

At the start of the SECR era much energy was going in to the development of telephone use, though at first this was used for control and administration rather than as an addition to signalling practice. Thus in early 1898 offices at London Bridge and Victoria were being connected by phone, this then being extended to include Folkestone, Dover, Charing Cross and other key points. A year later the Maidstone area was being connected, making it possible for staff at Tovil sidings to contact their superiors at Maidstone West. In April 1899 the SECR decided to install a complete network.

Much resignalling took place in connection with the widening of the ex-SER route into London and the re-arrangement of tracks approaching the London stations. In mid-1899 the SECR started work resignalling between Belvedere Road and Cannon Street West Junction, a new box at Belvedere Road being under construction in October and also at Surrey Canal Junction in December. Altogether seven boxes were renewed between London Bridge and New Cross, and also two boxes on the "Brighton" side of the viaduct were renewed - Blue Anchor and Up Croydon Line Junction. There were four "signal bridge" gantries at Coxson Place, Millstream Road, Perseverance Street and Abbey Street; three of these had special fog equipment and miniature repeating signals to improve working in foggy conditions. In 1903 new "signal bridges" were installed at St James' Road and Blue Anchor to control the Southwark Park to New Cross loop.

The contract for resignalling between St John's and Grove Park "B" in 1904 was for £17,000 and some Sykes electrical equipment was installed; by January 1908 this was proving expensive to maintain and the SECR felt it worthwhile to spend a further £6000 converting to mechanical operation.

Improvements for additional safety included the spread of Sykes electrical interlocking. During 1899-1900 this was installed between Stoat's Nest and Redhill as well as at Caterham, Perry Street Fork Junction and Farningham Road. Sykes treadles became standard in the London area soon afterwards as did "electrical fouling bars" to protect the signals. In 1901 it was decided that the traverser table that linked roads nos. 2 and 3 at Charing Cross should be linked to the Sykes system. In 1908 another innovation was the installation of electrical detectors on facing points such as at Herne Hill and Beckenham Junction.

During 1907-8 the signalling at Ashford was modernised as part of the station remodelling. A new box, "B" was opened at the junction between the ex-LCDR and ex-SER lines in 1907 and in the same year Ashford West Yard box was

Interior of Westcott signal-box near Dorking, one of the smallest boxes on the SECR and here in the care of a smartly-dressed young signalman. (Wakeman Collection, Ashford Library)

replaced by "C" box. The following year "D" box replaced Hastings Junction and Ramsgate Junction box, itself rebuilt in 1901, became "E".

Signalling was costly because of the man-hours involved. At Ladywell this had led to an unusual arrangement whereby the rails of the Mid-Kent line were interlaced with the "main" line for 260yds rather than join at the natural point; this meant that the actual junction was beside Ladywell signalbox, an arrangement which had been intended to save having an additional box but the double roads had proved difficult to maintain. Thus the signalbox was "moved" in 1903 to its proper place beside the points! The introduction of the electric tablet on the Westerham and Hundred of Hoo branches was proposed in 1903 to make economies possible, such as the closure of Cliffe signalbox saving £114 a year. The Westerham branch was equipped by 1905 but the Hoo line was not completed until 1926. In 1914 the old staff and ticket system of single-line working was replaced by Webb & Thompson's Electric Train Staff on the lines between Queenborough and Queenborough Pier, from the former to Sheerness Docks and from there to Sheer-ness-on-Sea; it was already in use between Middle Junction and Queenborough except for the Kingsferry bridge where a Sykes system was in use.

Some such schemes ran into trouble. In January 1910 the SECR decided to alter Lydd box so that Romney Junction box could be closed and the branch operated on the Tyers Electric Occupation system; this idea was blocked by the Board of Trade and a Key system used instead.

Money was also saved by partial closure of boxes. From 1911 Wandsworth Road box was closed on Sundays and between 10am and 6pm on weekdays; in February 1912 it was closed completely and its functions transferred to Factory Junction box. Some places were endowed excessively with boxes - quiet Elham had two until 1913, although one was just a gate box. In 1921, the Aylesford box at the Snodland end of the station was closed and a new one built at the Maidstone end, to save the additional cost of a gateman which had risen to £595 a year under the eight hour day rules. After 1920 there was also a trend of keeping some boxes only for goods workings, such as Winchelsea from April 1922. Here is a railway company increasingly conscious of staff costs as a factor in its profitability.

Boxes disappeared for other reasons too. The Medway Intermediate box between Hildenborough and Tonbridge burnt down in July 1917 and was not replaced whilst Deptford box closed in 1919 due to the reduced number of inner suburban trains. The boxes at Admiralty Pier were closed and their function transferred to the new "Turret" box in 1921.

Crossings became a growing problem as road traffic increased. In 1903 East Sussex County Council complained of delays at the crossings in Etchingham, Robertsbridge, Battle (Marley Lane) and Rye; the SECR agreed to alter the signalling, move the water cranes so that engines did not block the crossings for so long, and put red discs on the gates.

A significant safety improvement was the spread of fog signalling to replace men who had to stand beside the track and put detonators on the rails in foggy weather. In 1906 Clayton's fog-signalling apparatus was installed between Holborn Viaduct and Brixton, saving the use of eleven men, and electrical repeating signals were already in use on the widened lines from St John's to Orpington. The next year the system was expanded to cover Brixton to Victoria, Loughborough Junction to Bickley and Charing Cross to London Bridge. In 1920 the Clayton system was installed at Rochester, Chatham, Sittingbourne and Faversham.

Some situations were inherently unsafe. Chatham "A" box's down home signals were actually inside Fort Pitt tunnel - making them difficult to see, so a treadle-operated bell was put up to ring when the signals were at danger. This was unsatisfactory, so a klaxon was then tried before it was decided in 1920 to move the signals to the Rochester end of the tunnel.

Working in fog and in busy areas particularly was also made much safer by the use of track circuiting. This was installed at New Cross late in 1909 and extended to St John's in 1910, when the through roads at Ashford were also track circuited. Ludgate Hill was dealt with in 1911. However after this the system was not expanded any further, and so in January 1914 Pringle of the Board of Trade made it clear that he wished to see the whole Charing Cross, Cannon Street and London Bridge area so protected. Waterloo had been dealt with by February, but then war intervened although track circuits at Redhill were extended in 1918 due to the heavy goods traffic. Track circuits made operations more flexible: the use of them at Otford allowed carriages to be attached and detached out of the signal-man's sight for the first time. At Grove Park they made it possible to abolish the "B" box at a cost of £1150 which, as it was 1920, the Ministry of Transport paid 5% interest on.

The last major SECR signalling scheme originated from a decision in 1913 to replace the "Hole in the Wall" box at Victoria. It was decided to use a power signalling system and the assistant signalling engineer was sent to America to inspect systems in operation, though the contract was finally placed with the British Pneumatic Signal Co. at £32,000. A site adjacent to the "Hole in the Wall" was chosen for the box and in 1919 it was decided to extend the new system to the carriage sidings, the new box opening at the start of January 1920. A 1920 scheme to resignal Charing Cross and alter the track would have cost £130,000.

Other details of signalling changes authorised by the SECR include the following, not all of which were completed:
Ashford - new "B" and "C" SBs 1908; Battersea Pier Jct - renew SB 1909; Battle - close Station SB and enlarge Gate SB 1921; Bexleyheath - close Station SB and concentrate on goods yard SB 1918; Blackfriars - new SB at Hill Str and abolish Boro' Rd & Charlotte Str 1909; Bo-Peep - build new SB in fork to replace W St Leonards 1912; Canterbury E - new SB 1911; Canterbury Rd Jct - renew SB 1913, adapt for push/pull service 1914; Chambers Crossing SB - abolish this box between Faversham/Herne Bay 1922; Chatham - resignal 1909; Chelsfield - resignal 1900; Chipstead SB - to be closed except for goods 1921; Chipstead/Kingswood - extra SB for race traffic 1900; Crabtree Crossing - new SB 1907; Crowhurst - install track circuits and close partially "No 1" SB 1921; Denton - move SB nearer to crossing to dispense with gateman 1904; Dover Town - track circuits installed 1920; Farnborough - new "elevated" SB 1909; Folkestone Harbour - close "A" and "C", concentrate on "B" and use some ground frames 1922; Folkestone Jct - new SB built after ASRS complaint to BoT 1907; Hastings West - new SB and signals 1907; Holborn Yard - new SB opened Sept 1907; Kearsney - resignal 1914; Margate Sands - resignal 1909 and track circuits 1911; Maze Hill no2 - partial closure 1912; Minster - resignal 1900; New Beckenham - new SB 1903/4; New Cross "B" - move nearer St John's 1909; Perry Str Fork Jct - limited opening hours 1921; Plumstead - resignal 1900; Up Croydon Line Jct - rebuild SB 1902; St John's - new "B" 1911 and centralise New Cross "B" and Parks Bridge there (auth. 1919, not done until 1928); Shorncliffe - track circuits 1921; Shortlands - abolition of Station SB disc 1919, completed 1925; Strood Tunnel SB - track circuits 1921; Swanley Jct - abolish Park Lane SB 1919; Waterloo Jct SB - close on Suns and some daytime hours 1922; Whyteleafe - close one SB except for goods workings 1921.

Chapter 16:

Blood, Sweat & Tears

The employees of the SECR were always a major factor in the companies' management of their affairs, and an increasingly significant one from about 1906 onwards. In October 1902 the SECR employed 6323 people, with a weekly wage bill totalling £9532, although these figures are deceptive because there were many "casual" employees, such as the porters at Victoria, who earned no wage at all but subsisted on tips from the passengers. In 1907 staff wages came to about £1.5million a year. At the end of July 1909 staff figures were about 8000, with an increase of 800 being blamed by the Board on new Board of Trade regulations about hours of work. By September 1919 the number of employees was 25,204, an apparent huge increase being accounted for by changes in employment terms which had meant the bringing into the figures of many who previously existed on the fringes of the SECR empire.

One of the less well-known problems in the working union of the South Eastern and Chatham railways was that the two companies had distinct differences in their treatment of their workforces. The SER had become more progressive or even liberal during the 1890s, and responsive to staff feelings; in 1897 the conditions of the enginemen were "much improved" after a staff deputation. By the time the new Board discussed amalgamating the conditions of service in October 1899, there were obvious discrepancies - SER drivers had three days of paid holiday a year, rising to six after ten years service, whereas LCDR drivers had none. Invariably standardisation had to mean the more lenient condition, although a set week of sixty hours for footplate men and a maximum of eight shillings a day was hardly light.

Similar problems occurred with other grades such as goods guards; in 1896 the SER had set a maximum week of 72 hours, but there was no limit at all on the LCDR; the SECR settled on a 65 hour week, with a maximum wage of 30s. In June 1899 the ex-LCDR passenger guards claimed extra pay for Sundays to match their SER colleagues, but this was deferred as it would have added £800 to the wages bill. In September and October 1899 both the passenger guards and the Inspectors on the LCDR section received extra Sunday allowances. From 1 September 1904 Sunday pay became standard for all grades though this added an extra £16,000 to the annual wages bill.

Amazingly some staff differentials between the two companies lasted until October 1917. LCDR men in the Outdoor Locomotive Department's repairs team got double time for Sundays, Christmas Day and Good Friday which their SER colleagues did not. The same men got time and a quarter for nights, but no paid holidays. This was reorganised so that repair staff got three days paid holiday, rising to six after ten years with the SECR. At the same time LCDR platelayers were being paid time and a quarter to cut hay at the trackside, a benefit their SER

A Staff group was photographed on the platform at Folkestone Central, which by the SECR period was becoming the dominant station in the town, at the expense of Folkestone Junction. The view illustrates the variety of staff and grades employed at an important station. (Wakeman Collection, Ashford Library)

associates did not enjoy.

At the turn of the century the gradual reduction in working hours began to spread to all grades, at a time when the Amalgamated Society of Railway Servants was becoming more active - August 1900 was the start of the famous Taff Vale struggle. The Amalgamated Society of Railway Servants was active among the lower grades - which did not include the drivers; in July 1900 it had argued in the defence of two shunters at Bricklayers Arms who had been dismissed, claiming that a working day of over eight hours was too much for such duties. The following month the SECR joined other railways at a meeting at the Railway Clearing House to discuss the ASRS.

The July 1900, the SECR had reduced the hours of most "country" signalmen from twelve to ten as part of the policy of "assimilating" labour conditions, though the busy box at Ramsgate Junction, Ashford, had eight hour shifts; here was a clear case of a concession to the workforce having a strong safety incentive. Eight hours was almost the Holy Grail of the railway employee - even the lowly shunters at Bricklayers Arms were arguing for this limit in 1900 on the grounds that more was "arduous". Yet many worked much more - staff at Waterloo Junction in November 1899 were working a sixteen hour day on Sundays when the Board of Trade intervened on their behalf - in the interests of public safety; hours were reduced to twelve.

But wages were already becoming a key factor in the management of the

A LUXURIOUS HABIT

Philanthropist (to railway porter). '" Then what time do you get to bed ? "
Porter. " Well, I seldom what yer may call gets to bed myself, 'cause o' the night trains. But my brother, as used to work the p'ints further down the line, went to bed last Christmas after the accident, and never——"
[Train rushes in, and the parties rush off.

Working hours on the railways were a topic of popular debate - especially where "working the points" was concerned!

railway. In July 1905 Bonsor told a General Meeting that the fall in SECR profits was due to increased Sunday pay for outdoor staff - though in reality this would only have been a minor factor. Meanwhile George Wyndham, a director and also a MP was arguing that the SEC's unpaid porters - who existed off tips - should be given a wage. There were 254 in summer and 226 in winter, which Bonsor reckoned would cost the SECR £11,500 a year so the reform was rejected. The subject received further publicity in May 1914 when an unpaid porter was found hanging from a tree in Richmond Park, having been "harshly treated" by his foreman at Victoria; the Minutes noted that he received no wages.

In March 1907 the Board refused to meet Richard Bell, the Secretary of the ASRS, to discuss the men's conditions of service. By July 1907 *The Times* was able to report that all SECR permanent staff now had holidays with pay, which presumably excluded the porters who got no pay at all.

In October 1907 a delegation of Slades Green enginemen brought a list of changes to the Board, resulting in Hill suggesting improvements to their terms that would cost the SECR £3,500 a year. On 23rd October the Board decided that they would not change the pay scales, but were prepared to increase the percentage of drivers on eight shillings a day and said that firemen passed as drivers could be raised from 4s6d a day to 4s9d from 3rd November. Changes would be made to lodging allowances and drivers' holidays would be increased from three to six days with pay, and a pass for their families. Cleaners were only to get a family pass but rules were introduced to allow a cleaner to progress to become a fireman. The Company offered to further investigate other grievances such as meal times and long hours, and rather smugly commented on other railway companies complaining of a "Railway Crisis" due to militant labour conditions.

However the men came back for extra concessions in early November. The Board offered to raise grade D and E firemen to 4s6d a week, and then agreed this as a standard for all firemen after nine years service. This concession cost a paltry £300 a year. The firemen wrote to thank the Board for their help, but Bonsor had also been to meet "Mr Askwith" to discuss the Board of Trade's scheme for "Conciliation and Arbitration" between the railway companies and the trade unions.

Working hours improved only slowly. In February 1908 passenger guards were still working a 65 hour week, although it was conceded that they should earn overtime after 60 hours.

In March 1910 the SECR Conciliation Board met the men, who under the law would have been elected directly and so comprised a mixture of union and non-union personnel. Although a general increase of wages was refused, the SECR made a number of concessions on conditions such as a minimum of nine hours rest between shifts and overtime to be set at time and a quarter, with an extra quarter on top of that for Sundays, Christmas Day and Good Friday. Fireman were to receive a minimum 18s per week.

Negotiations dragged on for weeks and the settlement became effective from 3rd April. Men discharged through no personal fault were receive three months redundancy pay if they were of long service. Staff were to be paid at overtime rates if they had had less than nine hours rest. The list of "busy" signalboxes where staff worked eight hours rather than ten was extended, for example Penge Junction and Shortlands were added, and extra payments were also made. Gangers who worked in tunnels received extra whilst passenger guards received a rise from 28s to 30s a week. The head shunters at Hither Green and Stewarts Lane were to receive 28s, couplers at Herne Hill were to get 19s and a new grade of leading examiner was created at main stations. This complex arrangement, which cost £9000 per year, shows how obsessional the railways were at dividing their staff into ranks and grades.

With men on hourly rates the pressure could also be *against* reductions in time. In June 1911 the Longhedge staff complained at being reduced from 54 hours to 48hrs 45mins.

The SECR however was one of the more progressive companies and had maintained contact with representatives of its workforce when other railways had been cool and aloof, although it preferred the men's "own representatives" rather than ASRS officials; in May 1911, for example, it complained that "the ASRS are engineering this case" in connection with Driver Ewell, who had been receiving £1 a week since being injured in a 1906 accident.

The SECR policy paid off when the first national railway strike began on

18th August 1911 - largely as a result of the slow progress of the Conciliation Boards and lack of company recognition of the unions. Whereas receipts on the Great Western fell by 28.4% and on the London & North Western by 29.6%, the SECR suffered a loss of only 2.7% during the strike period. Support for the strike on the SECR was very patchy - in London 132 went on strike in the Coaching Department but only three in the Goods. The majority of strikers were in Locomotive, Carriage & Wagon Department - where 194 higher grades and 395 lower grades went on strike. There were 795 strikers altogether,

An agreement between the Railway Companies Association and the strikers was brokered by Lloyd George on 19th August, but the SECR declined to be involved as it felt its conditions were "so different" to the other companies.

In October 1911 the SECR awarded two days extra pay to all men who did not strike, and also gave increases to station clerical staff. However it still kept out of the RCA negotiations at the Board of Trade until mid-December, when Bonsor agreed to accept the terms for casual goods labourers.

The locomotive men seem to have been largely at a distance from all of this - as early as 1907 the Board had noted that some locomotive men wanted to look after their own affairs without ASRS representation as when the Ashford locomotive men discussed the pension fund issue. In December their stance was revealed when they became concerned about a new eyesight test - several drivers had failed this and been demoted to a cleaner's job on less than half the pay. W Stevenson, a Slades Green driver, led a deputation and informed the Board of his own opposition to the centralising tendency of Government and Unions which he felt "simply means the handing over of the responsible workmen to such forces as Tom Mann and Co and the Social Democratic Federation. Stevenson wanted a minimum 6s a day for men who had failed the test with 8s6d a day for drivers.

In March and April 1912 the country was hit by a national coal strike, which the SECR had planned for by arranging to coal its steamers in France. The strike began on 29th February but did not begin to affect the SECR until 2nd March, when it began to take steps to reduce coal consumption. Some trains ceased to be double-headed, for example the 10.45am Victoria to Margate which was banked out of Herne Hill instead. Staff were also offered an extra day's holiday if they took their leave during the strike while steam-heating was suspended except on Boat Trains..

Such measures had little effect and the laying off of staff became inevitable although men preferred the idea of "pooling" work so each got three days. On 11th March many "temporary" men were laid off in London but by 18th March the London Coaching Department had laid off 164 full-time staff. A total of 1,528 were stood off in the Traffic Department, losing pay of £442.

A number of SECR men joined the strike - 135 in the Traffic Department including fourteen guards at Victoria. A number of signalboxes were closed in the London area, and many staff laid off at Ludgate Hill including two of the female lavatory attendants.

On 23rd March the engineering workshops employed 1,610 but 1,461 of these were on short time. The same was true of most of the 2,400 permanent way

Mail bags piled high at Cannon Street during delays caused by the strikes of 1912.

staff. The savings from these actions were considerable - the Locomotive, Carriage & Wagon Department alone saved £10,532.

However the lengthy dispute forced the closure of Longhedge Works entirely from 4th March, which caused "considerable distress" among the men there. On 23rd March a deputation of the men went to see the General Manager to describe the threat of eviction for non-payment of rent that many faced. The Board decided that they would pay any money needed to avoid eviction. Two cases of hardship were reported in the *Daily* Express and the reporter visited the homes of some of the men. He found A Philpott "in a very weak condition...the house was a very poor one and the interior squalid. There were two young children without boots and stockings and the eldest, a boy of about 5, had only one eye." The reporter gave Philpott £1, which his wife used to get her boots and those of her husband and children from the pawnshop, as well as buying some clothes and food with what was left. The SECR (in the person of "CHJ") investigated the case and found that Philpott was £2-3s-6d in arrears with the rent of which £1-7s was due to the coal strike; he was advanced 15s. He had five children (aged 10, 7, 5, 3 1) and paid rent of 8s6d a week although they let out one room for 2s. On 27th March Bonsor decided to allow £1500 for the relief of the men; married men were to

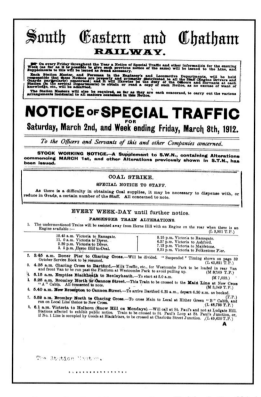

Various attempts were made to economise on workings during the coal strike, as this special traffic notice shows.

receive a basic 10s a week with extra if they had children. A charity concert also raised £76.

By April the situation was becoming acute. On 6th April (which proved to be the last day of the strike) the LC&W Department gave notice to 499 cleaners and 693 firemen alone. These two grades were hit badly, and a table of those stood off shows also the relative importance of the different depots:

In July 1912 the Board made further wage and conditions of service concessions which cost the SECR about £16,000 a year at the same time as £6700 was

Table 5: Staff laid off at SECR depots, April 1906

Depot	Cleaners	Firemen
Bricklayers Arms	80	146
Slades Green	49	89
Cannon Street	10	16
Orpington	21	36
Purley	7	18
Tonbridge	34	56
Redhill	21	16
Ashford	19	27
Dover/Folkestone/Deal	50	29
Maidstone W	12	15
Strood	16	29
Reading	20	23
Hastings	15	17
Battersea	60	90
Faversham	18	26
New Brompton	18	16
Margate West	9	8
Maidstone East	2	1
Dover Priory	20	10
Ramsgate Town	12	15

added due to the Government's Insurance reforms. Pay increases in 1913 added about £33,000 to the staff costs.

The Great War caused a sharp increase in the cost of living and so wages spiralled upwards. For example, in January 1917 all the clerical staff - including the women - asked for a 20% increase while two months later Shops and Running staff requested 10s a week extra. The same month it was agreed that the "War Bonus" should be converted into a war wage of an extra 15s a week for all men and women over 18 years old. War wages were further increased in November 1917.

There was some resistance to the wartime spread of women workers, perhaps because the men feared a reduction in wages. In May 1918 the men resolved "emphatically protesting against the proposed introduction of women to work passenger trains." The men argued that safety was their main concern, and that the work was not "suited" to women. However the SECR was not sympathetic as it had lost 24% of its trained staff to the armed forces. However in March 1920 it discharged many of the female clerical staff, who between them had £6251 worth of Company clothes. However not all female clerks were discharged, as in October 1920 the ones in London were given a 4s a week pay rise.

Shortly before the end of the War there was a strike affecting 42 staff - eleven Battersea and one Reading drivers, 28 Battersea firemen and two Reading guards. However their duties were light compared to the more prestigious stationmasters, who were working a seven day week; in October 1918 this was amended to give them alternate Sundays off by "pairing" stations.

The end of the War in November 1918 brought problems. Firstly, many men took the day off to celebrate and so were not allowed to have the SECR's extra day's pay which was awarded. The following month the SECR and the Railway Companies' Association were arguing against the Government's eight hour day policy, which became effective from 1st February 1919 and reduced the workshop men to a typical 47 hour week.

The War had resulted in a huge expansion of the wages bill. In 1913 the wages of staff in the "Conciliation grades" (those covered by the pre-war legislation) was £843, 649 - but in 1918-9 the year's cost was £2,345,531; for non-conciliation grades like those in the "shops" the costs had risen from £858,777 to £1,823,685. Companies were desperate to deflate these levels of pay, while the Unions fought a counter-battle. The result was the national strike of 26th September to 5th October 1919.

The strike was initiated by the National Union of Railwaymen and joined by the ASRS. The sudden start of the strike caused chaos when signalmen abandoned their duties at the appointed hour with trains still "in section"; this occurred at fourteen boxes mostly in London, but also at Maidstone East and Ashford, and nine trains were trapped including three goods trains trapped by the St Pauls signalman. The strike was solidly supported by all departments of the SECR:

Of 25,204 employees there were 19,992 on strike although the pattern varied between grades; 0.77% of clerks went on strike but 100% of greasers, 96% of both firemen and track staff, and 79.3% overall. Although stationmasters did not join

Table 6: Effect of 1919 Strike

Department	% Staff on Strike
Outdoor Locomotive	89
Engineers	93
Mechanics	97
London Coaching	86
London Goods	97
Northern	85
Eastern	85
Western	94
Horse	89
Marine	86

the strike in general, the humble "St Lawrence haltkeeper", as well as 227 women workers, did.

The SECR doubted whether the support for the strike was genuine, "At least 50% of the staff can be assumed to have left work without the least enthusiasm and entirely through fear." On 27th September only seventeen passenger and one goods trains ran and the SECR was able to run a mere ten locos with 733 staff at work. This gradually improved until it ran 307 trains with 101 locos over a total of 7,115 miles. A few goods trains were operated as well, with perishable traffic being given the priority. Quite a few volunteer staff were used, including ex-military men.

There were a few attempts at sabotage, starting at Crowhurst on 29th September when a tree trunk was placed on the line. On 1st October stones were thrown at the driver of the 1.50pm Victoria to Margate near Herne Bay. Two days later strikers defaced the house of the Yard Inspector at Ashford, whilst signal wires were cut at Eynsford and an obstruction placed on the line at Tadworth. The next day stones were thrown at trains at Belvedere and twice near Erith. There was a trickle back to work with 174 returning by 1st October and 922 back by 5th October.

1920 saw increasing Government involvement in wage levels. In June the Wages Board gave a rise of between 4s and 7s6d to London staff and in October a 3s a week increase to footplate men. These were part of a "cost of living" bonus scheme. In January 1921 the Ministry of Transport suggested that working hours should be reduced in order to help with unemployment, but the finances of the SECR were already struggling after a period of remorselessly increasing staff costs; since the outbreak of the Great War, the wages bill had risen from £1,750,000 p.a. to £6,070,000 causing costs to spiral and setting in train many problems for the future of Britain's railways.

The SECR seems to have had no real plans to control the cost of staff. Some desultory attempts were made to reduce the number of stationmasters: in July 1921 one man was placed in charge of Herne Hill, Loughborough Junction and Dulwich. The Chatham stationmaster also became responsible for Rochester and Gillingham on a salary of £400 - but the saving was £658. Beckenham Junction took care of Clock House, Kent House and New Beckenham whilst Folkestone Junction became Dover's responsibility. The London Bridge stationmaster took care of Spa Road and Southwark Park - an interesting decision as both had been closed since 1915.

Some respite came in 1922 when the "cost of living" bonuses began to be withdrawn, but one suspects the Southern Railway took over a line that still clung to Victorian staffing practices.

Unions such as the ASRS did not only concentrate on conditions of service, nor were they the exclusive representatives of the SECR workforce. Groups of men often combined together to defend their interests or to propose matters to the Board - in November 1906 a group of enginemen wrote to propose extra signals at Loughborough Junction. Sometimes safety could also be a useful lever in labour relations as the Secretary of the ASRS proved in May 1907 when he complained to the Board of Trade about inadequate signalling at Folkestone Junction: the result-ant new signal box cost the SECR £5291.

However the ASRS acted on behalf of its members when in trouble, such as Driver Skinner who was blamed for a collision at Bricklayers Arms on 24th No-vember 1905. As a result of their intervention, he was given a "shore" job instead of the sack. Sometimes staff even tried to use the Law as when William Lamb sued Inspectors Townsend and Smith for libel in 1907. Until 23rd June Lamb had been a "supernumerary porter" at Bricklayers Arms on £1 a week subject to twelve hours notice. On that day he arrived two hours late and then disappeared for an hour, after which he was noticed to be "unsteady". He was sacked for being drunk, but foolishly tried to contest the matter in the courts.

The Pension & Insurance Issues

The SECR had its own pension scheme for "indoor staff" in advance of the state scheme begun after the Liberals passed an Act in 1908. Some higher officials "outdoors" also seem to have had pensions - the Maidstone (SER) stationmaster retired in October 1898 on a useful pension of £200 a year. Sometimes the terms were even improved if the worker was especially deserving; a Mr Sewell retired in 1899 at the age of 75, having worked 36 years for the LCDR and 15 for the SER with a final salary of £104 a year - yielding a pension of £46 to which the SECR added an extra pound. However many grades of staff were not included whilst many eligible staff did not participate - thus there was always a tendency for some employees to continue working beyond normal ages. In 1904 the SECR acted to reduce this problem amongst its station masters, retiring J Bryan of Charlton at the age of 75 - he had 54 years service; the station masters at Chislehurst, aged 74, and Sandgate - 70 - soon followed.

Even at the start of the period the SECR had a substantial pension fund. In 1902 it paid out £22,295 in allowances and pensions to the retired and widows, of which the largest part - £5495 - was for former General Offices staff. Most staff were not covered at all, which the SECR felt was acceptable - in May 1902 it decided that the footplate men did not need pension provision since they were the best paid locomotive men in the country. In November 1906 a Pension Fund Com-mittee was set up and on 8th July 1908 the Board decided to proceed with the idea of an Outdoor Pension Fund, although they made no progress In December 1909 they decided to put off a start until at least February 1910 - when they did nothing again. By then they were actually paying £31,813 in the year for pensions and allowances outside the Pension Fund while the Fund itself had only 132 pensioners who shared £82,011 in the year.

However a Sick Fund did exist, although the rules were unclear and there were several occasions when the SECR refused to let a man have his money back when he left their employment. In 1902 this allowed for men to receive sick pay of 10s a week after the third week of illness. The LCDR locomotive men had set up their own Sick Club as early as 1862 which they ran themselves as a compulsory scheme, but it was affected by the Shop Clubs Act of 1902 and the Board realised there was some need for reorganisation. The Clubs also needed some protection - in January 1912 a man had to be sacked for "dishonestly handling" the LCDR Servants' Sick & Benefit Society funds.

The SECR was affected by the tide of social reform initiated by the Liberals between 1906 and 1914, including the 1908 Act which set up pensions for men and women over seventy. One of the most important reforms was the National Insurance Act of 1911, which became operative on 15th July 1912; the SECR estimated in advance that this would cost them £13,500 in employer contributions, of which £1500 was specifically for unemployment. This caused the Board to look again at the outdoor pension fund question, but in May 1912 they again deferred a decision. In January 1920 the SECR still employed 171 men over seventy and four who were over eighty!

Working Conditions

From about 1905 the SECR became increasingly concerned about the roles of its station masters, who were "on call" at all times. In these circumstances, it was desirable that all such officials should live at or near the railway station in their care although many still lived in lodgings or rented accomodation often a mile or more from the station. Thus the SECR commenced a scheme of building new station houses or buying property close to the station in order to ensure proper supervision by the station master.

It was unusual for a stationmaster to be permitted to live away from his base. A rare example is the Cannon Street stationmaster, who in November 1907 was given permission to live at St John's. Until 1918 the Victoria stationmaster was allowed to live at Herne Hill, but was then moved to 36 Belgrave Road. Some stationmasters still lived in poor conditions - in 1914 the official at Hildenborough was living in a wooden hut that had survived from the line's opening in 1868 until it was condemned by the local Sanitary Inspector.

Stationmasters were not the only staff to live in railway property. On Reculver Marshes were some ramshackle houses said to have been temporary huts erected in about 1858 for the navvies who built the line there. In March 1904 these were apparently still inhabited by some SECR "enginemen", although they were then pulled down and replaced by some cottages. Similarly the signalmen's huts at Harrietsham were condemned by the local authority in October 1904. Even more august staff lived in elderly buildings - in May 1909 it was decided to build houses for the stationmasters at Eltham and Sidcup as "the present residences are the original contractors' huts used when the line was constructed."

Staff at isolated sidings also needed somewhere to live, though this was often in the nearest village. The porter in charge of Miskin's Siding on the Hundred of Hoo line was provided with a house in 1911 - built on the site of some old uninhabited carriages. There was clearly a problem on this line, opened only in 1882, since in October 1913 it was reported that many of the staff cottages on it were uninhabitable and needed new ones at Wybournes Crossing, Stoke Creek, Stoke Siding and Grain Crossing.

In remote places such as these, the railway house was an essential part of the job and a poor house could lead to problems recruiting staff. At Kennardington Crossing the SECR could not get a gatekeeper in 1914 as the cottage had only two rooms and a scullery, so they were forced to add two new rooms.

Also in need of overhaul was the accomodation at Betchworth where "the stationmaster's apartments are on the first floor of the building and consist of five small, dark and damp rooms connected by a very narrow passage," the Board was informed in July 1909. In April 1916 the stationmaster at North Camp was living in "an old ground floor building situated on the up side of the line on land of a boggy nature and surrounded by marshy ground subject to floods..." It was re-solved to spend £700 providing him with a better home.

A number of houses had been built at Slades Green for the new depot there, but the staff were not entirely convinced about the merits of living there and in August 1900 applied for a rent reduction on the grounds that they were so far from the nearest market. No reduction was agreed, but the SECR gave a £2 bonus to each household and agreed to improve the cesspools, doors and to build an Insti-tute.

Sometimes it was not the actual condition of the house that was at fault. An outbreak of typhoid at Twydall Crossing in June 1909 was traced to the crossing-keeper's well. Rather bizarre was the situation of the refreshment room staff at Greenwich, who lived in rooms above the station which had no street access - when the station was locked at night they were locked inside!

Not all property used by staff was for habitation. From 1910 the Head Office clerks rented an arch at Waterloo for a miniature rifle club - for which the SECR charged them £90 a year.

Of course there was a world of difference between "working conditions" and "conditions of work" - or service, as the SECR tended to see it. Like most railway companies, the SECR had a strict disciplinary system reinforced with a rule book - when a new one was prepared in 1905 18,000 copies were printed. Questions of safety were treated very seriously, and any breach of the rules could be punished with dismissal. Clearly this was known to Inspector Daniels, who was in charge of a light engine running from Redhill to London Bridge in January 1914; he passed a signal at danger near Penge and then tried to get the signalman not to report the matter, but all to no avail - he was dismissed.

Offences connected with drink and insubordination were also punished se-verely. In March 1914 a goods guard at Queenborough managed to combine both when he left his train to go to the pub. On his return he was abusive to the Inspec-tor, so a sacking was inevitable. In October 1914 a clerk in the traffic department claimed that he had got drunk in his line of duty - he dealt with the theatrical trade. However this was his third offence so he was dismissed.

The country crossing at Gomshall seems to have been in the care of an elderly man and a young lad from this picture, but a house was provided and it was of a good standard compared to what many of the London staff would have had to endure. (Wakeman Collection, Ashford Library)

In July 1917 a shunter named Belsey was found playing cards with several other people while supposedly on duty at Reading. When challenged by the SECR policeman he became abusive and used obscene language - he was sacked.

However the SECR was not always stern. In August 1915 it had to solve a fracas at Cliffe, where stationmaster Potts has been accused of assaulting signalman Wilson. Potts' defence was that Wilson was "aggressive" and that he was under strain due to the illness of his wife; the SECR solved the problem by moving Potts to another position.

In July 1917 Driver Stevenson of Slades Green, who often represented the footplatemen, led a deputation to protest that the SECR was trying to alter the conditions of service. Following this the SECR agreed to provide extra working clothes and to take charge of washing them, as well as to provide special suits and clogs for the men who washed out the boilers.

Clearly this clothing was equipment for the job. In October 1917 the National Union of Railwaymen Purley branch wrote about SECR platelayers who had to provide their own tools for digging ditches and trimming hedges, whereas other railways provided tools.

Some minor fringe benefits are of interest. Platform staff, including stationmasters, were allowed to sell discarded newspapers found on trains until the rule was changed in January 1914; from thence on, the money was to go to the Benevolent Fund.

Criminal Tendencies

Many of the SECR staff were placed in positions of trust, where they had access to property of the general public, cash receipts or to goods consignments. Inevitably there were occasional failures of honesty, like the three Holborn Viaduct cloakroom attendants who were convicted of embezzlement in 1903. Carman Hemming was given three months in prison for stealing from the Holborn parcels office in December 1900. In December 1905 two goods guards were found guilty of theft in a trial at Guildford, receiving three and four years penal servitude each. However some staff were arrested but never found guilty, as happened to driver Suggett and two goods guards after the loss of some freight at Charing, although the case was confused by the failure of Suggett's solicitor to show him all the correspondence so that the ASRS had to intervene on his behalf although he did have compensation paid for wrongful imprisonment. William Osborne, a Tonbridge driver, was found Not Guilty of stealing £5 from a passenger's box even though no evidence was offered in his defence.

Small offences could be punished severely at a time when loss of a job was a difficult blow to recover from. In July 1916 a driver and fireman were sacked after stealing a sieve of cherries from a truck at Shortlands.

An unusual type of robbery was committed by J Jefferies, a SECR draughtsman, who managed to steal a mail bag containing £100 from the 5.04pm Cannon Street to Dartford. He received six months hard labour.

Misappropriation of cash was a common problem so that many staff were required to deposit a bond or surety. In May 1907 a deficit of £282 was uncovered in the goods accounts at New Brompton, but this was only discovered as the chief goods clerk there had committed suicide "some time ago". Pension payments to his widow were stopped.

Another problem revealed by a death surfaced when the Grove Ferry stationmaster died in March 1913, leaving a wife and eight children. A subsequent examination of the accounts revealed £73-7-6d missing, so that his family's allowance was reduced to 10s a week.

Staff responsible for checking goods consignments could easily cheat the company. Two collectors at Bricklayers Arms defrauded the SECR of £360 in 1899. J Long, a goods clerk at Sittingbourne in 1913, systematically defrauded the SECR's Lloyd's Paper account by giving the wrong weights and doctoring the invoices. He overcharged inwards traffic by £98 and outwards by £64. Long was sacked, as were several staff at Lloyd's who had colluded with him.

A very unusual case was heard at Lambeth in October 1909. Charles James, a former SECR carriage examiner, was charged with threatening to murder Harry Wainwright, the Locomotive, Carriage & Wagon Superintendent. It emerged that James had been sacked for assaulting a colleague at work, and that Wainwright had refused to reinstate him. James was bound over to keep the peace on a £5 surety, it being understood that he intended to go to Australia.

Blood on the Tracks: Railway Safety

It is a curious feature of British railway history that major disasters have attracted frequent historical studies, yet one form of endless carnage on Britain's railways has been largely ignored. This is the constant slaughter of railway workers who were killed in their daily work, either through momentary carelessness or because of a lack of sufficient safety standards.

The scale of the problem can be gathered from the following:

The vast majority of staff worked in the sidings, on the track and in the various depots of the companies. In these grades death and injury were almost routine aspects of the work, and a man's working life could be cruelly truncated at any moment. In order to help

Nervous Party. "The train seems to be travelling at a fearful pace, ma'am."
Elderly Female. "Yus, ain't it? My Bill's a-drivin' of the ingin, an' 'e *can* make 'er go when 'e's got a drop o' drink in 'im!"

Drunken engine-drivers were not usually a topic for jokes, and any such incident was likely to be followed by a period of unemployment!

the families of such workers, the Workmen's Compensation Act had been passed in 1895 - becoming effective just as the SECR was formed. This legislation laid down that the employer was liable to pay compensation for death or injury while at work; if the man died, then compensation should be paid to his wife or dependent family.

This law meant that the SECR Board discussed accidents to lower grade employees at regular intervals, since the compensation law meant the paying out of funds to the victims. The annual cost of payments rose to over £11,000 by 1914, giving safety an economic motive.

Most of the accidents were due to careless workmen or poor safety standards. In 1902, for example, a workman fell off the roof of Victoria station while doing some glazing and was killed; his "wife" claimed compensation, but was found to be only cohabiting with him although the SECR gave her £100 in any case. In cases where the husband and wife were separated, the SECR often refused to pay out at all. Two platelayers were killed at Corbetts Lane in February 1899 and their families received £187 and £171. However, these were small amounts - a Post Office employee injured in the accident at Chislehurst was awarded £1200 in 1903.

The carnage on the tracks in the late 1800s had attracted the concern of Parliament and led to the Railway Employment (Prevention of Accidents) Act of 1900, which became effective from 8 August 1903. This banned a number of practices regarded as dangerous by the Board of Trade's experts, of which "tow-roping" was a prime example, although they had already begun to abolish it at stations like Aylesford (1902) by installing new slip crossings. This meant that engines shunted trucks in adjacent sidings by the use of ropes, rather than by shunting round and coupling up. This was dangerous for the shunting staff, but when the law came into effect was still being done at 80 SECR stations. The Company decided to make changes at a cost of £40,470, but the work was completed slowly and led to some altercations with the Board of Trade; tow-roping was not abolished at Higham until 1907. The Act clearly identified goods sidings as a major location of death, and its other provisions included the fitting of brakes and levers to both sides of trucks, the labelling of both sides (quickly adopted by the SECR) and all yards where shunting occurred at night were to be lit. On the ground, point rods and signalling wires were to be repositioned to avoid men tripping over them while

PERMISSIVE SLAUGHTER

(*Five Thousand Shunting Accidents in Five Years!*)

First Shunter (with coupling-link, awaiting engine backing). " I saw poor Jack's wife and kids last night, after the funeral. Poor things, what will be done for 'em ? "
Second Shunter (at points). " Oh, the usual thing, I s'ppose—company's blessin', and a charity mangle!—— Look out, mate ! She's backin'! "

This cartoon seems to lay at least some of the blame for the death toll upon staff carelessness.

ground frame levers were to be kept at a safe distance from the track; the SECR estimated that it would cost them £12,520 to comply with these last two points..

The Act also made some changes to protect the locomotive men - boiler gauge glasses were to be protected and the locomotive toolbox had to be positioned where it could be reached easily. On the track, all platelayer gangs were to be protected by look-out men.

Some of these changes must have taken many years to effect. In 1904 the SECR decided to comply with the fitting of brakes and levers on both sides of its goods trucks at a rate of two hundred a year - but it had 11,438 trucks! Lighting of sidings was also installed slowly - in October 1907 the Board of Trade complained of the lack of lamps in the sidings at Penge, St Mary Cray, both Fawkham and Fawkham Junction, Farningham Road and Sole Street. In response to criticism, the SECR also began to improve Tonbridge East Yard in 1907 - it removed dangerous posts, put wires in trunking and slewed a siding to improve clearances.

In 1904 new Home Office regulations were introduced to improve safety at docks and wharves, such as the insistence on safety chains. These affected many parts of the SECR.

Table 7: SECR Staff Fatalities 1899-1921

Rank	Type of Work	Deaths
Platelayer	Track	57
Porter	Station area	38
Ganger	Track	30
Shunter	Goods sidings	26
Fireman	Footplate	15
Labourer	General	13
Guard	Train & sidings	12
Driver	Footplate	10
Soldier	Guard duty	10
Building worker	Construction	10
Goods guard	Train & sidings	10
Carriage cleaner	Sidings	8

Looking at the payments that the SECR was forced to hand out under the Workmen's Compensation Act, it seems doubtful that the new regulations improved safety by very much - compensation paid nearly doubled between 1909 and 1914:

Certain jobs seem to have carried a far higher risk than others. One dangerous task was the cleaning of points, which was often done by station porters between trains. Platelayers were exposed continuously to the danger of passing trains, but it was a bizarre accident that caused the death of a platelayer at Waterloo Junction in June 1914 - his arm got jammed in a check rail and he was unable to get out of the way of an approaching train. Goods sidings were especially dangerous, with numerous instances of men being "pinched" between truck buffers. This was also common when coupling up, such as the fireman at Hastings in January 1912 who was "pinched between the buffers" and "his heart torn from the blood vessels."

Perhaps basic first aid should have been essential for the men in the sidings. In August 1917 Frank Cox, a shunter at Ashford, was run over and his left foot cut off; he remained conscious long enough to explain to his colleagues how to bind up the shattered limb, thus saving himself from bleeding to death.

Apart from the goods sidings, there was a major problem on the running lines in the London area during fog. At such times men were stationed along the tracks to signal the trains by hand, but there was often too little room for them to do this safely. For example, a man was killed at New Cross in December 1904 after over ten hours of fog duty. In October 1906 the SECR finally decided to install fog repeater signals between Holborn and Brixton, where trains mostly ran over viaducts with no space for hand-signallers. Almost a year later this decision was revised to include the ex-LCDR line as far out as Bickley, and the SER section between Charing Cross and London Bridge.

There were a number of fatalities due to people being hit by non-railway objects. A goods inspector died in April 1909 as a result of a tin falling on him in the goods van - he contracted blood poisoning. A few months later the New Cross station-master was knocked down by a hop-picker and died from haemorrhaging of the bowel. A goods porter at Reading died in 1907 after a heavy case fell on him causing pelvic injuries and leading to death from "septic absorption." Cranes and hoists led to catastrophe as well - in December 1911 a Blackfriars goods loader was killed when he got trapped under the truck hoist and in July 1912 a driver was killed during coaling at Bricklayers' Arms when a skip of coal fell on him.

However the most appalling situation of all seems to have existed in Penge Tunnel, which was 2,200 yards long and poorly equipped with manholes in the side walls. The length of the tunnel meant that staff frequently worked inside during the passage of trains and it was often difficult to see. If a train was approaching, the standard procedure was therefore to lie down in the space between the up and down lines since it was usually impossible to get to one of the few manholes. The tunnel claimed lives regularly until more manholes were at last provided in 1915 at a cost of £4,700. The SECR had discussed the problem in 1910, but it took the loss of two more lives before the work was completed - compensation paid for a workman's death in the period 1910-15 averaged only £135. 200 recesses were built in 1910-11 at a cost of £4000. In fact another porter was killed in Penge Tunnel in January 1917. That manholes had not been a requirement can be noted from the fact that they were added to Bletchingley Tunnel in 1900.

On 1st February 1910 a driver was killed in the tunnel at Tunbridge Wells in circumstances which are also revealing of SECR working conditions. The driver had been doing some shunting and had stopped his engine inside the tunnel, where it was so smoky that he could not see whether the signals were set. He thus got down from his engine and walked along to see if the points were set instead, but was run over when his fireman restarted the engine.

Trying to see in a tunnel could be as dangerous as not seeing at all. In January 1906 Inspector Fagg was walking through Abbots Cliff Tunnel at Dover when he was knocked down by an inspection trolley. He fell and upset his lamp, so that the naphtha from it burnt his face and hands leading to death from septic poisoning. The jury at the inquest declared the lamps to be a "death trap" and advised their immediate replacement with something less hazardous.

Footplate men were usually less prone to accident, but it was still not a "safe" profession. On 22nd June 1900 a fireman on the "Granville Express" was killed when his head hit a bridge near Faversham and in November 1902 a fireman died when he fell off the train at Canterbury West. Generally the former type of accident seems to have been the most common; for example, at Charing Cross in November

1911 a fireman was killed when his head hit a signal girder at Charing Cross - he was working on the coal; a month later a driver was found dead on the coal by his fireman - though it was believed that on this occasion the man had climbed up to retrieve his cap. In April 1905 a driver was killed when he fell off the footplate near Newington. An incident showing the alarming lack of safety provision occurred at Bickley in April 1914, when a driver fell against the firebox and burnt his face badly. Septic poisoning set in and, with penicillin yet to be discovered, he died. A driver and an Inspector were also killed when they jumped off the footplate seconds before the collision at Tonbridge on 6 March 1909. It is also remarkable that boilersmiths sometimes worked on engines that were in steam - one died at Longhedge in 1908 after trying to tighten a tube and being scalded to death.

It was not always the trains that caused the danger. In February 1904 a gateman at a crossing near Sheerness was run over by a car in the charge of a Major-General. As the car belonged to the War Department, the SECR attempted to force the Government to pay the man's compensation - with a degree of success; he was awarded £65 from the WD and £35 from the SECR. Another bizarre incident occurred in July 1914, when a "boarhound" en route from Hemel Hempstead to Chatham escaped at Holborn. It headed off along the down line to Elephant & Castle, chased by Stephen Murphy, an 18 year old porter. Murphy was knocked down and killed by a light engine near Walworth Road station.

The SECR also employed many "Marine" staff on its ferries from Dover and Folkestone. Many of these were involved in accidents too, such as the coal-trimmer who went ashore at Dover in January 1906 to vote. Returning to the ship on a ladder stretched across from the dockside, he fell in and drowned.

However the two worst incidents that occurred during the period did not involve railway traffic. On 5 December 1905 the roof collapse at Charing Cross station caused the death of four workmen and a further two people at the Avenue Theatre. Four men employed by the contractor Rigby were killed at Margate West on 18 March 1914, when undercutting a wall during extension works.

When non-railway staff were required to work on the line, there were often problems. In June 1907 PC Harryman was killed at the mouth of Gillingham Tunnel when on guard duty for the royal train. This sort of incident became a major problem with the start of the Great War - Private O'Neill being killed on guard duty at Rochester Bridge on 30 July 1914 - before the war had started. Eight other soldiers were killed within the next year, including the Captain in charge of the guards at Folkestone. The War also brought female employees into types of work previously dominated by men, such as goods portering at Bricklayers Arms; the first female to require compensation was a portress who was injured when a barrow there overturned in 1916. The first woman to have been killed seems to have been Emma Hill, a carriage cleaner at Victoria, who was crushed in 1918 though this job was performed by women long before the War.

Other "non-railway" staff were killed when they had no excuse for being on the line, such as the professional photographer killed at Blackfriars Goods in April 1907 when trying to persuade some goods staff there to commission him to do a "working group" photo.

Yet even this catalogue of misery does not touch on all aspects of the blood shed on SECR tracks. There was also a continual carnage on various "occupation" crossings and where footpaths crossed the track. At one crossing in Sydenham six people were killed between 1906 and 1911 and some crossings had to be replaced with expensive bridges. As well as this, suicides on the railway averaged at least one a fortnight in the years leading up to the Great War.

Rank	Type of Work	Deaths 1899-1921
Platelayer	Track	57
Porter	Station area	38
Ganger	Track	30
Shunter	Goods sidings	26
Fireman	Footplate	15
Labourer	General	13
Guard	Train and sidings	12
Soldier	Guard duty	10
Goods Guard	Train and sidings	10
Driver	Footplate	11
Building worker	Construction	10
Carriage cleaner	Sidings	8

We know little about industrial diseases connected with railway employment. One of the few cases in SECR records concerns a paint grinder at Ashford, who died of lead poisoning in 1919; his family was paid £300 compensation.

Sources and Acknowledgments

As ever I am grateful to my fellow members of the Railway & Canal Historical Society for their help and support with this text. I must mention especially Alan Jackson, Edwin Course and Roger Kidner who have read and checked my manuscript valiantly and assiduously. John Creed and Peter Kay have also helped greatly.

The majority of research has taken place at the Public Records Office, Cambridge University Library and Ashford Library; I am grateful to these institutions for their facilities.

The most significant sources are those classified under RAIL633 in the Public Records Office, which are too extensive to list in detail here. However other class references also contain material, such as RAIL116 (Chipstead Valley), RAIL635 (LBSC & SEC Joint), RAIL145 (Crowhurst, Sidley & Bexhill), and RAIL414 (Oxted).These, together with some of the periodicals listed below, have been my principal sources for this work.

Periodicals:

Backtrack
Journal of the Railway & Canal Historical Society
Railway Gazette
Railway Magazine
The Times

Other Published Sources:

Ashford: The Coming of the Railway, G Turner, Maidstone, 1984.
Biographical Dictionary of Railway Engineers, J Marshall, Newton Abbot, 1987.
Britain's Railways & The Great War, E A Pratt, London, 1921.
Britain's Railways in World War One, J A B Hamilton, London, 1967.
British Coal Trade, H S Jevons, London, 1917.
The Caterham Railway, J Spence, Headington, 1986.
Cement Railways of Kent, R W Kidner, Lingfield, 1973.
Dictionary of Business Biography, D J Jeremy, London, 1984.
Dictionary of National Biography.
The East Kent Railway, A R Catt, Tarrant Hinton, 1975.
Gateway to the Continent, E W P Veale, London, 1955.
Harold Laski, A Political Biography, M Newman, London, 1993.
Sir Herbert Walker's Southern Railway, C Klapper, London, 1973.
History of the Southern Railway, M Bonavia, London, 1987.
History of the Southern Railway, C Dendy Marshall, Middlesex, 1963.
Industrial Archaeology of SE England, A J Haselfoot, London, 1978.
Locomotive History of the SECR, D L Bradley, London, 1980.
London's Termini, Alan A Jackson, Newton Abbot, 1969.
Men & Women of the Time, various, London, 1899.
Military Railways in Kent, R M Lyne, Maidstone, 1983.

The Oxted Line, R W Kidner, Tarrant Hinton, 1972.
The Railwaymen, P S Bagwell, London, 1963.
The Railways of Southern England (3 vols.), Edwin Course, London, 1973.
Reading to Tonbridge Line, R W Kidner, Tarrant Hinton, 1974.
Richborough Port, R Butler, Sandwich, 1993.
South Eastern & Chatham Railway, O S Nock, Middlesex, 1961.
South Eastern & Chatham Railway in the 1914-18 War, D Gould, Tarrant Hinton, 1981.

A number of other works are referred to in the footnotes and I should also mention the voluminous works of Vic Mitchell and Keith Smith, published by Middleton Press (see back page). These books contain a wealth of pictorial, cartographical and factual information. However the major source for railway history, as for this book, must always be the original materials in the keeping of the Public Records Office which are too numerous to list individually here - but a visit is recommended!

Middleton Press albums illustrating the SECR and associated routes

In ISBN order - please enquire regarding availibility
** 0 906520   + 1 873793*

* Steaming through Kent
* Branch Line to Tenterden
* Eastbourne to Hastings
* Branch Lines to
        Tunbridge Wells
* Hastings to Ashford
* Tonbridge to Hastings
* Reading to Guildford
* Ashford to Dover
* East Croydon to Three Bridges
* London Bridge to
        East Croydon
* East Kent Light Railway
* Branch Line to Allhallows
* Guildford to Redhill
* Branch Line to Hawkhurst
* Redhill to Ashford
* Charing Cross to Dartford
* Dover to Ramsgate

* Holborn Viaduct to Lewisham
* Crystal Palace (High Level) and
        Catford Loop
* Sittingbourne to Ramsgate
* Lewisham to Dartford
* Charing Cross to Orpington
* Victoria to Bromley South
+ Orpington to Tonbridge
+ Faversham to Dover
+ Strood to Paddock Wood
+ Branch Lines around Sheerness
+ London Bridge to Addiscombe
+ Bromley South to Rochester
+ Caterham and Tattenham Corner
+ Dartford to Sittingbourne
+ Swanley to Ashford
+ Croydon to East Grinstead
+ Branch Lines around Canterbury
+ Ashford from Steam to Eurostar

INDEX OF CHARACTERS

INDEX OF COMPANIES Etc.

INDEX OF PLACES

MP Middleton Press

Easebourne Lane, Midhurst, West Sussex. GU29 9AZ Tel: 01730 813169 Fax: 01730 812601
... WRITE OR PHONE FOR OUR LATEST LIST ...

BRANCH LINES
Branch Line to Allhallows
Branch Lines to Alton
Branch Lines around Ascot
Branch Line to Ashburton
Branch Lines around Bodmin
Branch Line to Bude
Branch Lines around Canterbury
Branch Line to Cheddar
Branch Lines to East Grinstead
Branch Lines to Effingham Junction
Branch Line to Fairford
Branch Line to Hawkhurst
Branch Lines to Hayling
Branch Lines to Horsham
Branch Line to Ilfracombe
Branch Line to Longmoor
Branch Line to Lyme Regis
Branch Line to Lynton
Branch Lines around Midhurst
Branch Line to Minehead
Branch Lines to Newport (IOW)
Branch Line to Padstow
Branch Lines around Plymouth
Branch Lines around Portmadoc 1923-46
Branch Lines around Porthmadog 1954-94
Branch Lines to Seaton & Sidmouth
Branch Line to Selsey
Branch Lines around Sheerness
Branch Line to Southwold
Branch Line to Swanage
Branch Line to Tenterden
Branch Lines to Torrington
Branch Lines to Tunbridge Wells
Branch Line to Upwell
Branch Lines around Wimborne
Branch Lines around Wisbech

SOUTH COAST RAILWAYS
Ashford to Dover
Brighton to Eastbourne
Chichester to Portsmouth
Dover to Ramsgate
Portsmouth to Southampton
Ryde to Ventnor
Worthing to Chichester

SOUTHERN MAIN LINES
Bromley South to Rochester
Charing Cross to Orpington
Crawley to Littlehampton
Dartford to Sittingbourne
East Croydon to Three Bridges
Epsom to Horsham
Exeter to Barnstaple
Exeter to Tavistock
Faversham to Dover
Haywards Heath to Seaford
London Bridge to East Croydon
Orpington to Tonbridge
Sittingbourne to Ramsgate
Swanley to Ashford
Tavistock to Plymouth
Victoria to East Croydon
Waterloo to Windsor
Waterloo to Woking

Woking to Portsmouth
Woking to Southampton
Yeovil to Exeter

COUNTRY RAILWAY ROUTES
Andover to Southampton
Bournemouth to Evercreech Jn.
Burnham to Evercreech Junction
Croydon to East Grinstead
Fareham to Salisbury
Frome to Bristol
Guildford to Redhill
Porthmadog to Blaenau
Reading to Basingstoke
Reading to Guildford
Redhill to Ashford
Salisbury to Westbury
Strood to Paddock Wood
Taunton to Barnstaple
Wenford Bridge to Fowey
Westbury to Bath
Woking to Alton
Yeovil to Dorchester

GREAT RAILWAY ERAS
Ashford from Steam to Eurostar
Clapham Junction 50 years of change
Festiniog in the Fifties
Festiniog in the Sixties
Isle of Wight Lines 50 years of change

LONDON SUBURBAN RAILWAYS
Caterham and Tattenham Corner
Clapham Jn. to Beckenham Jn.
Crystal Palace and Catford Loop
East London Line
Finsbury Park to Alexandra Palace
Holborn Viaduct to Lewisham
Kingston and Hounslow Loops
Lines around Wimbledon
London Bridge to Addiscombe
Mitcham Junction Lines
North London Line
South London Line
West Croydon to Epsom
West London Line
Willesden Junction to Richmond
Wimbledon to Epsom

STEAM PHOTOGRAPHERS
O.J.Morris's Southern
Railways 1919-59

STEAMING THROUGH
Steaming through Cornwall
Steaming through East Sussex
Steaming through the Isle of Wight
Steaming through Kent
Steaming through West Hants
Steaming through West Sussex

TRAMWAY CLASSICS
Aldgate & Stepney Tramways
Barnet & Finchley Tramways
Bath Tramways
Bournemouth & Poole Tramways

Brighton's Tramways
Bristol's Tramways
Camberwell & W.Norwood Tramways
Croydon's Tramways
Clapham & Streatham Tramways
Dover's Tramways
East Ham & West Ham Tramways
Eltham & Woolwich Tramways
Embankment & Waterloo Tramways
Enfield & Wood Green Tramways
Exeter & Taunton Tramways
Gosport & Horndean Tramways
Greenwich & Dartford Tramways
Hampstead & Highgate Tramways
Hastings Tramways
Holborn & Finsbury Tramways
Ilford & Barking Tramways
Kingston & Wimbledon Tramways
Lewisham & Catford Tramways
Liverpool Tramways 1. Eastern Routes
Maidstone & Chatham Tramways
North Kent Tramways
Portsmouth's Tramways
Reading Tramways
Seaton & Eastbourne Tramways
Southampton Tramways
Southend-on-sea Tramways
Southwark & Deptford Tramways
Stamford Hill Tramways
Thanet's Tramways
Victoria & Lambeth Tramways
Waltham Cross & Edmonton Tramways
Walthamstow & Leyton Tramways
Wandsworth & Battersea Tramways

TROLLEYBUS CLASSICS
Croydon's Trolleybuses
Bournemouth Trolleybuses
Maidstone Trolleybuses
Reading Trolleybuses
Woolwich & Dartford Trolleybuses

WATERWAY ALBUMS
Kent and East Sussex Waterways
London's Lost Route to the Sea
London to Portsmouth Waterway
Surrey Waterways

MILITARY BOOKS
Battle over Sussex 1940
Blitz over Sussex 1941-42
Bombers over Sussex 1943-45
Bognor at War
Military Defence of West Sussex
Secret Sussex Resistance

OTHER BOOKS
Betwixt Petersfield & Midhurst
Brickmaking in Sussex
Garraway Father & Son
Index to all Stations
South Eastern & Chatham Railways
London Chatham & Dover Railway

SOUTHERN RAILWAY VIDEO
War on the Line